BENCHMARKING
THE USER EXPERIENCE

A Practical Guide to Benchmarking Websites,
Software, and Product Experiences

Jeff Sauro

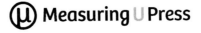

Notices

Knowledge and best practices in this field constantly change. Based on new research and practical experience, it may become necessary to change research methods or professional practices. Practitioners must rely on their own experience and knowledge when using the information and methods described in this book, being mindful of their own safety and the safety of others.

To the fullest extent of the law, neither the Publisher nor the author assumes any liability for any injury and/or damage to persons or property as a matter of products liability, negligence or otherwise, or from any use or operation of any methods, products, instructions, or ideas contained in the material herein.

CONTENTS

DEDICATION

To my three children: Nicholas, Chase and Josephine who exceed all my benchmarks.

ACKNOWLEDGEMENTS

A book doesn't write itself and it certainly doesn't edit itself into a presentable format. I'd like to thank my editor Sarah Harris for diligent and detailed work to help get the manuscript to print. Thanks to Jim Lewis and Kim Oslob for finding time to review and providing helpful comments. I'd also like to thank Jennifer Lam for getting the layout right and Daniel Ankele for getting all those images looking a lot better for the reader.

INTRODUCTION

Welcome to *Benchmarking the User Experience*. This is a practical book about how to measure the user experience of websites, software, mobile apps, products, or just about anything people use. This book is for UX researchers, designers, product owners, or anyone who has a vested interest in improving the experience of websites and products.

In this book, I use practical examples gleaned through my years of experience to illustrate what benchmarking is and how you can use this technique to measure users' experiences. I use examples of studies that the team at MeasuringU, a quantitative research firm that I founded, have worked on to give you constructive information that will help you formulate and/or understand your benchmarking studies, which ultimately helps you understand your audience and customers.

If you are new to benchmarking, you'll find the introductory chapters will provide a thorough background and overview of the primary impetus underlying common benchmarking concepts, methods, and metrics. If you are familiar with in-person usability studies, many of the chapters compare and contrast moderated versus unmoderated benchmarks and should have many familiar concepts and examples.

Chapters 2, 3, and 4 provide guidance on the common "how much," "how long," and "how do we" questions and practical advice on making the most of your benchmark. If you are familiar with benchmarking and looking for guidance, you'll find Chapter 5 useful for providing a thorough overview of task- and study-level metrics. Chapter 6 explains how to determine and justify the sample sizes you choose.

The latter chapters on analysis provide several step-by-step guides on gathering raw benchmark data, graphing benchmark data, and using some best practices for statistical analysis and reporting. The free downloadable

MeasuringU Benchmark Calculator (see Chapter 10) can help even the most seasoned researcher more efficiently analyze their benchmark data. Appendix A contains a checklist for conducting a benchmark study, and Appendix B contains best practices for competitive benchmarks, referencing relevant chapters for more details.

Benchmarking studies also elicit many of the same common questions for any study that aims to quantify the user experience:

- How do I get started? Chapter 2 and 3
- How much and how long should I plan for a benchmark study? Chapter 4
- What metrics do I use? Chapter 5
- What sample size do I need? Chapter 6
- How do I find enough participants? Chapter 9
- What statistical test do I use? Chapter 10 and Chapter 11

My goal with this book is to make benchmarking more accessible and encourage more frequent use. The more we understand how a user experiences a design or product, the more we know what to fix and if all those design and product changes actually make a quantifiably better experience!

CHAPTER I

AN INTRODUCTION TO USER EXPERIENCE BENCHMARKING

User experience (UX) benchmarking is an effective method for understanding how people use and think about an interface. Whether it's for a website, software, or a mobile app, benchmarking is an essential part of a plan to systematically improve the user experience.

There are many aspects involved in conducting an effective benchmark study. To start, benchmarking the user experience effectively means first understanding both what benchmarking is, what the user experience is, and then progressing to methods, metrics, and analysis.

WHAT IS USER EXPERIENCE?

Few things seem to elicit more disagreement than the definition of user experience and how it may or may not differ from user interface design or usability testing. While I don't intend to offer an official definition (there's some health in the debate), here's the definition I use: The user experience is the combination of all the behaviors and attitudes people have while interacting with an interface. (This definition is similar to the definition that Tullis and Albert use in their book *Measuring the User Experience: Collecting, Analyzing, and Presenting Usability Metrics*.) These include but aren't limited to the following:

- Task completion
- Task time
- Clicks
- Ability to find products or information
- Attitudes toward visual appearance
- Attitudes toward trust and credibility
- Perceptions of ease, usefulness, satisfaction

These are also many of the classic usability testing metrics, but this list also includes broader metrics dealing with attitudes, branding, loyalty, and appearance. As such, we borrow heavily from usability testing methods and terminology when discussing a user's experience.

WHAT IS BENCHMARKING AND WHY DO IT?

A benchmark is a standard or point of reference against which metrics may be compared or assessed. This definition provides a good sense of the purpose of benchmarking. The word "benchmark" has an interesting etymology: It originally comes from land surveyors who would cut a mark into a stone to secure a bracket called a "bench." This would be used as a point of reference for building.

With computers, a benchmark is usually an evaluation that assesses the performance of software or hardware to set standards for future tests or trials to gauge performance against (such as CPU or database performance). Similarly, UX benchmarking involves evaluating an interface using a standard set of metrics to gauge its relative performance.

FIGURE 1.1: A mark used by surveyors to place the "bench" or leveling-rod for setting the correct elevation. Photo credit: en.wikipedia.org/wiki/Benchmark_(surveying).

A UX benchmark is something akin to getting a checkup at the doctor. You get your blood pressure, weight, height, and cholesterol checked among other things measured. These metrics help describe quantitatively how healthy you are. They can be compared to existing criteria (e.g., relatively high blood pressure or cholesterol) and tracked over time. If there's a problem, you create a plan to improve your health.

One of the hallmarks of measuring the user experience is seeing whether design efforts actually make a quantifiable difference over time. A regular benchmark study is a great way to institutionalize the idea of quantifiable differences. Benchmarks are most effective when done on a regular interval (e.g., every year or quarter) or after significant design or feature changes. Figure 1.2 shows the same tasks from an automotive website across three years.

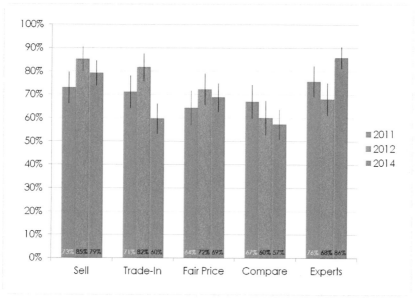

FIGURE 1.2: Completion rates for five tasks from a UX benchmarking study for an automotive website.

A good benchmark indicates where a website or product falls relative to some meaningful comparison. A benchmark can be compared to the following:

- Earlier versions of the product or website
- The competition
- An industry
- An industry standard (such as an NPS or conversation rate)
- Other products in the same company

TIP:

Conducting a benchmark study involves a lot of effort and coordination. To make a line, you need at least two points. The same can be said for benchmark studies. While many benchmark efforts start as stand-alone studies to get an idea of how good or bad an experience is, benchmark studies are often more effective when compared against a competitor, earlier version, or an industry standard (e.g., at least 90% completion rates).

WHAT CAN YOU BENCHMARK?

While just about anything can be benchmarked, the most common interfaces that have benchmark evaluations are the following:

- **Business to business (B2B) and business to consumer websites (B2C):** examples include the shopping experience on walmart.com, costco.com, or ge.com
- **Desktop software (B2C and B2B):** QuickBooks, Excel, or iTunes
- **Web apps:** Salesforce.com or MailChimp
- **Mobile websites:** PayPal's mobile website
- **Mobile apps:** Facebook, Snapchat, or the Chase Mobile app
- **Physical devices:** remote controls, in-car entertainment systems, or medical devices
- **Internal apps within a company:** expense reporting applications or HR systems
- **Service experiences:** customer support calls or out-of-box experiences (OOBE)

TWO TYPES OF BENCHMARKING STUDIES

There are essentially two types of benchmark studies: retrospective and task-based.

Retrospective: Participants are asked to recall their most recent experience with an interface and answer questions. At my company, MeasuringU, we use this approach for the Consumer Software and Business Software Benchmark reports we produce—see, for example, "Net Promoter & UX

Benchmark Report for Consumer Software (2017)," available online at measuringu.com/product/consumer-software2017/.

Task-based: Participants are asked to attempt prescribed tasks using the interface that is being evaluated, which simulates actual usage in a controlled setting. This is the common usability test setup and is what we used when we created a benchmarking report for Enterprise's company website, enterprise.com (this company provides rental cars, more information on this project later).

Pros and Cons of Retrospective vs. Task-Based Benchmarks
Deciding which approach to take is a matter of trading the pros and cons of each and balancing the goals of the benchmark. For retrospective studies, the main pros are the following:

There is no need for app access. You don't need to have access to a working system, like enterprise software or a competitor's product. This can be especially helpful when you don't have access to a working system.

There is no need for task scenarios. Instead of contriving task scenarios for participants to complete (which you hope are representative and realistic), you can have participants reflect on what they did.

The main cons of retrospective studies are the following:

There are no task interactions. You don't have a record of how difficult or easy specific task experiences are; you only have high-level self-reported data. This can make diagnosing the root cause of a poor experience difficult.

Only existing users' data is available. By definition, you can only have existing users reflect on their most recent experience and therefore aren't capturing a new user's experience.

Memory decay is fallible. The more time that passes from when users actually worked with the system, the less salient the experience is and consequently the metrics collected may be less accurate. Some preliminary data we've collected suggests users tend to provide higher metrics in retrospective studies than those in a usability test.

No task data is available. Without a record of what users are doing, you can't see the rich data you get from a task-based study—the errors, hesitations, or problems users might encounter.

Retrospective and task-based studies focus on different experiences as shown in Figure 1.3.

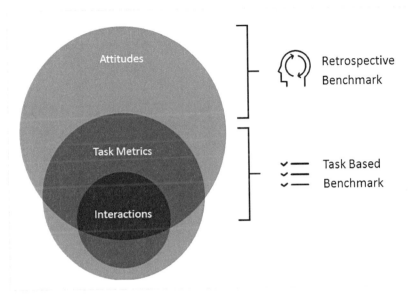

FIGURE 1.3: Retrospective and task-based benchmark studies focus on different parts of the experience: existing attitudes about prior use (retrospective) and current attitudes and actions from interacting through simulated use (task-based).

Fortunately, UX benchmark studies can use a mix of retrospective and task-based studies. We take this approach whenever we can by having participants reflect on their experiences, and then we have another mix of new and existing participants attempt tasks on a website or product.

We used the mixed approach with our hotel UX benchmark study. (For more information on this study, see the article "User Experience Benchmarks for Hotel Websites" at measuringu.com/hotel-ux/). We had 405 participants reflect on their usage of one of five hotel websites and answer a set of questions about their experience, which included completing the Standardized User Experience Percentile Rank-Questionnaire (SUPR-Q). Another 160 participants who had booked *any* hotel online were randomly assigned to complete two tasks on the same hotel website.

Combining both the retrospective and task-based studies gave us a more complete picture of the user experience than if we had used only one type of study.

I've included a summary of the pros and cons of retrospective and task-based benchmarks in Table 1.1.

Pros & Cons	Task-Based	Retrospective
Need Access to Interface	−	+
Need to Write Realistic Tasks	−	+
Task Interaction Data	+	−
Mix of New and Existing Users	+	−
Memory Decay	+	−

TABLE 1.1: Pros and cons of retrospective vs. task-based benchmark studies. Plus signs indicate a pro, and minus signs indicate a con.

DIFFERENT MODES OF UX BENCHMARKING

When conducting a task-based UX benchmark, you need to choose between the different types of modes: moderated (lab-based or remote) or unmoderated testing.

Moderated testing: Moderated testing requires a facilitator/moderator with the participant. Moderated testing can be conducted in person or remotely using monitoring software such as GoToMeeting or WebEx.

Unmoderated testing: Unmoderated testing is similar to a survey. Participants essentially self-administer the study by following directions to answer questions and attempt tasks. Software, such as our MeasuringU Intelligent Questioning (MUIQ) platform, Loop11, or UserZoom, help automate the process and collect a rich set of data, including timing, clicks, heat maps, and videos. There are also some low-cost, lower-tech solutions, such as using a survey platform like SurveyMonkey, to have participants complete tasks and then reflect on the experience (but at the cost of no automatically collected metrics and no videos).

While there are many advantages and disadvantages to moderated or unmoderated testing, the major difference is that unmoderated testing allows you to quickly collect data from more participants in more locations. However, this can sacrifice the richness of a one-to-one interaction, but often for many benchmarking studies, it's worth sacrificing that interaction to get larger numbers of participants.

 TIP:

> Combine multiple methods to fully understand a customer's experience with a website or software. For example, you can have 300 users complete tasks using the remote unmoderated method, and then have 10 to 15 users come into a lab so you can follow up on interesting interactions or problems.

Table 1.2 shows the pros and cons of each of the three usability testing methods.

Attribute	Lab-based	Remote moderated	Remote unmoderated
Geographic diversity	Con: Limited to one or a few locations.	Pro: Users from anywhere in the world can participate. Con: Time zone difference can limit participation.	Pro: Users from anywhere in the world can participate whenever it is convenient.
Recruiting	Con: More difficult because the geographic pool is limited.	Pro: No geographic limitation.	Pro: No geographic limitation.

(continued on pg. 9)

Attribute	Lab-based	Remote moderated	Remote unmoderated
Sample quality	Con: Limited to people willing to take time out of their day.	Pro: Able to recruit specialized users at less of an inconvenience.	Con: More likely to attract people who are in it for the honorarium.
Qualitative insights	Pro: Direct observation of both interface and user reactions. Facilitator can easily probe issues.	Pro: Direct observation of interface and limited user reactions. Facilitator can ask followup questions and engage in a dialogue.	Pro: If session recorded, then direct observation of interface. Con: If no recording, insights are limited to answers to specific questions.
Sample size	Con: More restricted due to geographic limitation and time.	Con: Restricted by time to run studies but usually more flexible hours of scheduling for participants.	Pro: Easy to run large sample sizes (100+).
Costs	Con: Higher compensation costs for users and facilitator time.	Pro: User compensation is lower and requires less facilitation time.	Pro: Compensation is cheap and doesn't require facilitation or lab costs.

TABLE 1.2: Comparison of the difference between usability testing methods (lab-based, remote moderated, and remote unmoderated).

Benchmark Metrics

Benchmarks are all about the metrics they collect. Benchmark studies are often called summative evaluations where the emphasis is less on finding problems but more on quantitatively assessing the current experience. That experience is quantified using both broader study-level metrics and granular task-level metrics (if there are tasks). A detailed review of benchmark metrics is available in Chapter 5; here is a general overview.

Study-based metrics

One or more of the following metrics are typically collected during a study (either task-based or retrospective):

- **The Standardized User Experience Percentile Rank-Questionnaire (SUPR-Q)** provides a measure of the overall quality of the website user experience plus measures of usability, appearance, trust, and loyalty.

- **The Standardized User Experience Percentile Rank-Questionnaire for mobile apps (SUPR-Qm)** is a questionnaire for the mobile app user experience.

- **The System Usability Scale (SUS)** is a measure of perceived usability; good for software.

- **The Net Promoter Score (NPS)** is a measure of customer loyalty for all interfaces; best for consumer-facing ones.

- **The Usability Metric for User Experience (UMUX-LITE)** is a compact measure of perceived usefulness and perceived ease.

- **Brand attitude or brand lift** has a significant effect on UX metrics. Measuring a user's attitude towards a brand before and after a study helps identify how much of an effect the experience has (positive or negative) on brand attitudes.

Task-level metrics

For studies with tasks, the following are the most common metrics collected as part of the task or after the task:

- **Attitudes:** perceptions of ease (e.g., the Single Ease Question, SEQ) and confidence (collected after the task)

- **Actions:** completion rates, task times, errors (collected from the task)

CHAPTER SUMMARY AND TAKEAWAYS

In this chapter, I discussed the concepts of what a benchmark is and how it applies to the user experience:

- A UX benchmark provides a quantifiable measure of an interface, such as a website, mobile app, product, or software.

- A good benchmark indicates how the performance of the interface scores relative to a meaningful comparison from an earlier point in time, competition, or industry benchmark.

- Benchmarks can be retrospective (participants reflect on actual usage) or task-based (participants attempt tasks in simulated or actual use).

- Collecting data for UX benchmarking involves the same modes as usability testing: moderated or unmoderated approaches.

- Benchmarking data should come at the study level (SUPR-Q, SUS, NPS) and, if there are tasks, at the task level (completion rates, time, errors, SEQ).

CHAPTER 2:

PLANNING AND DEFINING YOUR STUDY

You've made the decision to benchmark. Congratulations. Now it's time to get into the details. In this chapter we'll start with defining the broader goals of a benchmark study, the best benchmarking method, and whether to approach the benchmark as a stand-alone or comparative study.

In addition to these major details, there are other logistical details you'll want to sort through prior to testing your first participant. We've found that one of the best ways to organize your study and address as many details as possible upfront is by using what we call the project booking form.

The project booking form is basically a simplified study plan; it's what we use during the initial call with a client to help focus the conversation. It's a guide to outline the questions you need to answer before even thinking about testing a user. Once we gather this information in the booking form, a researcher can use the information to start building an online research platform which will serve to collect data for the benchmarking study. You can see an example of a booking form in Appendix D.

The following sections provide an overview of the type of information we gather in our booking form. To illustrate the rationale for determining how we plan and define our studies using the booking form, I give practical examples of how the team at MeasuringU does it.

DEFINING STUDY GOALS

Most benchmark studies have the core goal of obtaining a measure of the user experience. However, there are usually other underlying reasons why companies want to gain the information provided by a benchmark study. It's important to clearly define the goals and understand the background of why the client wants the study. Using questions to gather information to define the goals and understand the background is an effective tool that can help guide the questions and tasks (if it is a task-based benchmark) used in a benchmark study.

The questions can be general, like the following examples:

- Does the website have a better experience than the closest two competitors?
- Can at least 70% of users find information on the first attempt?
- Do users provide overall SUPR-Q ratings at the 80th percentile or higher?

Or they can be more specific:

- What are the biggest problems with users finding the performance of a mutual fund?
- Is the information on the product detail page helpful? Does the product page need to be redesigned?
- Does the product filter design help or hurt the experience of picking the right products? Is it better or worse compared to how two competitors filter?

HOTEL EXAMPLE: Is there a significant difference in the user experience between the Best Western and Marriott websites? Does either website offer a best-in-class experience for reserving a hotel or exceed an industry benchmark metric such as at least 75% on the SUPR-Q?

Rationale: For the hotel study, like most benchmarks, we wanted to quantify the experience of the hotel website. Hotel websites compete with aggregator sites like Hotels.com so it's important for the experience to be as good or better to attract and retain customers (and consequently reduce booking fees from aggregator websites). We also wanted to see how good the experience was relative to an industry leader, like Marriott.

PICKING THE METHOD

As introduced in Chapter 1, benchmarking involves one of two approaches: a retrospective approach, where participants recall their experience and answer questions, or a task-based approach, where participants attempt prescribed tasks in a contrived setup. The right approach here will be the one that accomplishes the following:

- **Satisfies the study goals:** If you need detailed information on both the performance and what to improve, you may need a task-based benchmark.

- **Stays within the budget:** If you want to benchmark 30 products, you may not have the budget for a comprehensive task-based evaluation and instead will need to conduct a retrospective benchmark.

The following two examples highlight how we determined which benchmarking approach would be appropriate to use based on either our goals or our client's needs and goals.

HOTEL EXAMPLE: TASK-BASED BENCHMARK

Rationale: We wanted to make comparisons at the task level to understand if either of these popular websites had a better way of finding and booking a hotel. This dictated a task-based benchmark.

CONSUMER AND BUSINESS SOFTWARE EXAMPLE: RETROSPECTIVE BENCHMARK

Rationale: We use the SUS and the NPS to gather data for our regular benchmark of 20 consumer and business software products. Because we aren't interested in necessarily improving any single product, the data gathered for this retrospective benchmark provide reference points of popular products like iTunes, Excel, and Dropbox using industry standard measures of SUS, NPS, and UMUX-LITE.

STAND-ALONE OR COMPARATIVE STUDY

A lot of benchmark efforts start as a stand-alone study with data being collected for just one experience, like a single website, software product, or prototype. Two common reasons for considering a comparative benchmark study are the following:

- To provide more meaning and answers to the question: Compared to what? The "what" can be data from one or more key competitors.

- To evaluate the cost effectiveness of a study, as a lot of effort goes into the setup and execution. If this is a comparative study, is it between (different users in each group) or within subjects (same users in each group)?

The following examples highlight how we determined whether a stand-alone or comparison study was needed to accomplish our client's goals.

HOTEL EXAMPLE: COMPARISON STUDY

Rationale: We didn't have any external data on how difficult or easy the tasks we selected would be. Deciding to compare the tasks using at least one competitor allowed us to better interpret task metrics like completion and perceived difficulty.

FINANCIAL SERVICES EXAMPLE: COMPARISON STUDY

Rationale: We worked with a financial services company who had never conducted a UX benchmark study. They were unsure if competing sites' data visualizations were superior. Developing a comparison study made the tasks used in the study much more meaningful.

ACCOUNTING SOFTWARE EXAMPLE: MODERATED STAND-ALONE

Rationale: In working with a company that provides accounting software to the construction industry, we recommended a moderated (remote and in-person) benchmark. This was primarily because participants would need to log in to a remote account system with fake data. The study required a lot of time to set up and execute tasks and required a very specialized population of participants (the customers of this company who were very busy), which made it a challenge to get the 20 participants we needed.

Within vs. Between Subjects vs. Mixed

If you decide to run a comparative study (which we recommend if you can), then you'll next need to weigh the pros and cons of a within- versus between-subjects design.

While the between-subjects approach is the more familiar one to researchers, you'll see that the within-subjects approach has some important advantages. The right choice however is based on considering a few factors: sample size and power, carryover effects, impact on attitudes, comparative judgement, preference, and the study duration.

Sample size and power

By far the biggest advantage to using a within-subjects approach is that you can detect differences between design metrics with a fraction of the users as compared to a between-subjects approach. In other words, you can use a much smaller sample size. The cost of recruitment, honorariums, and facilitator time are usually the biggest costs of a study, so reducing the time and cost creates a strong appeal for choosing within-subjects studies.

In measuring human behavior, the differences between people often outweigh the differences between designs. But a within-subjects study design effectively eliminates the differences between people. For example, if you happen to have a few particularly slower participants in a study, that same slowness is applied equally to all designs they interact with—essentially "controlling" for it.

Depending on the difference you want to detect, a within-subjects approach requires just 33% to 2% of the sample size that a between-subjects study does. See Chapter 6 for more details on sample size computations and weighting a within- vs. between-subjects approach.

 TIP:

> Every within-subjects design actually contains a smaller between-subjects design given proper counterbalancing. For example, if 100 participants attempted tasks on two websites (Website A and Website B) and were randomly assigned one first, you can compare the 50 participants that received Website A first and the 50 that received Website B first as a between-subjects study (albeit with less statistical power).

Carryover effects

People learn and get better with practice. However, you usually don't want participants applying these learnings (also called sequence effects) from one design to the next. Participants get faster and more accurate; subsequently, their first impressions change with more exposure. Consequently, the first designs often have poorer metrics than later designs (called recency and primacy effects). This is usually the biggest concern researchers have when implementing a within-subjects approach.

Fortunately, there's an effective way to reduce many (but not all) of the negative consequences that carryover effects bring through counterbalancing. Counterbalancing varies the presentation order of the designs systematically so not every participant sees the designs in the same order. For example, if you're testing two designs (A versus B), half the participants get A first and half get B first. Counterbalancing ensures that carryover effects are equally applied to both designs.

Impact on attitudes

Counterbalancing can minimize many of the unwanted sequence effects, but it doesn't erase the participants' memories. If you want to benchmark how people think about a brand or design experience, exposure matters. Participants' ratings are impacted by what you expose them to, and not always in predictable ways.

For example, we often see exaggerated ratings in within-subjects designs. If you give participants one relatively mediocre design (or website) and one really bad design (or website), participants tend to rate the mediocre design much higher than if it were rated in isolation. They also tend to rate the lesser of the designs as much worse.

We saw this effect when we did a within-subjects benchmark of the websites for the Enterprise and Budget car rental companies. Budget scored much higher than Enterprise on both task and study metrics like the SUPR-Q. When we tested both sites in isolation (using a between-subjects approach), Budget and Enterprise actually scored similarly.

If you want to benchmark how people think about a brand or design without being impacted by another design or brand they just experienced, a between-subjects approach is likely the better way to go (if you can handle the larger sample size!).

If you go with a within-subjects approach, you can get a between-subjects comparison from a within-subjects study by restricting the analysis to the participants' first experiences. In other words, every within-subjects design contains a between-subject design when properly counterbalanced and analyzed.

Comparative judgment

Having an impact on attitudes isn't necessarily a bad thing. People have an easier time making relative versus absolute judgments. It's a lot easier for participants to answer how satisfied they are with a design if they can say, "Well, it's a lot better than the other design you just showed me." If you're looking to identify a winner between alternative designs (even bad designs), a within-subjects approach is usually the way to go.

Preference

Another important advantage of within-subjects setup is the ability for participants to make direct comparisons between the experiences. At the end of a study, participants are asked which experience they preferred, which is an opportunity for practical feedback. For example, when we conducted a comparative benchmark study between car rental websites, participants often had preferences for one experience over the other. This piece of information—do users prefer my website over my competitors—is often the first thing stakeholders want to know.

Participant study duration

All other things being equal, a within-subjects study takes longer for the participant. If you have five designs to test and want participants to attempt multiple tasks and answer many questions, the study duration might just be too long, even for the most vigilant participants. If you can't cut down the number of designs or reduce the number of tasks, you may need a between-subjects study to fit in everything.

Summary of within vs. between subjects—and an alternative solution—mixed

The following table summarizes the pros and cons of within-subjects and between-subjects studies.

Factor to consider	Between	Within
Sample size and power	-	+
Carryover effects	+	-
Impact on attitudes	+	-
Comparative judgment	-	+
Preference	-	+
Participant study duration	+	-

TABLE 2.1: Factors to consider when deciding between a within- or between-subjects study. Plus signs indicate a pro, and minus signs indicate a con.

If you can't decide—just as with many research methods—there is a compromise. You can use a combination of between-subjects and within-subjects approaches. For example, all participants can get the baseline design and one of three alternate designs.

This sort of analysis is a bit more complicated to analyze, as you'll need to switch statistical tests depending on the combination of designs you're comparing. It does, however, strike a balance; you can keep the test short while getting data on multiple designs and still allow for many questions and tasks.

HOTEL EXAMPLE: BETWEEN SUBJECTS

Rationale: We wanted a benchmark of how participants felt about the website without them directly comparing it to another hotel website. Even though using a within-subjects study would increase our statistical power, we chose to use a between-subjects approach because we didn't want our participants to rate the website relative to the other websites tested.

FINANCIAL SERVICES EXAMPLE: WITHIN SUBJECTS

Rationale: We worked with a financial services company who had never conducted a UX benchmark but wanted to understand how the process of selecting funds (a core task) differed across competitors. The cost for the specialized sample (financial advisors) was high so we needed to keep sample sizes to a minimum. Using a within-subjects approach allowed us to get task data for three websites but limited us to two tasks per website (six tasks total).

EMAIL MARKETING: MIXED SUBJECTS

Rationale: When benchmarking the email marketing platform, Constant Contact, we had all participants use Constant Contact, and they were assigned to one of three other competitors. This solved two issues: it allowed us to collect preference data for the product the client most cared about (theirs) and ensured we had a large enough sample size for future benchmarks, which would not be competitive and only measure their product over time.

CHAPTER SUMMARY AND TAKEAWAYS

In this chapter, I covered the first steps in planning a benchmark:

- Start with defining benchmark study goals. These can be broad (Is the website a better experience than a competitor?) and/or more specific (Are the new product filters helping visitors find the right products faster?).

- Pick the method, a retrospective benchmark or a task-based benchmark, that best addresses the study goals (and is the most feasible).

- Decide between a stand-alone or comparative benchmark. Many first-time benchmarks start as stand-alone but morph into comparative as the comparative benchmark puts the metrics into a better context.

- Weigh the pros and cons, if running a comparative benchmark, of a within- (same participants on multiple products) or between-subjects study (different participants on each product).

- Detect statically significant differences with a much smaller sample size; this is the biggest advantage to a within-subjects study. However, its major drawback is it adds time to the study and adds carryover effects (which for the most part can be reduced with proper counterbalancing).

CHAPTER 3:
WORKING THROUGH STUDY DETAILS

With a general idea of the study goals and whether the study will be stand-alone or comparative, you can focus on more of the details of the study. In this chapter we'll cover the interface that will be evaluated (which isn't always obvious), the tasks (if applicable), and task participants.

DEFINE THE INTERFACE(S)

Even if you're testing a public facing website, while it may seem simple, you'll quickly see the need to think about which platforms to use (desktop, tablet, mobile) and to figure out how participants will access the interface for task-based benchmarks (for example, if the site is password protected) and if they need to use their own accounts.

Platforms
The major platforms you'll need to consider for benchmarks include the following:

Desktop: The most common benchmark used for websites and business or consumer software is conducted via a desktop computer (non-mobile). When benchmarking you'll need to consider the operating system (usually Windows and/or iOS) and web-browser type (e.g., Chrome, Internet Explorer).

Phone and tablet: As mobile benchmarking continues to grow, you'll need to think about operating systems (iOS, Android, and Windows) and how they relate to the mobile experience. This may vary depending on the country: While iOS and Android have around equal market shares in the US, Android tends to be the dominant phone operating system outside the US.

Internet of things (IoT): While it's still a bit early to tell, it's likely we'll see more testing on IoT devices like watches and smart fridges.

Hardware: Benchmarking physical products, like remote controls, smart TVs, or medical devices, requires having all the right pieces in place and a setting that mimics actual use (a living room, doctor's office, or automobile).

Mixing: In-car navigation/infotainment systems and TV accessories (like Roku, cable boxes, and on-screen guides) require the proper planning of both physical spaces and products and the software that goes with them. Be sure all these are well defined, as different combinations may lead to different results (e.g., small vs. large TV screens with participants situated close vs. across the room).

Interface Access

For enterprise software or even mobile apps, users tend to customize their experiences, which gives you the task of figuring out how they access the interface. This is common for enterprise systems like financials, HR, payroll, or sales-automation software, which are extensively customized by an organization. Determining which interface to use in a benchmark study can be a challenge. The following information details the considerations to take into account for the four types of interfaces used in benchmarking studies.

Publicly accessible: Consumer website benchmarks (e.g., walmart.com, united.com) that offer generally the same experience are usually easily accessible by anyone in the world and are the easiest interfaces to benchmark (which is why we benchmark them every quarter at MeasuringU). These interfaces are easily accessible from any platform, and there are fewer privacy concerns.

 TIP:

Consumer websites increasingly conduct "experiments" by presenting different content, images, or other changes in the design that may mean some participants will have differing experiences. Having session recordings of what the participant sees will help disentangle these potentially confounding effects.

Participant's own system/account: For any system with customization or configurations, such as accounting systems, advertising accounts, or bank accounts, participants will be most familiar with an interface populated with their data to get the most realistic product experience (because it's what they use on a daily basis). There are two problems you'll need to account for with this approach. First, the different setups for each participant means it will be difficult to have standard tasks (such as checking a report), as customers will have different data and may likely expose them to different usability issues (and some may be idiosyncratic to their system). The second issue is privacy and data integrity. Customers will be reluctant to add journal entries, hire a fake employee, or add leads to their sales system, as this work will need to be undone (or worse, cause additional problems). Sensitive information, like bank accounts, payment information, or other employee data, can make testing challenging or at least make participants reluctant. Despite these drawbacks, it may be the way to go for your benchmark, and tasks will need to be crafted to account for the differences across participants and any impact on their accounts.

Demo/canned system: Most enterprise and consumer software apps have a demonstration version or one with "canned" data. These systems are usually fully functioning complete with all the features. Some benefits for conducting a benchmark study using these systems are that you avoid problems with privacy, customer data won't be affected, and all participants in the benchmark are exposed to the same system, allowing for more standard and consistent task experiences. The major drawback is participants won't be familiar with the details, and this may artificially affect the experience. At its worst, if stakeholders don't think the experience was authentic, they may dismiss the results of the benchmark—something you want to avoid.

Prototypes: In the absence of access to the customers own app or a demo version, a final alternative is to mock up part or all of the task experience using prototyping software. You get access (even remote access) to an experience, and you don't need to worry about customer privacy or affecting their data. But, like the demo system, you'll have it prepopulated with canned information the participants won't be familiar with. As with any prototype testing, you'll also now have to deal with the effects of limited functionality and less realistic experiences. Fortunately, many task and study metrics are still reliable indicators. While not a first choice, if you're unable to use the real product, it is better to use this type of interface than to not benchmark at all when you need to get some task-level data.

TIP:

Table 3.1 summarizes the pros and cons of selecting the different ways the interface can be accessed.

Factor to consider	Publicly accessible	Participant's own account	Demo system	Prototype
Realistic experience	++	++	+	-
Data privacy	++	--	+	+
Affecting customer data	++	--	++	++
Functionality	++	+	-	--

TABLE 3.1: Factors to consider when deciding what interface to use in the benchmark. Plus signs indicate a pro, and minus signs indicate a con.

USING THE QUICKBOOKS DEMO VERSION

One of the first benchmark studies I worked on was at QuickBooks—the accounting software for small businesses. Customers configure their accounting software based on their organizations, different vendors, customers, and bank accounts. With the problem of both the wide variability in setups and the issue of privacy, we created a demo version of the software. It was prefilled with dummy customers, banks, and invoices. This allowed us to have a controlled experience but at the cost of knowing it wouldn't be exactly like users' experiences. After each task, we asked each participant how similar the setup was to their own version of QuickBooks. When the rating was lower, we used more caution when interpreting the results.

Platform and Interface Access Examples

Here are some examples to illustrate how we, at MeasuringU, select different platforms and figure out ways participants should access the interface for our benchmarking studies.

HOTEL EXAMPLE: DESKTOP WEB EXPERIENCE

> **Rationale:** We started with the desktop experience knowing we could advance to mobile later if we wanted. Anyone with a web browser can access the websites, making it an easy test.

ACCOUNTING SOFTWARE EXAMPLE: DESKTOP VERSION USING A DEMO ACCOUNT

> **Rationale:** We used the desktop version of the accounting software because users generally use this platform to access the accounting software. To protect our participants' customer data and privacy, we used a demo-version of the software that could be accessed using a virtual private network (VPN).

ONLINE ADVERTISING PLATFORM EXAMPLE: PARTICIPANTS' OWN ACCOUNTS

> **Rationale:** An online advertising provider wanted to benchmark the user experience for users who manage advertising budgets. The stakeholders were concerned a demo account would not make sense to participants and not provide the data they needed. The tasks were carefully created to prevent participants from accidently submitting a new ad campaign or increasing or decreasing a campaign budget. We also notified the participants about using their own accowunts.

IDENTIFY THE TASKS

If this is a task-based benchmark, you should identify the task-topics (from a high level at this stage— the actual scenario with task-success criteria is presented in a subsequent chapter). The tasks you select should also address the study goals. For example, if you are focusing on the new user experience, tasks should be things new users to the product or website would do, such as registering, configuring, or setting up. If one of the goals of the benchmark is to determine how well participants use a product filter, tasks should expose participants to the filter.

Rationale: We wanted to use what we think are the quintessential tasks for the hotel experience that would be applicable for both first-time and experienced users: browse for available rooms and search for prices.

ACCOUNTING SOFTWARE EXAMPLE: ENTER, CHANGE, RESPOND, AND PRINT

Rationale: There were multiple modules that we couldn't access, so we focused on the most common payables tasks: enter a batch of five invoices, change an invoice, respond to vendor requests, and print a check.

Determining the Tasks

There is a finite amount of time participants spend on tasks in a benchmarking study. For moderated studies this is usually around an hour, and for unmoderated studies this is usually less than 30 minutes. You're therefore limited to how many total tasks you can have participants attempt. For benchmarks there are usually two ways to select tasks: pick the top tasks and/or pick the less-used tasks that address study goals.

Top tasks: While every software app, product, or website often supports hundreds to thousands of features and tasks, there are a smaller number that disproportionately account for usage. Identify these top tasks and include them. For example, on a third-party automotive website, the product team identified 94 pieces of content. After conducting a top-tasks analysis, one task was the most popular: finding the miles per gallon for a car. This became the key task we benchmarked across the website (and over time). See the next section "Finding Top Tasks" for more information on how to conduct a top-task analysis.

Tasks that address goals: Even if tasks aren't the top ones, they may merit space in your benchmark study. If a feature was just redesigned (or is being considered for redesigning) or has potential problem areas, tasks that expose participants to this functionally may be worthy of inclusion. For the financial services example mentioned in Chapter 2, we had a task that asked participants to find detailed information about a mutual fund. We anticipated this task would lead participants to a product filter that stakeholders thought may be causing problems (which we later did confirm in the study).

Finding Top Tasks

While there are hundreds to thousands of things users can accomplish on websites and software interfaces, there are a critical few tasks that drive users to visit a website or use a software or product.

Think of all the features Microsoft Word provides. It supports document editing, mail merging, desktop publishing, and a full range of HTML. By one estimate, it has around 1,200 features. Now think of the most important features that you need when you create or edit a document—the features you couldn't live without. These features likely support your top tasks.

Prioritizing tasks is not a new concept. Having users rank what's important is a technique that's been used extensively in marketing and conjoint analysis. But having users force-rank hundreds or thousands of features individually would be too tedious for even the most diligent of users (or even the most sophisticated, choice-based conjoint software).

The following sections outline the essence of conducting a top-tasks analysis.

List the tasks

Identify the features, content, and functionality you want people to consider. The tasks can be specific to a website or to a class of websites. For example, here are a few tasks you can do on a healthcare insurance company website:

- Look up the address of a doctor.
- Find the office hours of a doctor.
- See if a healthcare provider accepts your insurance.

 TIP:

> Avoid internal jargon as much as possible and make sure tasks are phrased in a way that a person can relate to and in a way that is actionable.

The total number of tasks you need depends on the scope of what you are testing. A broader experience (e.g., an entire ecommerce website) will have more tasks compared to a more focused experience (e.g., on-demand videos for a cable provider). You might have as few as 20 tasks or as many as 150.

Have representative participants select the tasks

Recruit a representative set of users or prospective users to determine the top tasks (typically between 30 and 150 participants). As with all sampling methods, you'll want to be sure the participants who assist with your study share the same characteristics as the larger customer base you are making inferences about.

In top-tasks analysis, most items will actually only be selected by a small percentage of users, making the sample sizes on the high side for most of the items. In other words, this is a worst-case scenario sample size. However, sample sizes as low as 20 customers can still provide valuable insights.

Randomizing and Limiting

Present the list of tasks in randomized order to representative users. You want to randomize because users don't consider tasks individually; they scan the list for recognizable key words. With a randomized list, tasks have an equal chance of being near the top or bottom of the list, which are the top locations where most users tend to scan.

 TIP:

> You can use software to randomize the order of your tasks. We use our MeasuringU Intelligent Questioning (MUIQ) platform or you can use SurveyMonkey. The important part is that the software allows you to randomize.

Have users pick their top five tasks from the list. There's nothing sacred about picking five; it's just a good number that works when you have 50 or more tasks. With fewer tasks, say 20 to 30, you can adjust the number down to three tasks for users to select. This ensures users are forced to choose the really important tasks over the nice-to-have tasks.

 TIP:

> It's hard to know every task a customer would like to accomplish. Therefore, include an "Other" option so customers can provide their own top task.

Separate the top tasks from the trivial tasks

Count the votes for each selected task and divide that by the total number of participants who voted. This gives you the percent of times a task was selected. Sort them in descending order. The characteristic shape of the top-task graph is the "long neck" of the vital few tasks your users care about. Figure 3.1 shows an example. Notice the handful of tasks that really stand out near the left side of each graph? These are the top tasks.

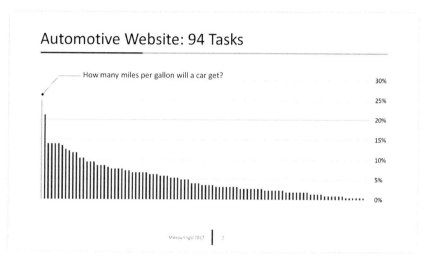

FIGURE 3.1: Example of top tasks from an automotive website top-task analysis.

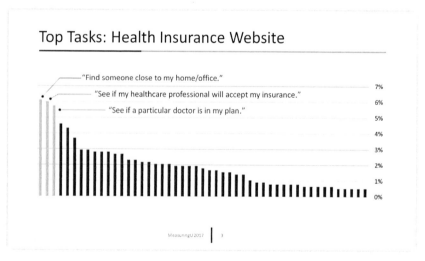

FIGURE 3.2: Example of top tasks from a health insurance top-task analysis.

You'll also see the long tail of the tasks that are less important. Of course, you can't just stop supporting your less important tasks, but you should be sure that customers can complete the top tasks effectively and efficiently. These top tasks should become the core tasks you conduct benchmark tests around and the basis for design efforts.

TIP:

It's common that teams will have too many tasks for participants to complete in a benchmark. Having a prioritized set of tasks provides a good input for how to cut tasks if there are too many.

DEFINE PARTICIPANTS

Understanding who your users are is a book in itself. While I won't provide an extensive overview of how to define your users, we will cover some essentials on selecting users for a benchmarking study.

Benchmarking, like many UX methods, relies on input from participants. It doesn't matter how sophisticated your analysis is if you're drawing conclusions from the wrong type of participants in your study. There are two common ways of defining your participant pool: attributes and behaviors.

Attributes: The classic demographics of age, gender, income, education level, and geography are all attributes of user populations. While you'll likely need to collect many of these variables, they are usually incidental aspects of your customers.

Behaviors: What people have done or knowledge they have is usually a much more differentiating factor. This includes prior experience with a product (such as accounting software or a mobile app) and domain knowledge (such as a financial advisor or IT decision maker).

TIP:

Don't rely heavily on attribute data. Minimize relying on attributes like demographics (age, gender, education) when defining your participant profile. These are often the symptoms and not the reasons for why people do or don't use a product or service.

Rationale: We felt that having a group of participants who had booked a U.S. hotel online in the last year was a minimum qualification level. Having a mix of new and experienced participants would be indicative of the typical hotel user. Note that this was based on participants' behavior, not just attributes like gender or age.

Rationale: We needed participants who had specific software knowledge and who were familiar with a particular payables module, as the tasks covered this module.

Defining Subgroups

It's rare that users of a product or website are homogenous. At the very least you need to consider prior experience with the website, domain, or product. If you have different subgroups, this may affect the questions you ask, the tasks you present, and the overall sample size. One of the most common subgroups is based on prior experience with a product or domain. This can be new versus existing, such as the following:

- Existing online grocery customers vs. those interested in trying the service
- Owners of a Linksys router vs. owners of other routers
- Current users of Uber vs. users of Lyft vs. prospective ride sharing users

It can also be subgrouped by the amount of experience and frequency of use such as with the following examples:

- Purchase from Amazon weekly vs. a few times per year
- 5+ years using AutoCAD vs. less than 5 years
- On Facebook multiple times a day vs. a few times per month

And there are, of course, the more common subgroups by demographics:

- Men vs. women
- Younger vs. older
- US vs. international
- By persona (or predefined customer segment)

Rationale: We were open to knowing we'd get a mix of people with or without experience. We collected prior experience with each brand to understand how, if at all, this prior experience would impact the task and study metrics. We also wanted to have participants from only the US.

FINANCIAL SERVICES EXAMPLE: CONSUMERS AND FINANCIAL ADVISORS

Rationale: Two distinct subgroups we tested for the within-subjects financial services study were between consumers with investible assets and financial advisors—the latter group has a lot of knowledge of funds and investing relative to consumers and was a significant source of the website visitor traffic.

ENTERPRISE SOFTWARE EXAMPLE: HR PROFESSIONALS VS. ACCOUNTANTS VS. ADMINISTRATORS

Rationale: MeasuringU conducted a benchmark for an international B2B software company with three distinct subgroups who each attempted different tasks: HR professionals (e.g., hiring/onboarding), accountants (e.g., payroll processing and compliance), and administrators (e.g., granting and revoking access).

CHAPTER SUMMARY AND TAKEAWAYS

In this chapter, I covered the next steps in planning a benchmark, which include the following steps:

- Define the interface(s) to benchmark, which often include combinations of desktop and mobile devices or versions of physical products.

- Consider how the interface will be accessed for task-based benchmarks. For public facing websites it's usually easy (use the website), but for enterprise software it can be more challenging and participants may need to use their own system or you'll need to set up a demo system or prototype.

- Define realistic tasks for participants to attempt when conducting a task-based benchmark. Select tasks that are considered top tasks or ones that address the study goals.

- Use a top-task analysis to find the most important tasks for participants by having them select a small number from a longer list of tasks.

- Define the participant characteristics for the benchmark. These are usually a combination of attributes (e.g., demographics) and behaviors (e.g., prior experience with a product), with the primary focus on behaviors.

- Consider any distinct subgroups you'll want to include, for example, users from a certain geographic area or new versus existing users of a product or service.

CHAPTER 4:

PLANNING AND LOGISTICS

In this chapter I address many of the how, how long, and how much questions that arise when a decision has been made to benchmark and after many of the details in Chapters 2 and 3 have been settled. In this chapter, I discuss typical timelines, the types of unmoderated platforms, and the costs involved.

COMMERCIAL UNMODERATED RESEARCH PLATFORMS

In 2010, when Albert, Tullis, and Tedesco's book *Beyond the Usability Lab: Conducting Large-scale Online User Experience Studies* came out, it listed four commercial options for unmoderated studies. I would have expected to see twice as many options eight years later. Instead only two of the original platforms featured still exist (Loop11 and UserZoom). Since then, UserTesting and Validately also offer the ability to collect data quickly but are primarily meant for smaller-sample, think-aloud videos and don't offer much of the customization needed for effective benchmarks (we'll see if that changes).

Because we weren't satisfied with the capabilities and flexibility available in any of the unmoderated platforms, we built the MeasuringU Intelligent Questioning (MUIQ) platform. The MUIQ platform provides the key features we need to conduct an unmoderated benchmarking study. The following are the main features we need to consider when conducting benchmarks; you can use this list as a checklist when selecting an unmoderated commercial platform:

- **Task-based:** This is the ability to display a taskbar along with a website (Figure 4.1). There is a benefit if you can configure the taskbar so it doesn't interfere with key elements on the page (Figure 4.2).

- **Branching and logic:** When different segments of a company's population (e.g., customers vs. financial advisers) are included in the same benchmark study, you'll want to display only relevant questions to each participant segments and branch or add conditionals to keep studies smooth and short for each segment.

- **Question screen outs:** You need the ability to find participants' answers to specific demographic questions, such as their prior experience, brand, income, or age to ensure you're targeting the right type of participants for your study. This is especially important when using online panels.

- **Quotas on questions:** To manage the right balance of participants (e.g., 50% experienced and 50% new users), you need to have question-level quotas. This simple feature is surprisingly absent from most unmoderated platforms (but available with MUIQ).

- **Screen recording:** Having a recording of a participant's screen for both desktop and mobile web, and ideally mobile native apps, is one of the best ways to understand interactions and validate task successes.

- **Participant selection:** There seems to be a trend in bundling participants with commercial providers (e.g., UserTesting and UserZoom are increasingly bundling this cost with the platform), but you'll want the ability to select your own panel or participants.

- **Click paths:** Knowing where participants click allows for building many different types of visualizations, such as heat maps and click maps, that show how participants move through a website. Though, collecting clicks usually requires a plug-in and only works on some browsers (usually Chrome and Firefox).

- **Mobile:** If applicable to your study, you'll want all the previously discussed features available for mobile web devices and, as much as possible, for mobile native apps.

- **Multiple browser support:** As of this writing, Chrome is the dominant browser (around 60% of the desktop market), but not everyone uses it, especially at large businesses. You'll want the ability to let participants use different browsers (Firefox, Edge, Safari), even if this means click-data won't be collected.

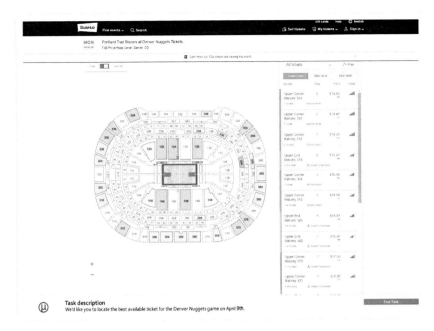

FIGURE 4.1: Task-question at the bottom position of a tested web page using the MUIQ platform.

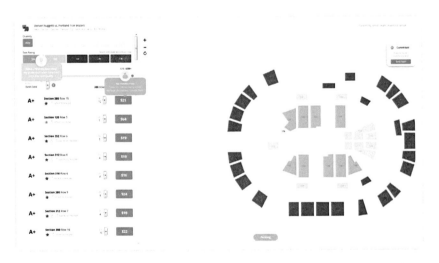

FIGURE 4.2: Using MUIQ, the task question is less conspicuous with a floating, right-side starting position.

Do-It-Yourself or Survey-Only Based Platforms

Not all researchers have the budget or are able to use the benefits of a commercial unmoderated platform. Fortunately, there are some other do-it-yourself ways to conduct an unmoderated study. The main sacrifice you'll be making is the loss of rich task-based metrics, clicks, and videos. For some studies, though, this do-it-yourself approach may be sufficient. You can use a survey platform like SurveyMonkey or Qualtrics to administer tasks as survey questions. Present tasks as text-only questions, for example: "We'd like you to locate a blender for less than $40 with at least a four-star average rating. Open the Target.com website and find the brand of blender that matches these criteria and return to this survey when you feel you have complete the task."

After participants return to the survey, they answer post-task questions, including verification questions (e.g., "What was the name of the blender you found?") and perceptions of ease using the SEQ. See *Beyond the Usability Lab* by Albert et al. for more ideas on do-it yourself systems.

Remote Moderated Software

For remote, moderated benchmark studies, there's usually less need for a robust, all-in-one platform. Do-it-yourself and low-tech solutions often suffice. To perform this type of benchmark study, you'll need to consider meeting and screen recording software, such as GoToMeeting and WebEx (which are around $350 a year for a license) or using a cheaper/free version such as join.me or BlueJeans. All of these options require some sort of download. For now, we've found GoToMeeting the most compatible and least painful (albeit not free from problems). Most platforms record the screen and sometimes the participant's face via a webcam (albeit at generally low quality).

 TIP:

> Have a second method for recordings. Unfortunately, we've found the recordings from meeting software like GoToMeeting can become corrupted or don't encode properly. We use Open Broadcast Software (OBS) Studio for our main recordings and use GoToMeeting recordings as a backup for this reason.

In-Person Moderated Software

For in-person, moderated lab studies, you can be as low tech as paper, pen, and a watch, but you may want to consider some software, such as the following, to help gather screen recording data.

- Camtasia is a popular screen recording software (around $200) that generates high quality video of a participant's screen.

- Morae is a more advanced version of Camtasia. It will both record the screen of the participant and broadcast it over Wi-Fi to a moderator's computer. Morae also includes some automated metrics collection and video clip creation.

- OBS Studio, which is what we often use and is free and open-source, records the screen like Camtasia and broadcasts a live stream video to YouTube.

- Ovo Studios offers a "lab in a box" that includes screen and face recording plus logging capabilities.

Anticipating Complications

Even with access to commercial unmoderated platforms, a large budget, and a generous timeline, you'll likely encounter some foreseen and unforeseen challenges for both moderated and unmoderated benchmark studies. The following sections detail some challenges that we've experienced.

Authentication problems

When benchmarking web apps, websites, or software that requires users to login or create an account, it can be difficult to use the standard features of unmoderated software. For example, we conducted a competitive benchmark for an email editing platform. Participants were asked to create a login and generate an email newsletter. The tasks were broken down into small steps (e.g., adding an image, link, or contacts) so we could more precisely measure and diagnose the usability of each task. Unfortunately, the task-based plug-ins of the unmoderated software would log participants out or reset their position in the flow. Our workaround was to have participants keep the study instructions available in a survey in the MUIQ platform while having them complete the tasks in a separate browser tab using the unmoderated software. Our advice is to pretest your setup and anticipate needing workarounds like the one we came up with.

Privacy concerns

Asking participants to log in, make a purchase, or use personally identifiable information (PII) can cause anxiety for them as well as for the company collecting the data. Whenever possible, try to avoid asking for PII. When you can't avoid it, such as when registration or purchasing are needed as tasks for a benchmark, find ways to not record or safeguard and destroy any compromising information. It reduces your liability and assuages concerns for your participants.

Making purchases

For websites that support ecommerce, a significant part of the experience is making purchases, such as groceries, airline tickets, hotels, or event tickets. Benchmarking the checkout experience often involves asking participants to make a purchase, which opens the door to complications around using PII and the logistics involved to reimburse people for making purchases. To avoid problems when benchmarking a checkout procedure, be sure participants know what will be expected (e.g., having a credit or debit card) and whether they can keep the items they purchased (more information on this subject later).

 TIP:

> When asking participants to login or make a purchase in unmoderated or moderated benchmarks, we disable recording devices to prevent recording PII, such as names and credit card information.

Multiple concurrences

One workaround to avoid using personally identifiable information is to use a dummy account (see Chapter 3 on defining the interface). However, for most systems, you can't have multiple participants accessing the account simultaneously, as in an unmoderated study. For example, in the benchmark we conducted for Constant Contact's email marketing platform, we had participants use their own accounts because creating a dummy account would mean some participants would be creating an email campaign while other participants would start the study with the email already created, which would not collect the appropriate benchmark data.

Benchmarking with credit cards and personal data

For many ecommerce websites, benchmarking the checkout experience is essential to understand an important part of the user experience. This needs to be balanced with a participant's reluctance to provide personal information, including their credit card. When we know we need to benchmark a checkout experience or have participants make purchases or register their personal information for moderated or unmoderated studies, we consider the following approaches: simulating purchases, actually making the purchase, or using a mockup or demo account.

Simulating purchases

You can choose one of two ways to simulate a purchase:

- **Have participants stop before the purchase.** If you're looking to benchmark the "cart" process of a website, ask participants to locate an item, add it to their cart, and complete the purchase stopping before they click "submit." Or, if you don't want them to complete the checkout form, you can have them stop at the "buy" button. This is by far the most common approach taken when benchmarking ecommerce websites. Note: If participants enter their own payment details, be prepared for some to accidentally click "buy" instead of stopping, so have ways of cancelling orders or reimbursing participants.

- **Use a fake confirmation screen.** Participants may be reluctant to provide personal information, even if it isn't being submitted. The more personal, the more reluctant participants become— from names and addresses to income, credit card numbers, drivers' licenses, and social security numbers. One way to offset this reluctance is to provide a fake credit card number or account details that will prevent participants from making the purchase but allows them to progress all the way through the checkout process.

 TIP:

> A commonly used test number for Visa cards is 4111 1111 1111 1111 which may work if you need to provide some value.

Making purchases

Sometimes you need to test the entire checkout experience, from finding to carting and then to checking out. This will allow you to examine confirmation screens and error messages. If you want participants to actually make a purchase, you'll first need to decide whether you'll want them to pick a product or if you're going to pick one for them at a set price. The route you choose depends on the scenario you're more interested in modeling and speaks to different stages of the customer journey (e.g., researching vs. ready to purchase). The following options can help guide the purchasing process:

- **Pick a product.** The advantages of picking a product are that you can validate whether participants select the right one, the browsing time is reduced, and you have more control over the budget. The major disadvantage is that you force participants to purchase a product they may not want. An additional factor to watch out for if you pick a specific product is that it may sell out. Even with 20 participants, products can sell out quickly and create inconsistent experiences.

- **Set a fixed price.** Participants in benchmark studies generally like being able to pick their own product, as it allows them to search for something they are interested in, creating a more natural checkout context. Things like colors, sizes, reviews, pictures, and search results all matter more when participants know they'll be receiving a product. The disadvantage is that we've found many participants will spend a lot of time browsing to find something they like.

- **Set a time limit.** What we've found that has helped with this issue is to let participants know they have a set time limit (say 10 minutes) or to instruct them ahead of time to think of a type of product to search for. While it may not be necessary to have a budget, especially if there are a limited number of products on the website, it's probably a good idea to keep budgets low and expectations set.

With either a fixed-price or fixed-product approach determined, you'll then want to decide if participants will use their own payment method or one you provide. Here are some tips to guide the decision:

- **Provide prepaid cards.** You can give participants the numbers of prepaid debit cards to use when they make a purchase. The major advantage is that participants don't have to provide their own information, and it will therefore be easier to recruit participants. You'll need to be sure you have enough money loaded on one card or multiple cards and that the bank security safeguards will allow multiple purchases to go through from the same website (often within minutes of each other).

  One unforeseen problem we had when using this approach was in one study, dozens of participants used the billing information from the prepaid card as the shipping information. The card issuer then received dozens of products! To avoid this problem, automatically provide the billing information, and then participants can ship the product to their houses or a friend's house.

- **Have participants purchase items and then reimburse.** While gift cards and prepaid debit cards will get users through the purchase process, it won't be as realistic as when participants use their own form of payment and billing information. Selecting payment methods (PayPal, credit, debit) and dealing with idiosyncratic shipping details are all common pain points in the checkout process. Asking participants to use their own payment method will make recruiting more difficult and costly, but we've done it several times and include the reimbursement as part of the honorarium. We've done this for both in-lab tests and unmoderated remote tests. It's easier to reassure people in person that you're not going to steal their information, so you'll need to add extra assurance when conducting an unmoderated study.

- **Cancel orders.** Instead of incurring the costs of reimbursing participants, you can cancel their orders if you have sufficient control over the inventory system or if you are able to cancel them manually from emails or confirmation numbers. This can be difficult to do, as most ecommerce websites have complex and quick automated fulfillment processes. When we tested rental car websites, we asked participants not to submit the reservation. Due to a massive usability problem, dozens of participants accidentally reserved a car. Because we had all participants use a fake email address, we were able to log in to the account and manually cancel the reservations.

- **Have a subset of the sample purchase.** A hybrid approach is often a good compromise for budgets and logistics. You can have a larger sample simulate the purchases and have a smaller sample (say 10 to 30 people) actually go through with the purchase. It's fewer people to recruit and requires a smaller budget for reimbursing. You can use the same metrics as the larger sample (time, completion rates, and perceived difficulty) then see if there are differences between simulated and actual purchasing. Our previous experiences with this approach indicate some measures remain consistent whereas others diverge. In one study, participants spent a lot more time browsing when they had to purchase a product versus locating one they didn't get to keep.

Using mockups and demos

Sometimes you can't use the live system because of security reasons, such as participants using their own bank or credit card accounts. In such cases you might consider mocking up part of system or the entire system or using a test or demo version.

- **Use a demo or test system.** For credit card systems, bank accounts, and other systems that require an account, there's often a demo or test version (as we discussed in Chapter 3 when defining the interface). Demos usually contain canned data, so there are limits on errors and some functionality, but it's surprising how even these fake systems provide valuable insights on the navigation, form fields, and flow. Test systems are often staging "sandboxes" for the developers to ensure fixes and features are working. Test systems usually allow participants to encounter real errors and messages, realistic load times, and full functionality with fake account credentials. Watch out for unanticipated downtime and bizarre errors—both of which are the price to pay for using the test environment.

- **Use a dummy account.** In both live systems and test systems there's often a dummy account that the developers create for testing. It can be either a dummy login or dummy credit card, which will simulate all functionality. If it allows for concurrent logins and access to full functionality, it becomes another alternative.

- **Mock up the whole flow.** If you need to test a competitor's system that requires an account and you can't have dozens of participants accessing simultaneously, you might consider mocking up a high-fidelity version using software like Axure or InVision. You can use screenshots as backgrounds and just enable form fields and navigation to get a good representation of the experience. Keep in mind that this approach won't simulate load times or error messages, which can have a significant impact on the user experience.

- **Mock up some screens.** Often mocking up just part of a task or set of screens will accomplish your goal for benchmarking. This may work if participants stop before purchasing and you want to test the confirmation screen. Split up the experience across tasks, have the participants pretend to make the purchase on one task, then show the mocked-up confirmation screen for the next task. You can also do this using prototyping systems, screenshots, or some simple HTML with hotspots.

DO-IT-YOURSELF VS. OUTSOURCING YOUR BENCHMARK

After you've decided to conduct a benchmark, you should consider whether to conduct it internally within a company or outsource all or part of the design, data collection, and analysis to an external firm—like MeasuringU. The following are major factors to consider when deciding which route to take.

- **Cost:** Outsourcing will cost more money for the professional services, access to expertise and software, and help with recruiting participants. (See the "Budgeting for Your Benchmark" section in this chapter.)

- **Time:** Having an external company conduct the benchmark usually means it will get done faster than doing it yourself. Internal teams can focus on interpretation and buy-in instead of dealing with the minutiae of unmoderated platforms, recruiting, and graph/PowerPoint manipulation.

- **Expertise:** Depending on the firm you hire, you should get access to a company that has experience conducting benchmarks for similar websites, products, and within and across industries.

- **Purchasing testing software and licenses:** External companies usually have invested in the infrastructure of testing and recruiting, which often means you don't have to commit to expensive software you may not use very often.

- **Recruiting and panel relationships:** Finding qualified participants remains one of the more challenging parts of benchmark studies (especially for hard to find profiles). External companies often have their own panel or existing relationships with vetted national panels and recruiting firms which will allow for faster and more targeted recruiting.

- **Product familiarity:** Even the most experienced third-party firm is unlikely to know as much about the product or website being tested compared to the internal product team.

- **Objectivity:** An external company isn't privy to all the internal debates detailing what's working and what's not. Being free from these political influences means the results are often seen more objectively by stakeholders.

- **Company and stakeholder buy-in:** There can be a negative attitude in some companies for externally conducted research. This "not invented here" attitude is the opposite problem of the benefit of objectivity.

Table 4.1 provides a summary of the pros and cons of conducting your own or outsourcing your benchmark.

Factor to Consider	Internal	Outsourced
Time	-	+
Cost	+	-
Expertise	-	+
Objectivity	-	+
Purchase testing platforms	-	+

Factor to Consider	Internal	Outsourced
Recruiting panel relationships	-	+
Product familiarity	+	-
Internal buy-in	+	-

TABLE 4.1: Factors to consider when deciding between outsourcing and an internal benchmark. Plus signs indicate an advantage, and minus signs indicate a disadvantage.

 TIP:

> Sometimes outsourcing part of a benchmark gets you the best of both worlds—less cost, some objectivity, faster time, and access to software with the buy-in.

HOW LONG DO BENCHMARK STUDIES TAKE?

In our experience *most* benchmarking studies last between 4 and 12 weeks. Few can be properly conducted quicker than 4 weeks, but some can take a lot longer than 12. At a minimum, it usually takes a week to plan the tasks, questions, and study details and to get buy-in from stakeholders.

Typical Phases and Durations

While it depends on the number of participants, complexity of the study script, and availability of the stakeholders, the following sections give an idea of the typical phases and timelines we see at MeasuringU. Keep in mind that by the time we're approached by clients, a lot of work has already been done on getting buy-in and ideas for the tasks and objectives have begun to be discussed.

Planning and study design

During this phase, the details in the booking document are refined (the competitors, type of tasks, participants, devices, and metrics). The study script is written from the booking document details. Task and question wording gets reviewed and refined with stakeholders. Then, for unmoderated benchmark studies, a researcher programs the platform that is going to be used.

Duration: 1 to 4 Weeks

Participant recruitment and data collection

Faster data collection comes from unmoderated benchmark studies with general consumer populations for relatively small sample sizes (<200 participants). In many cases the data can be collected in 1 to 2 days. However, it can take weeks to find qualified participants, such as harder to find participations (e.g., small business owners in Brazil) and larger sample sizes. You will need to build participant recruitment into the schedule for data collection.

For moderated benchmarks you'll have to plan for both recruiting time, which is usually 2 to 4 weeks, and facilitation time, which is usually 1 week for 20 participants to 6 to 10 weeks for 80 participants, for example.

Duration: 1 to 4 Weeks

Analysis

Once all the data is collected, it typically takes our team 1 to 2 weeks to have all the data analyzed and graphed and statistical calculations made. If lots of crosstabs are needed (e.g., task metrics by experience) or we need to review session recordings to validate task success or find root-causes of problems, it takes longer.

Duration: 1 to 4 Weeks

Presentation and road shows

Most benchmarking presentations contain a lot of metrics and details that describe the experience. This can often be overwhelming for product stakeholders who are less familiar with the intricacies of UX evaluation. You (or your agency) will need to create an executive, high-level presentation that may only contain key study or task metrics and core problems. Presenting the findings (often to multiple teams) means tweaking the information for each audience and working with the busy schedules of product owners and executives.

Duration: 1 to 4 Weeks

Planning table

As you can see, the quicker benchmarks can be accomplished around 4 weeks and the longer ones around 12 weeks. Table 4.2 is a checklist that will help you plan for what factors lead to longer benchmark studies. Start with a benchmark baseline of 4 weeks, and for each section you check, add another week.

For example, checking "Lots of script revisions" and "Hard to find/recruit participants" will add two weeks, so plan for 6 weeks total. Moderating participants will add a week for every 10 to 20 participant sessions.

Factor that increase duration	Add I week for each check
Lots of script revisions	
Busy stakeholders	
Lots of participants	
Hard to find/recruit participants	
International study	
Moderating study	
Analysis complexity	
Many types of presentations and revisions	

TABLE 4.2: Factors that increase the duration of a benchmark study.

TIP:

We've found the most common delays in benchmark studies are not usually finding participants or the analysis time, it's usually just the availability of stakeholders to answer questions about a product or website. The back and forth over emails and scheduling meetings with busy stakeholders adds anywhere from days to weeks to a benchmark study.

BUDGETING FOR YOUR BENCHMARK

All the good things in life are free...except benchmark studies, which do take time and money but are definitely good for measuring the user experience.

With the testing mode and the number and type of participants in mind, you can create a budget. If you are outsourcing your benchmark to a firm like MeasuringU, the bulk of the cost will be the professional service time needed to develop the study plan, to host/program a study and/or to facilitate the sessions, to analyze and compile the results, and to pay for participant recruiting and honorariums.

Fully outsourced benchmarks typically cost between $20K and $80K (U.S. dollars). A lower cost project, for example, would be for a 10- to 20-minute study on a single website on a desktop experience with generally easy to find and compensate participants (e.g., general consumers). A cross-platform (mobile + desktop) competitive benchmark in three countries will be closer to the $80K price point.

The major drivers are technology platform costs, participant recruitment/honorariums, and professional service costs for facilitation and analysis. Similar to the duration table, Table 4.3 shows the variables that tend to increase the cost. The more items you check, the more the cost.

Factor that increase cost	Increases cost
Platform technology licenses	
Competitive/comparative studies	
Mobile and desktop	
Large sample sizes	
Hard to find/recruit participants	
International study and translation	
Moderated study	
Analysis complexity	
Many presentation options and revisions	

TABLE 4.3: Factors that increase the costs in a benchmark study.

Unmoderated Technology Costs

For unmoderated studies a major cost to consider will be either the license fee to use a commercial platform or the cost of the service that includes the platform (as is the case with MUIQ). Prices will differ depending on the platform needed (desktop and/or mobile), sample sizes, and features. Many companies continue to bundle platform access, participants, and professional service costs.

Commercial platforms typically range from around $1,000 for a simple web-based-only study to $100K+ for a one-year license to conduct multiple studies on desktop and mobile devices, along with some participant and professional service and training costs. Table 4.4 provides some idea about the range of costs and comparisons for unmoderated platform options.

Platform	Cost	Features	Notes
SurveyMonkey/ Do-it-yourself	$	-	Limited to retrospective benchmarks or with simple task instructions (no metrics).
Loop11	$	-	Good for simple, low-cost studies (not much branching, logic, or customization) but doesn't work for all websites (may require JavaScript on a website).
MUIQ	$$	++	No license is required, includes service fees to program, host, and analyze.
UserTesting	$$$	+	Limited customization options and difficult to find specialized users. Panel of potential participants are well trained "professional users."

(continued on pg. 51)

Platform	Cost	Features	Notes
UserZoom	$$$	++	Fully featured but expensive and requires an annual license that starts at $50K.
Validately	$	-	Similar to UserTesting, but limited in the number of available questions and tasks.

TABLE 4.4: Unmoderated commercial platform comparison.

Moderated Technology Costs

For a moderated benchmark you may need to consider the costs of a facility location (if needed) and screen recording and logging software (both optional).

Facility/lab rental: A spare conference room can work for a low/no-cost option. A rented conference room or hotel room will work for a medium price option. A more premium option is a usability lab rental, which typically runs $1,000 to $3,000 a day for the room and the software needed for facilitating.

Screen recording and video editing software: These can be free (open-source options) to $1,500 a year for more sophisticated integrated recording and screen-sharing solutions like Morae.

Logging software: Free (for simple Excel workbooks) to $1,500 for Morae or more expensive integrated options from Ovo Studios ($5K+).

Participant and Recruiting Costs

The cost of finding and paying people to participate in your benchmark study can range from a trivial cost to a substantial one. The cost depends on how hard it is to find the participants, how much you need to pay (the honorarium), and how many you need. For most benchmarking studies, the participant costs range from $2,000 to $20,000.

Unmoderated recruitment costs

For unmoderated studies in which you need dozens to thousands of participants, you'll need to consider many sources and the first is probably the help of an online panel.

Online panels: There are dozens of companies that provide participants willing to take online surveys and, by extension, participate in unmoderated benchmarking studies. The cost per participant will range from between $5 and $10 for a general consumer profile in the US to higher for targeted groups (e.g., income > $75K), and go up substantially to $40 to $100 for more difficult to find groups (called low incidence rate or IR), such as financial advisors, physicians, IT decision makers, or small business owners. Many participant panels also have a minimum project amount (usually $1,500) and may charge a project management or setup fee.

International studies also increase cost and have limited availability. We work with Op4G (Opinions 4 Good) regularly and have also used Toluna and Harris Interactive as panels. Amazon's Mechanical Turk and SurveyMonkey's survey platform can be good do-it-yourself options for general consumers (if you're OK with dealing with some technical components yourself). Look to get multiple quotes, as cost will vary with some panels being able to fill harder to find profiles. For example, we conducted an international study on Android phones in the US, Thailand, the Philippines, and Egypt. The price ranges we received for these countries ranged by an order of magnitude; some quotes we received for the same country were $25 to $75 per participant. (See Chapter 9 for more on using online panels.)

Internal lists: Using customer lists can be less expensive than online panels, but you are by definition using only existing customers who have opted in to be contacted (hopefully!). This means they'll likely be less objective for competitive benchmark studies. You'll need to be careful about depleting this sample—you don't want to over-survey your customers. You can pay participants directly using digital gift cards (typically $20 to $50 for online studies) or set up a lottery, for example, to give away two iPads.

Advertising: You can post ads to Facebook or Google Ads to recruit participants. You'll have to pay a cost per click and either pay each participant or pay for the cost of a raffle/giveaway.

Bulk mail costs: If you are looking to email your customers directly, you'll need to have a bulk mail provider do the mailing or your email address and even domain will get blacklisted by Internet service providers (ISPs). Bulk email providers like Decipher (now part of FocusVision), MailChimp, and Constant Contact have relationships with ISPs to ensure your message isn't marked as spam (and they will ensure you aren't a spammer too!). The cost varies depending on the size of the list, but we often spend $1,500 to $3,000 mailing 5,000 to 50,000 customers to ask for their participation. There is usually a project management cost, a cost per email address, and a cost per delivered email.

Moderated recruitment costs

For moderated studies you can pull from existing customer lists, advertisements, or use the help of a professional recruitment firm.

Internal lists: As with unmoderated studies you can ask people who have opted in to a customer panel or list to participate for the more involved moderated studies. You should plan on paying participants between $50 and $200 for an hour or so of their time (in person or remote).

Advertising: You can post ads on Craigslist, Facebook, Google, or other platforms to attract qualified participants. This will take a budget for advertising costs (usually a few hundred dollars) and a lot of time screening for qualified participants (often days to 2 weeks).

Professional recruiting: Companies like Plaza Research and Fieldwork will find participants for in-person studies in most major cities in the US and for many international locations too. They tend to charge between $100 and $300 to find each qualified participant and charge a project management fee. The more you need, the quicker you need them, and the harder to find the participants, the more you should budget. For a moderated benchmark with 20 participants with some qualifications (e.g., "work for a large company"), you should expect to pay between $12K and $15K for recruitment costs and honorariums (usually cash or check).

Professional Services Costs

When outsourcing your benchmark study, the biggest cost will be paying for other professionals (ideally experts) to assist. This will involve aspects of design, collecting the data, and analysis.

The design phase involves writing the study script and working through details of tasks, metrics, and wording. For collecting the data, you need to manage online panels for unmoderated benchmarks or to recruit and facilitate sessions for a moderated benchmark. For the analysis portion, you will need to prepare your data for presentation (see Chapter 10), run the appropriate statistical analyses (Chapter 11), and then interpret the findings for the stakeholders.

Costs for each phase can range from $10K to $20K. It takes careful planning to have a third party manage part of a benchmark study. Outsourcing the analysis can be easier because the data has been collected, whereas outsourcing the collection in a moderated study represents the bulk of the work and can be the most difficult and expensive to outsource.

CHAPTER SUMMARY AND TAKEAWAYS

In this chapter, I addressed many of the logistical issues of how, how much, and how long questions that typically come up when planning a benchmark study:

- Decide if you need a commercial unmoderated platform or if you can use a do-it-yourself (internal) solution (which comes with limited features). A good unmoderated benchmark platform should support task-based questions, branching and logic, session recording, mobile and desktop support, and screen outs and quotas.

- Determine the type of screen-sharing software (e.g., GoToMeeting) that should be used for a remote moderated benchmark study. A software that also records screens is beneficial too.

- Consider using a screen recording software for moderated studies. Moderated benchmark studies aren't as reliant on technology as unmoderated or remote benchmark studies, but software such as Morae or OBS Studio provide screen recording and help with metric collection.

- Anticipate complications. All benchmark studies come with technical complications, such as authentication issues or privacy concerns. These can be made more challenging when participants need to login or make a purchase.

- Consider whether to conduct a benchmark yourself or outsource all or part of it to a third party. Outsourcing usually costs more but can usually be done quicker and with expertise. Some third parties have access to their own software, meaning it may be cheaper to hire a third party with their software instead of purchasing a software license.

- Establish a timeline. Most benchmark studies take between 4 and 12 weeks to complete. Often the biggest delay is the availability of stakeholders to answer questions about a product or website.

- Calculate the costs. Fully outsourced benchmarks typically cost between $20K and $80K (U.S. dollars). The major drivers are technology platform costs, participant recruitment/honorariums, and professional service costs for facilitation and analysis.

CHAPTER 5:
BENCHMARK METRICS

In this chapter I provide more detail on many of the metrics used at a study and task level for benchmarks.

STUDY METRICS

For both retrospective and task-based benchmarks you'll need core study-level metrics. These metrics are typically collected at the end and/or beginning of a study. The most common study metrics are the SUS, SUPR-Q, and NPS. Additional metrics may include ratings about the quality of the content or features or customer reviews. The following sections provide more details about popular study-level metrics.

The System Usability Scale (SUS)

The SUS is the most commonly used measure of perceived usability. It's a 10-item questionnaire originally developed in 1986 (and published in 1996 by John Brooke: "SUS: A Quick and Dirty Usability Scale" in *Usability Evaluation in Industry*). It was originally created as a "quick and dirty" scale for administering after usability tests on systems.

The SUS is technology independent and has since been tested on hardware, consumer software, websites, cell-phones, IVRs, the yellow-pages, and even a pair of scissors. It has become an industry standard, with references in over 1,200 publications ("SUS: A Retrospective" by Brooke, 2013), and has accounted for 43% of post-test questionnaires since 2009 ("Correlations among Prototypical Usability Metrics: Evidence for the Construct of Usability" by Sauro and Lewis, 2009). We use the SUS in our regular retrospective benchmarks for business and consumer software. To view our reports, please see measuringu.com/b2c-ux2017/.

The following are the SUS's 10 items along with its 5-point response options as shown in Figure 5-1.

1. I think that I would like to use this system frequently.
2. I found the system unnecessarily complex.
3. I thought the system was easy to use.
4. I think that I would need the support of a technical person to be able to use this system.
5. I found the various functions in this system were well integrated.
6. I thought there was too much inconsistency in this system.
7. I would imagine that most people would learn to use this system very quickly.
8. I found the system very cumbersome to use.
9. I felt very confident using the system.
10. I needed to learn a lot of things before I could get going with this system.

Strongly Disagree 1	2	3	4	Strongly Agree 5
○	○	○	○	○

FIGURE 5.1: SUS response format.

Use the following information to score the SUS:

- For odd items, subtract one from the user response.
- For even-numbered items, subtract the user responses from 5.
- This scales all values from 0 to 4 (with 4 being the most positive response).
- Add up the converted responses for each user and multiply that total by 2.5. This converts the range of possible values from 0 to 100 instead of from 0 to 40.

The raw scores themselves can then be converted into percentile ranks and even interpreted with a letter grade, from A to F. Table 5.1 shows the raw scores to percentile ranks and corresponding grades.

SUS score range	Grade	Percentile range
84.1 – 100	A+	96 – 100
80.8 – 84.0	A	90 – 95
78.9 – 80.7	A-	85 – 89
77.2 – 78.8	B+	80 – 84
74.1 – 77.1	B	70 – 79
72.6 – 74.0	B-	65 – 69
71.1 – 72.5	C+	60 – 64
65.0 – 71.0	C	41 – 59
62.7 – 64.9	C-	35 – 40
51.7 – 62.6	D	15 – 34
0.0 – 51.6	F	0 – 14

TABLE 5.1: SUS score to grade and percentile rank.

More details on using the SUS are available in *A Practical Guide to the System Usability Scale: Background, Benchmarks & Best Practices* (Sauro, 2011) and *Quantifying the User Experience: Practical Statistics for User Research, 2nd Edition* (Sauro and Lewis, 2016).

Standardized User Experience Percentile Rank-Questionnaire (SUPR-Q)

When I started systematically measuring website usability over 10 years ago, I started with the SUS as a key metric. However, after observing enough website interactions and hearing the problems and concerns participants had, it became clear that the website user experience was more than just the narrow construct of usability addressed by the SUS.

Usability is, of course, a critical part of the website user experience. If participants can't complete their goals on a website, they can quickly find an alternative. But I needed a questionnaire to address the broader attitudes that affect the quality of the website user experience while keeping it to as few items as possible. The result is the Standardized User Experience Percentile Rank-Questionnaire (SUPR-Q), an 8-item psychometrically validated questionnaire specifically designed to measure the quality of the website user experience.

In addition to a global UX score, it includes the following four subscale scores:

Usability

1. This website is easy to use.
2. It is easy to navigate within the website.

Credibility/Trust

1. The information on the website is credible.
2. The information on the website is trustworthy.

Loyalty

1. How likely are you to recommend this website to a friend or colleague?
2. I will likely visit this website in the future.

Appearance:

1. I found the website to be attractive.
2. The website has a clean and simple presentation.

There are five response options for seven of the items. You can randomize the order of the responses as long as you keep track of the item number when scoring the responses. In Figure 5.2, Amazon is used as an example website; substitute the name of your website when using the SUPR-Q.

Please rate your level of agreement to the following statements about the Amazon website.

	Strongly Disagree 1	2	3	4	Strongly Agree 5
I will likely return to the Amazon website in the future.	○	○	○	○	○
It is easy to navigate within the Amazon website.	○	○	○	○	○
The information on the Amazon website is credible.	○	○	○	○	○
I find the Amazon website to be attractive.	○	○	○	○	○
The information on the Amazon website is trustworthy.	○	○	○	○	○
The Amazon website has a clean and simple presentation.	○	○	○	○	○
The Amazon website is easy to use.	○	○	○	○	○

FIGURE 5.2: SUPR-Q response format.

Not at all Likely 0	1	2	3	4	Neutral 5	6	7	8	9	Extremely Likely 10
○	○	○	○	○	○	○	○	○	○	○

FIGURE 5.3: NPS response format.

The item "How likely are you to recommend this website to a friend or colleague?" has 11 response options and can be displayed like the example shown in Figure 5.3. The option scale needs to start with a 0 and end with a 10 and have both end-points and the middle option labeled. This is the question you need to also generate the commonly used Net Promoter Score.

One of the main advantages of the SUPR-Q is it has a curated database of 150+ websites. The raw SUPR-Q scores are then re-scaled relative to this "normed" database, and scores are expressed as percentile ranks from 1% to 99%. So, an average score has a percentile rank of 50%, meaning half the websites score above and below this point. A score below the 50th percentile would be below average. A SUPR-Q score of 75% means the website is scoring above average (higher than 75% of scores in the database). The SUPR-Q is a licensed questionnaire with the licensing fees funding quarterly updates.

Why I recommend the SUPR-Q over the SUS for website benchmarks

If your organization uses the SUS, there's no reason to immediately ditch it. But when you are measuring the website user experience, the SUPR-Q is likely a better alternative for the four reasons discussed in the following sections.

The SUPR-Q measures more than usability

Measuring the user experience of websites is more than just asking about perceptions of usability. Users that don't trust a website (the brand, the information, the payment system, how their data is used) tend not to purchase, return, or recommend. What's more, the appearance of the website also affects attitudes towards the brand and even attitudes toward usability itself. The SUPR-Q captures these sentiments of trust and appearance in separate factors, which helps you understand how these factors affect purchase intent and likelihood to return and recommend.

A normalized score is more meaningful

One of the main advantages of using the SUPR-Q is that it has a normalized (also called standardized) reference database of 150 websites: The S in SUPR-Q stands for standardized. This normalized database shows how a raw SUPR-Q score compares to others for both the overall score and the sub-factors of usability, appearance, trust, and loyalty. The scores in the database are updated quarterly and include some of the most common websites to provide familiar reference points to stakeholders. Maintaining regular updates means the SUPR-Q database isn't free like the SUS, but we think the timely and relevant benchmarks justify that cost.

While the SUS has a reference database (I helped put it together), its 500 scores include a mix of physical products and software, and not just websites—making the benchmark less relevant. The best benchmarks are those that are tailored specifically for the domain or type of interface.

You get more with fewer items

Not only does the SUPR-Q measure more than the SUS, it does so with fewer items. Participants' time is scarce. We need participants to spend as much time interacting with interfaces as possible and less time answering redundant items. While some redundancy is good in a questionnaire, there is a diminishing return. When developing the SUPR-Q, we winnowed down the items to just two essential items for each factor (eight items overall). Two items are the minimum number you need to analyze a factor structure using factor analysis.

The SUS's 10 items were intended to measure only the single construct of usability. And it does this well. In both its original research and follow-up research, the SUS, despite being shorter than other questionnaires (like the SUMI and PSSUQ), was found to be reliable (consistent responses) and valid (usable products had higher SUS scores than unusable products). But even at 10 items, there's a fair amount of redundancy and an opportunity to reduce the number of items.

There is a price to pay, albeit a small one, for using fewer items for both usability and the user experience. The overall SUPR-Q score and usability scores tend to have slightly lower reliability scores than the SUS (.86 and .88, respectively). The SUS typically has a high reliability score (a Cronbach alpha of around .90 to .91). But the slight reduction in reliability is a small price to pay for needing only 20% of the items when measuring perceived usability and measuring more constructs with fewer items.

You can predict SUS scores from the SUPR-Q

The two-item usability subscale on the SUPR-Q can predict SUS scores quite accurately because they are highly correlated ($r = .87$). We wanted to retain as much continuity to existing SUS data, so when we created the SUPR-Q, we made sure that the usability factor correlated highly.

For example, we collected SUPR-Q data for a retail benchmark comparison study using the two-item usability questions. Our SUPR-Q results showed a correlation to the SUS scores: Amazon had a SUPR-Q usability score in the 98th percentile (better than 98% of websites) and a SUS equivalent score of 85. A SUS score of 85 places Amazon in the 97th percentile relative to 500 other interfaces, showing the two items on the SUPR-Q have strong agreement with the 10-item SUS.

In the same benchmark study, Best Buy and Nordstrom had SUS equivalent scores of 77, derived from SUPR-Q usability scores at the 72nd percentile (also showing the close agreement). The difference in percentile ranks reflects the different reference databases—the SUS scores are compared to all types of products, whereas the SUPR-Q scores are compared to only websites. The linkage between the SUS and SUPR-Q allows teams to easily transition from the SUS to the SUPR-Q, as I did years ago.

Net Promoter Score (NPS)

The NPS is a popular (some would say notorious) measure of customer loyalty. Increasingly companies are adopting the NPS as *the* corporate metric. In many organizations, all metrics and activities (including user experience metrics) tend to revolve around the NPS, which may or may not be a misguided tendency.

The NPS is based on a single question: How likely is it that you'll recommend this [product or service] to a friend or colleague? The response options range from 0 (Not at all likely) to 10 (Extremely likely). Responses are then collected into the following segments.

Promoters: Responses from 9 to 10

Passives: Responses from 7 to 8

Detractors: Responses from 0 to 6

FIGURE 5.4: The likelihood-to-recommend question used to compute the Net Promoter Score.

Subtracting the proportion of detractors from the proportion of promoters and converting it to a percent gets you the Net Promoter Score. For example, 100 promoters, 30 passives and 80 detractors, gets you a Net Promoter Score (NPS) of 9.5% (20 divided by 210). This means there are 9.5% more promoters than detractors. An NPS of -10% means you have 10% more detractors than promoters.

> NOTE: Our friends at Satmetrix want us to remind you that Net Promoter and Net Promoter Score (NPS) are trademarks of Satmetrix Systems, Inc., Bain & Company, and Fred Reichheld.

Fred Reichheld, in his 2011 book *The Ultimate Question 2.0: How Net Promoter Companies Thrive in a Customer-Driven World* (p. 28), pointed out that this likelihood-to-recommend question was the best or second-best predictor of repeat purchases or referrals in 11 out of 14 industries (79%). However, I would say that despite the popularity and enthusiasm for the NPS being the "ultimate" question, there might be better questions for your company or industry. There are many measures of customer satisfaction and customer loyalty, for example, the likelihood to revisit, repurchase, or reuse—these might be better indicators of customer loyalty for your product or industry.

Because the NPS—the likelihood-to-recommend item—continues to be popular, we felt that it should be included in the SUPR-Q (in the loyalty subscale) and in our software and website benchmark reports.

Satisfaction

By far the most common and fundamental measure of customer attitudes is customer satisfaction. Customer satisfaction is a measure of how well a product or website experience meets customer expectations. It's a staple of customer analytic scorecards as a barometer of how well a product or company is performing.

You can measure satisfaction on everything from a brand, a product, a feature, a website, or a service experience. While measuring customer satisfaction alone isn't going to do much, it's an essential metric to collect when you want to gauge your customers' sentiments and prioritize around what's working and not working. Many companies still use customer satisfaction as a Key Performance Indicator (KPI), and we'll often include it in our benchmark studies (especially for product experiences).

In general, you should measure two levels of customer satisfaction: general (or relational) satisfaction and a more specific attribute (or transactional) satisfaction.

General satisfaction

Asking customers about their satisfaction toward a brand or organization is the broadest measure of customer satisfaction. It's often referred to as a relational measure because it speaks to a customer's overall relationship with a brand. It encompasses repeated exposure, experiences, and often repeat purchases.

To measure general satisfaction, ask customers to rate how satisfied they are with a brand or company using a rating scale. Figure 5.5 shows an example of a satisfaction question where participants were asked to rate their level of satisfaction with a company on a 7 point scale.

FIGURE 5.5: Satisfaction question example and response format.

Because customer satisfaction is such a fundamental measure for gauging your company's performance with your customers, a number of firms offer a standardized set of satisfaction questionnaires and reports to allow you to compare your satisfaction scores with your competitors and industry.

One of the most common industry surveys of general satisfaction (at a company level) is the American Customer Satisfaction Index (ACSI). The ACSI uses a standard set of questions to survey thousands of U.S. customers each year on products and services they've used. They provide a series of benchmark reports across dozens of industries, including computer hardware, hotels, manufacturing, pet food, and life insurance to name a few.

The ACSI provides benchmark reports that allow you to see how satisfied U.S. customers are with your company. In some cases, the satisfaction benchmarks are also provided at a more specific product level. In most cases you'll want to collect your own data, but where possible, look at the index for your industry, product, or service. Because the data in the ACSI reports have been vetted for reliability, this index provides you with valuable data that you can use to compare your results from your own studies to these validated, available reports.

Attribute and product satisfaction

While customer satisfaction provides a broad view of a customer's attitude, you'll also want to find out whether your website or product is or is not exceeding expectations.

To generate more specific and diagnostic measures of customer attitudes, ask about the satisfaction with features or more specific parts of an experience—usually of a website or product. This is often referred to as attribute or transaction satisfaction because customers are rating attributes (features, quality, ease of use, price) of a product or they are rating the most recent transaction. Examples of attribute satisfaction include the following:

- Check-in experience
- Registering a product
- Download speed
- Price
- Product (for brands with multiple products)
- The website
- In-store experience
- The online checkout process

To measure attribute satisfaction, use the same type of scale and question(s) as you used to measure general satisfaction, but direct respondents to reflect on the specific attribute you're interested in (e.g., the check-in experience, the search results page, the download speed).

In addition to collecting closed-ended rating-scale data from customers, offer a space for them to add a comment about their attitudes. You can use these comments to help understand what's driving high or low ratings. You can even turn these comments into quantifiable data. See the "Understanding the 'Why' Behind the Metrics" section in Chapter 11 for more information.

Brand Attitudes

Two important pieces of data you can collect about a brand are people's attitudes about and satisfaction with a product or service. Although there is a slight difference between the two, they are both highly related and both tend to predict customer loyalty. Here's how to remember the difference: Potential customers have an attitude toward a brand or product they've never used, and actual customers rate their satisfaction after having experienced a brand or product.

For example, customers can rate their opinion toward Apple before ever being a customer (attitude), their level of satisfaction with Apple after making a purchase (general satisfaction), their satisfaction with iTunes (product satisfaction), and with synching iTunes with their iPhone (attribute satisfaction).

If you're interested in the beliefs, ideas, and opinions of prospective customers, you have to measure attitudes. For example, in our competitive benchmark of two rental car websites, participants were asked about their attitudes toward the most common U.S. rental car companies.

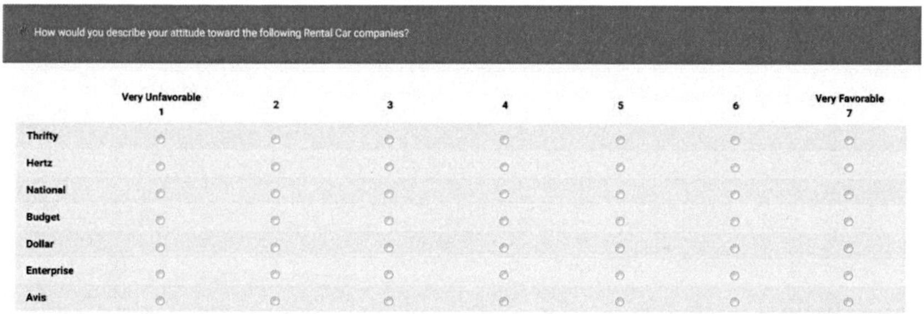

FIGURE 5.6: Example question for assessing brand favorability (for rental car companies).

One benefit of asking customer attitudes at the beginning of a survey is that you can screen out participants who have a very strong negative attitude toward your brand. While you don't want to ignore these customers—in fact, you'll want to follow up with them in the future—in most cases, you want to hear from prospective customers who are at least willing to use your product or service in the near-term.

Brand Lift

Customer attitudes shift based on product and website experiences. One way to understand how particular experiences impact attitudes is to measure lift.

Lift is the general name used to describe the difference between attitudes before and attitudes after some stimulus. Lift can be both positive (an improved attitude) or negative (a reduced attitude, often referred to as brand drag).

Brand lift is one of the more common lift measures, but almost any attitude can be measured: satisfaction, perception of usability, attractiveness, likelihood to recommend, and likelihood to purchase, to name a few. See the "Understanding Brand Lift and Drag" section in Chapter 11 for more detail on computing brand lift.

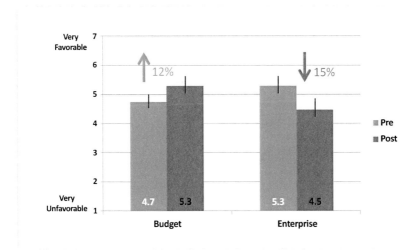

FIGURE 5.7: Example of brand lift and drag from a survey for car rental companies.

Usability Metric for User Experience (UMUX)-LITE

Despite being short—10 items—the SUS has a fair amount of redundancy, given it only measures one construct (perceived usability). While some redundancy is good to improve reliability, shorter questionnaires are preferred when time in a usability study is limited or when a measure of usability is needed as part of a larger survey (which may already be too long).

In response to the need for a shorter questionnaire that produced SUS-like scores, Kraig Finstad introduced the four-item Usability Metric for User Experience (UMUX) in 2010. Other researchers modified the UMUX to a condensed version using a two-item questionnaire. This is called the UMUX-LITE. The following are the two-items in the questionnaire; both items have a 5-point and 7-point response option variation:

- [This system's] capabilities meet my requirements.
- [This system] is easy to use.

Across multiple studies the UMUX-LITE has been found to be highly correlated with the SUS, often explaining over 85% of the variance. In many cases there is only a 1% difference in SUS scores when using the two-item UMUX-LITE instead of the full 10-item SUS. The UMUX-LITE may be a viable substitute for the SUS when brevity is a need.

To use the UMUX-LITE, administer it just like the SUS using a 5- or 7-point agree/disagree scale (we use the same 5-point scale as the SUS). We've found the UMUX-LITE particularly helpful for benchmarking many internal IT products—it's short and easily fits into surveys.

Standardized User Experience Percentile Rank-Questionnaire for mobile apps (SUPR-Qm)

The SUPR-Qm is a 16-item instrument that measures the perception of the mobile app user experience. As its name (and logo) suggest, it is an extension of the SUPR-Q introduced earlier.

We started with the SUPR-Q as a measure of the user experience for websites but immediately knew a new reference database would be needed for mobile apps instead of desktop websites. We also wanted to verify that the subconstructs of usability, appearance, trust, and loyalty were the differentiating factors for mobile apps. This was particularly challenging because of the variety of apps available in the Apple and Google stores (gaming, social media, and productivity apps). For example, a particularly delightful and satisfying gaming app that outperforms competitors on meaningful metrics, like number of unique downloads, may have very different characteristics than a similarly satisfying and successful mobile banking app. Perhaps for this reason, measures of the mobile app experience are often domain specific.

Like the SUPR-Q and UMUX, we wanted a short questionnaire, as participants would likely be taking the questionnaires on their mobile devices. However, instruments like the SUS and UMUX focus on a narrower definition of perceived usability, and the UMUX-LITE seems more relevant to productivity apps.

While these domain-specific metrics are useful, a common instrument would allow developers the ability to compare the mobile app user experience across domains. Thus far, mobile phone user experience measures have focused on relatively high-level constructs such as ease of learning, efficiency, emotional responses, and memory load. The following are the 16 items in the SUPR-Qm (only a subset, usually 4 to 6 are needed when administered using an adaptive questionnaire (available in the MUIQ platform).

1. I can't live without the app on my phone.
2. The app is the best app I've ever used.
3. I can't imagine a better app than this one.
4. I would never delete the app.
5. Everyone should have the app.
6. I like discovering new features on the app.
7. The app has all the features and functions you could ever want.
8. I like to use the app frequently.
9. The app is delightful.
10. This app integrates well with the other features of my mobile phone.
11. I will definitely use this app many times in the future.
12. The design of this app makes it easy for me to find the information I'm looking for.
13. I find the app to be attractive.
14. The app's capabilities meet my requirements.
15. It is easy to navigate within the app.
16. The app is easy to use.

While the SUS, SUPR-Q, and all UX and usability questionnaires have been developed using a technique called classical test theory (CTT), the SUPR-Qm was developed using a more recent and advanced technique called item response theory (IRT). Whereas CTT tends to identify items that optimized around the average level of a construct like ease, IRT optimizes around a fuller range of the construct, from low to high, not just around the average (and is why only a subset are needed when administered adaptively).

IRT generally has two main advantages over CTT:

- It allows us to select items that cover a broader range of a construct (from low to high attitudes around a user experience, for example).
- We can use the item information to create a "bank" of pre-calibrated items.

TIP:

See measuringu.com for more information on licensing and using the SUPR-Qm.

TASK METRICS

Studies with tasks should generally have a measure of effectiveness (usually task completion), efficiency (task time), and some perception of the experience (a post-task questionnaire).

Task Completion Rate

Completion rates are the fundamental usability metric. If participants can't achieve their intended goals, not much else matters. For each task you should define the task success criteria (see the "Writing Task Scenarios" section in Chapter 7 for more information). Task completion should be coded as a binary measure:

- Code a 1 if participants meet the success criteria.
- Code a 0 if participants fail to meet the success criteria.

Task Time

Task times are the quintessential measure of efficiency. Long or highly variable tasks times are often symptoms of interaction problems with an interface. Task time is an ideal metric for benchmarking studies, as it is sensitive to more subtle changes in an interface. Consequently, you often need smaller sample sizes to show statistical improvements over time (see Chapter 6 for more on sample sizes).

There are typically three ways to report task time data in benchmark studies:

- Average task completion time: This is the median time from participants who completed the task.

- Average time on task/engagement: This is the median time from all participants (those who succeeded and failed a task). This can provide an overall time it took to complete the task.

- Average time till failure: This is the median time of participants who failed a task. This can help the researcher understand how long participants spend trying to accomplish their tasks before failing.

We typically report the average task completion time for benchmark studies (see Chapter 10 for more information on reporting task-time data).

Task Ease

You'll want to measure a participant's attitude toward the experience immediately after the task. We've examined a number of questionnaires over the years and found a single item question works about as well or better than longer and more sophisticated ones (see "Comparison of Three One-Question, Post-Task Usability Questionnaires" by Sauro and Dumas, 2009).

The one item questionnaire is aptly named the Single Ease Question (SEQ). It has a 7-point rating scale to assess how difficult users find a task and is administered immediately after a user attempts a task. (as shown in Figure 5.8).

FIGURE 5.8: Response format for the Single Ease Question (SEQ).

 TIP:

Keep the SEQ in this format so you can compare your SEQ score to its global average, which is around 5.1. See the "Post-task ease" section in Chapter 10 for analyzing the SEQ.

Single Usability Metric (SUM)

Post-task metrics of completion rates, time, and perceived ease tend to correlate with each other. That is, participants who complete a task and complete it quicker tend to find the task easier. Aggregating these metrics into a composite score can provide a good overall measure of the task experience for dashboards or when you need a summary of effectiveness, efficiency, and satisfaction. This is an aggregation of existing metrics, so no additional items are needed to present to participants. See the "Summarize the data to a Single Usability Metric" section in Chapter 10 for more information.

ADDITIONAL TASK LEVEL METRICS

While you don't want to bog down participants with too many items to respond to after each task, there are additional metrics that can help describe the task experience.

Confidence

Even if users are completing tasks or finding items in a navigation structure correctly, it doesn't mean they are 100 percent sure that what they did was correct. Asking participants to rate how confident they are that they completed a task successfully provides another measure to diagnosing potential interaction problems. It can also serve as a benchmark between competitors, alternate designs, or between tasks. To get a reading for a participant's task confidence, we use a 7-point rating scale like the SEQ.

FIGURE 5.9: Response format for asking about confidence.

Understanding how confident users are that they completed a task is one of many ways of diagnosing interaction problems and providing a benchmark for comparisons between tasks or versions. (Note: This measure of confidence is different than a confidence interval, which is a statistical procedure to put the most plausible range around a sample mean or proportion)

Disasters

Completion rates are the gateway metric. If users can't complete tasks on a website, not much else matters. The only thing worse than participants failing a task is participants failing a task and thinking they've completed it successfully. This is called a disaster. The term was made popular by Gerry McGovern and is discussed in his book *The Stranger's Long Neck: How to Deliver What Your Customers Really Want Online* (2010). Disasters are anathema to websites and software.

The most effective way of measuring disasters is to collect binary completion rates (pass and fail) and ask users how confident they were they completed the task successfully. We use the confidence scale shown above, but you could use a 5-, 9-, or 11-point scale too.

Disasters are when users fail the task and yet report they are extremely confident they completed it successfully (e.g.,7's on a 7-point scale). See the "Additional task metrics" section in Chapter 10 for more on reporting disasters.

Open-Ended

While not a metric per-se, after each task we have participants briefly describe the task experience with a question: "Briefly describe why you chose the number you did." This type of information can be used to provide details that stakeholders may not have even been aware of. See the "Verbatim Analysis" section in Chapter 11 for more information on analyzing these comments.

Task Specific Metrics

When you need to gather information about a specific task, such as measuring how satisfied a user is about the information on a product page, defining task specific metrics can be valuable. These task-specific metrics are a snapshot of how users perceive a product or web page. For example, if a task has participants working with the product-detail page (as part of the benchmark goals), you may want to include specific questions such as the following for these tasks:

- Rate the level of the detail of the search results page (7-point scale).

- How satisfied were you with the detail on the product page?

- What is your impression of the amount of time the task took (1 = much longer than I expected to 7 = much less time than I expected).

For a comprehensive view of UX metrics, see Tullis and Albert's *Measuring the User Experience* and Chapter 8 of my book with co-author Jim Lewis, *Quantifying the User Experience*.

EXAMPLES OF APPLYING THE METRICS

Here are examples of how these study-level metrics were incorporated in some MeasuringU benchmarking studies.

HOTEL EXAMPLE: STUDY LEVEL: SUPR-Q, NPS, BRAND ATTITUDE; TASK LEVEL: COMPLETION, TIME, EASE, AND CONFIDENCE

> **Rationale:** We used the SUPR-Q (which includes the NPS metric) as a measure of the quality of the website user experience. Brand attitude provided us with some idea about how brand attitude may increase or decrease the SUPR-Q scores.

ACCOUNTING SOFTWARE EXAMPLE: STUDY LEVEL: SUS, UMUX-LITE, AND NPS; TASK LEVEL: COMPLETION, TIME, EASE, CONFIDENCE, AND SUM.

> **Rationale:** The SUS is appropriate for software and allowed us to provide a relative comparison to the historical data. The company also used NPS and compared this NPS to their own data. UMUX-LITE was new to this client, but we showed them how it could be compared to our internal data set of 24 business and consumer products for both usability and usefulness.

CHAPTER SUMMARY AND TAKEAWAYS

In this chapter we covered benchmark metrics at the study level and the task level:

- Benchmark metrics are collected at the study level (collected once) or at the task level (collected for each task).
- The SUS, SUPR-Q, and NPS are the most common study level metrics for retrospective and task-based benchmarks.
- Other study level metrics include satisfaction, brand attitudes, and the SUPR-Qm (for mobile apps).

- The UMUX-LITE is a newer benchmark metric that can act as a substitute for the SUS, but it has only two items compared to the SUS's 10 items.

- The most common task-based metrics are completion rates, task time, task-ease, and an aggregated SUM.

CHAPTER 6:
SAMPLE SIZE PLANNING

One of the most common mistakes we see in benchmarking studies is using an insufficient sample size. Many practitioners are used to conducting smaller, more formative studies (find and fix studies) with 5 to 10 participants. Benchmarking studies, however, have a different goal than formative studies and therefore require a larger sample size and a different way of computing it.

DO YOU ONLY NEED 5 PARTICIPANTS?

It is true that with just five participants in a study, you will generally see most of the obvious issues and problems. More technically, if a problem exists in an interface and affects at least 31% of all the users, then if you test with five participants, you'll have an 85% chance of seeing this problem at least once. Benchmark studies however aren't primarily intended for uncovering problems, but rather for describing the experience using metrics. For these studies, you'll need a larger sample size.

For more background on when having five participants is and isn't sufficient in UX research, see "5 Reasons You Should and Should Not Test With 5 Users" (measuringu.com/five-for-five/), and for a thorough discussion on sample sizes estimation for problem discovery studies, see Chapter 7 in *Quantifying the User Experience, 2nd Edition* (Sauro and Lewis, 2016)

While there seems to be a lot of controversy and confusion around the right sample size (I get questions weekly on this topic), there are fortunately some generally scientific and straightforward answers for benchmarking studies.

To determine what sample size you need, you'll need to start with whether it is a stand-alone study or comparative study (which by now you should have defined). You can then use one of two sample size tables, Table 6.1 or Table 6.2, to determine the optimal sample size. More detail and precise calculations are available in Chapter 6 of *Quantifying the User Experience, 2nd Edition* (Sauro and Lewis, 2016). These tables provide a good approximation for almost all benchmarking studies and are what we use when scoping most benchmarking projects for clients.

Sample Size for Stand-Alone Studies

When conducting a stand-alone study, you are essentially using a sample of participants to make inferences about a larger population of users. As such, the sample size you need is a function of how precise you want to be. Your sample size is based on the desired margin of error. This is the same approach marketers or pollsters use when computing sample size requirements for their surveys.

There are four topics you need to consider:

- **The metric:** UX benchmark studies include a mix of discrete binary (success/fail) and more continuous measures (time and rating-scale questions). Discrete binary measures have less fidelity than continuous measures (it's all success or failure, nothing in between) and so require a larger sample size to achieve the same level of precision. That is why, unless completion rates will not be part of the study, we use the binary completion rate as the metric for determining the appropriate sample size.

- **The variability:** The more variable the thing you are measuring, the larger the sample size you need. For example, if people all generally rate an experience high on a 7-point scale, take around the same amount of time to complete a task, or most if not all complete the task, then each sample will have relatively consistent results. In contrast, if there are some very high and low responses on a 7-point scale, some very fast and slow times, and half the users complete the task and half fail, you have high variability and each sample will be less consistent. In our experience, most practitioners don't have an estimate of the variability for the task or study they are measuring (it's often their first measure). In such cases, you use the highest level of variability (a conservative approach) and use a 50% completion rate for the binary metric.

- **The level of confidence:** The outcome of your benchmark metrics will include a mean/percentage with a corresponding confidence interval (see the "Conducting Statistical Tests and Interpreting *P*-Values" section in Chapter 11). The result will be statements like "We are 95% confident that between 60% and 70% of users can complete the task." The 95% in that statement is the confidence level. The more confident you need to be, the higher the confidence level and therefore the larger the sample size needed to maintain the same level of precision. The confidence level is typically 90% or 95% but can be adjusted up or down.

- **The precision:** Of course, you'd like to have no uncertainty in your estimate (perfect precision), but that would require including every possible user in your benchmark. It's a waste of money and time. Like polls, instead of surveying everyone, you survey enough to get a reasonable level of precision to address your study goals. To know how precise you need to be, answer the question (or have your stakeholders answer the question): If we know 50% of participants completed the task, but that figure could fluctuate by 20% (so it could be as high as 70% or as low as 30%), is that precise enough? How about 50% +/- 10%, so the actual completion rate could fluctuate between 40% and 60%? The more precision you need, the larger the sample size, but there is a large diminishing return when you use too many participants. To cut your margin of error in half, you need to approximately quadruple the sample size. Table 6.1 shows this relationship.

Table 6.1 shows you the sample size needed for the specified level of precision for either 90% or 95% confidence intervals (see the "Conducting Statistical Tests and Interpreting *P*-Values" section in Chapter 11). This table makes two assumptions: The first is that the information in the table uses the binary metric (e.g., a completion rate), and the second is that the metric is at the highest level of variability—50%. This level of variability is the most conservative assumption but one that is generally recommended in the absence of other data.

This also greatly simplifies calculations. To use the table, perform the following steps:

1. Start with the desired margin of error on the left column (for example, 10%).

2. Find the sample size needed based on the level of confidence in the second (90% confidence level) or third columns (95% confidence level). For 90% confidence, the sample size needed is 65.

3. Interpret the findings. To be 90% confident that an observed completion rate of 50% won't fluctuate by more than 10%, you should plan on a sample size of 65.

Margin of error (+/-)	90% Confidence sample size	95% Confidence sample size
24%	10	13
20%	15	21
17%	21	30
15%	28	39
14%	32	46
13%	38	53
12%	45	63
11%	54	76
10%	65	93
9%	81	115
8%	103	147
7%	136	193
6%	186	263
5%	268	381
4%	421	597
3%	749	1,064

TABLE 6.1: Sample sizes for a stand-alone benchmark studies for 90% and 95% levels of confidence (using a binary completion rate at 50%).

Practice using the table

Here are three more examples to practice with this table. Remember, focus on the level of precision (the desired margin of error) and pick the confidence level (default to 90% unless stakes are high or conventions dictate otherwise—e.g., publications). The answers are at the end of the chapter.

- To be 95% confident, you've estimated completion rates to within +/-5%. What sample size should you plan for?

- If you only have the budget to moderate 20 participants, what level of precision can you expect at 90% confidence?

- What sample size should you plan for to have a margin of error of no greater than 15% (90% confidence)?

Sample Size for Comparison Studies (Within and Between)

We'll use a similar approach for computing sample sizes for comparison studies. Because we're dealing with two estimates (the definition of a comparative study), we have more variables to work with and consequently we'll need larger sample sizes. While most of the functions of a sample size is similar to stand-alone studies, for comparison studies you also have two more factors to keep in mind: statistical power and the decision to use either a between- or within-subjects approach. To accurately decide on a sample size for a comparative study, consider the following factors:

- **The metrics:** Just as with stand-alone studies, you work with the metric with the most variability—the discrete binary metric.

- **The variability (of both samples):** You can again assume the highest variability for both binary metrics is 50%.

- **Level of confidence:** Again, confidence levels typically default to 90% or 95%. However, in this case, do not compute a confidence interval; instead, determine if the difference observed is greater than random noise. To do this, conduct a statistical test; the outcome will be a p-value. The confidence levels of 90% and 95% correspond to what's called the alpha values of .10 and .05, which I cover in Chapter 11.

- **The detected difference:** Instead of the level of precision, what you're primarily interested in here is the size of the absolute difference you hope to detect (if one exists). This difference can be expressed as a percentage. For example, you may anticipate needing to detect a 10% difference in completion rates (e.g., Sample 1 = 50% and Sample 2 = 60%) or a 5% difference (Sample 1 = 50% and Sample 2 = 55%). As with the level of precision, the smaller the difference you hope to detect, the larger the sample size will need to be.

- **Statistical power:** This is the ability to detect a difference if one exists. It's like the confidence level, except it's for when you think there is no statistical difference. For example, when analyzing the data, in a statement like "The 12% difference in completion rates was not statistically significant, $p = .19$," your statistical power is how confident you can be that when you are saying there's no difference, there actually isn't a difference. Power is a complicated topic. See Chapter 6 in *Quantifying the User Experience, 2nd Edition* (Sauro and Lewis, 2016) for more background. Fortunately, we can use a conventional starting point and set the power to 80%, for example. Like a confidence level, we can adjust it up or down depending on how confident we need to be that when we see no difference, it's not just because our sample size is too low.

- **Within- vs. between-subjects approach:** The final variable to consider is whether you'll be using a within-subjects approach (same participants on both interfaces) or a between-subjects approach (different participants using different interfaces). You'll see from Table 6.2 that a within-subjects approach allows you to use much smaller sample sizes for the same percentage of difference to detect. In most cases, the sample size requirement for a between-subjects approach will be "at least four times larger than a within-subjects approach (which can vary considerably depending on the needs of your study)."

HAVE ENOUGH POWER

One of the biggest problems we see with comparative benchmark studies is insufficient sample sizes. More technically, this means a statistical power that is too low. It's a waste of money and effort to conduct a study knowing you have very little ability to differentiate real differences from random noise. Ensure you have enough statistical power before conducting your benchmark by using the tables in this chapter and by reviewing Chapter 11 on how to interpret statistical significance.

Table 6.2 shows the sample size needed for the specified level of precision for within- or between-subjects. These tables make three assumptions: The first is that they are using the binary metric for both samples (e.g., a completion rate). Second, the binary metrics are at the highest level of variability—50%. This is the most conservative assumption but one that is generally recommended in the absence of other data. Third, the tables use a 90% confidence level and 80% statistical power level.

Using a table also greatly simplifies the lookup process. For more precise calculations (including varying power, confidence intervals, and the variability of the metrics), see Chapter 6 in *Quantifying the User Experience, 2nd Edition* (Sauro and Lewis, 2016). To use the table, perform the following steps:

1. Start with the difference you want to detect between samples from the first column, for example, 10%.

2. Find the sample size needed based on whether it is a within-subjects sample (second column) or between-subjects sample (third column).

3. Interpret to be able to find a 10% difference (if one exists) as statistically significant between completion rates. Plan on a sample size of 115 for a within-subjects approach and a sample size of 614 for a between-subjects approach (307 for each interface).

Difference to detect 90% confidence and 80% power	Sample size within-subjects	Sample size between-subjects (each group)
50%	17	11
40%	20	17
30%	29	32
20%	50	75
12%	93	213
10%	115	307
9%	130	380
8%	148	481

(continued on pg. 84)

Difference to detect 90% confidence and 80% power	Sample size within-subjects	Sample size between-subjects (each group)
7%	171	629
6%	202	857
5%	246	1,234
4%	312	1,930
3%	421	3,433
2%	640	7,726
1%	1,297	30,911

TABLE 6.2: Sample sizes for comparison benchmark studies for within- and between-subjects study benchmarks (using 90% confidence and 80% power).

Practice using the table

Here are three more examples to practice with this table. Remember, focus on the level of precision (the desired margin of error) and pick the confidence level (default to 90% unless stakes are high or conventions dictate otherwise, e.g., scientific publication usually requires 95% confidence in reported outcomes). The answers are at the end of the chapter.

- What sample size would you need to detect a 5% difference between completion rates between two websites with the same participants attempting two tasks on both websites?

- What is the percentage of difference that you can detect if you only have budget and time to moderate 40 participants in a benchmark study?

- If you want to compare four websites with different participants assigned to each website, how many should you plan on testing to detect an 8% difference?

With information on how to compute sample sizes for stand-alone or comparison studies, here are two examples of how we calculated the sample sizes for these benchmark studies.

ACCOUNTING SOFTWARE EXAMPLE: 20 PARTICIPANTS, STAND-ALONE MODERATED BENCHMARK STUDY

> **Rationale:** For a moderated study, budget, time, and participant availability often dictate sample size. This gave us a level of precision of at least +/-17% at the 90% level of confidence for binary metrics and higher for SUS, NPS, and SEQ.

HOTEL EXAMPLE: 30 PARTICIPANTS, UNMODERATED COMPARATIVE BENCHMARK STUDY

> **Rationale:** This was an exploratory study. We wanted to look for large differences between the hotels and wanted to collect the data in 1 day.

 TIP:

> While this chapter has hopefully made clear that one sample size does not fit all, here are some minimum sample sizes guidelines for benchmark studies. For moderated benchmarks you'll want *at least* 20 participants, and for unmoderated studies, aim for *at least* 65. For comparison studies go for 100+ participants to have a decent chance of detecting medium to large differences in the metrics.

Sample Size for Comparing Against an Industry Benchmark

Even if you don't have a comparison website or product to use for your comparison benchmark study, there still can be value in comparing your stand-alone scores to an industry benchmark, such as a completion rate or SUS score. For example, some organizations we've worked with set a goal of having their internal systems achieve a SUS score of at least an 80 when compared to other similar systems that have publicly available data (which would put their system in the top 10%). In other cases, a company might want to show that a particular task has exceeded a minimum completion rate of 90%, for example, by comparing their stand-alone benchmark study to an industry benchmark.

The sample size that would enable you to accurately claim that a metric exceeds an industry benchmark is similar to the sample size needed for a comparison study. However, you won't have to consider the between- or within-subjects approach as it will only have one sample. When our team compares a stand-alone benchmark to an industry benchmark, I use both completion rates and the SUS for computing sample sizes. Consider the following points and use Table 6.3 for guidance when comparing your benchmark data to industry benchmarks:

- **The metrics:** Discrete binary metrics (completion rates) have the most variability and continuous metrics like the SUS have less (and require a smaller sample size).

- **The variability (only a single sample):** The highest variability for binary metrics is at 50%, so the closer a sample and benchmark are to 50%, the higher the sample size needed. For the SUS, we can use the historical standard deviation of 21 (on a 100-point scale). For more information on sample sizes and using the SUS as a benchmark, see my book *A Practical Guide to the System Usability Scale: Background, Benchmarks & Best Practices* (2011) for more on the historical standard deviation and using SUS as a benchmark.

- **Level of confidence:** Again, the typical default for confidence levels is 90% or 95%.

- **The detected difference:** Similar to comparison studies, specify the size of the absolute difference between your observed data and the benchmark. For data like the SUS, you can use points (e.g., 5-point difference). For completion rates, you can specify the percentage of difference (e.g., a 10% difference) and the benchmark (e.g., 75%). In other words, if you observe an 85% completion rate in the data, what sample size would you need to ensure at least 75% of *all* users can complete the task?

- **Statistical power:** This is the ability to detect a difference if one exists. It's like the confidence level, except it's for when you think there is no statistical difference. You can use the same conventions for comparison studies and set the power to 80%.

Table 6.3 shows the sample size needed for comparing an observed completion rate against a benchmark. This table uses a 90% confidence level and 80% power level to derive the needed sample sizes for three common benchmark thresholds: 50%, 75%, and 90%.

For more precise calculations see Chapter 6 in *Quantifying the User Experience, 2nd Edition* (Sauro and Lewis, 2016). To use the table, perform the following steps:

1. Start with the benchmark you want to achieve, for example, at least 50% of all users can complete a task.

2. Select a completion rate to target from your sample data to determine the needed sample size. For example, if your sample of participants achieves a 55% completion rate (a 5% difference from the benchmark of 50%), you would need a sample size of 450 to exceed the 50% benchmark with at least 90% confidence. If 85% of the participants completed a task and you wanted to exceed the benchmark of 75%, you should plan on a sample size of 72.

Sample completion rate	Benchmark		
	50%	75%	90%
	Sample size needed		
99%	3	7	23
95%	4	13	122
90%	6	28	
85%	8	72	
80%	11	314	
75%	17		
70%	27		
65%	49		
60%	112		
55%	450		

TABLE 6.3: Sample sizes needed for comparing an observed completion rate to a benchmark.

TIP:

The closer your sample estimate is to the benchmark, the greater the sample size must be to claim you have exceeded the benchmark. Another way to look at this is to ask (1) What is the benchmark? and (2) What is the required level of precision? The more precision required (e.g., the closer the sample result is to the target), the larger the required sample size. If your target is 75% and precision requirement is 5%, then you need to look at the intersection of a sample completion rate of 80% (75 + 5) and benchmark of 75%, which is $n = 314$. If your target is 75% and can accept precision of 20%, then look at the intersection of 95% sample completion and 75% benchmark, which is $n = 13$.

Table 6.4 shows the sample size needed for comparing an observed SUS score against a benchmark SUS score. This table use a 90% confidence level and 80% statistical power and uses the historical SUS standard deviation of 21 points.

SUS point difference	Sample size needed
13	13
12	15
11	18
10	22
9	26
8	33
7	42
6	57
5	81
4	126
3	223
2	499
1	1,990

TABLE 6.4: Sample sizes needed to exceed a SUS benchmark by number of SUS points.

Use Tables 6.3 and 6.4 to find the sample size:

1. Start with the benchmark you want to achieve. For example, the average SUS score should be at least a 68 (a historical average).

2. Select the number of points higher from the benchmark you expect to obtain from the sample to determine the needed sample size. For example, if your sample of participants achieves a mean SUS score of 75 (7 points higher than the benchmark of 68), you would need a sample size of 42 to exceed the 68 benchmark with at least 90% confidence (see the row in Table 6.4 that starts with 7). If the mean SUS score obtained is an 82 and you wanted to exceed a SUS benchmark of 80 (a high SUS score), you should plan on a sample size of 499.

Practice using the tables

Here are three more examples to practice using Tables 6.3 and 6.4. The answers are at the end of the chapter.

- What sample size would you need to ensure at least 75% of all users can complete a task if 85% of the sample completed the task?

- If you want to ensure a product achieves a SUS score above 80 and you plan on testing with 80 participants, what average score would you need to observe?

- If you want to ensure at least 90% of users can complete a task on their first try and you expect around 95% in your sample will, what sample size should you plan for?

Here is an example of setting minimum sample sizes for benchmarking with the SUS.

ENTERPRISE IT SOFTWARE EXAMPLE: A large company wanted to ensure all its IT products had at least a SUS score of 80 (a high bar) and used a survey to assess current attitudes of the usability. A minimum of 33 responses per product were recommended for comparing against an industry-standard SUS benchmark.

Rationale: If at least 33 participants responded per product and a mean of 88 was achieved, the product would have evidence (at the 90% level of confidence) that it exceeded the SUS score benchmark of 80, placing it in the top 10% of historically measured products.

CHAPTER SUMMARY AND TAKEAWAY

In this chapter we discussed how to compute the sample size for a benchmark study. Consider these factors when determining your sample sizes:

- One sample size does not fit all, and your resulting sample size will definitely be more than five users.
- Sample size is computed one way for stand-alone benchmarks (a measure of precision) versus comparative benchmarks (detecting the size of the difference) and again differently for comparing against a historical benchmark.
- For stand-alone benchmarks, the variables that affect sample size are the following:
    - the metric type being used (binary versus continuous)
    - the variability of the data
    - the level of confidence
    - the level of precision (margin of error/confidence interval width)
- For comparison benchmarks, you have all the same factors that affect the sample size as stand-alone benchmarks, but also two more—the last two in this list:
    - the metric type being used (binary versus continuous)
    - the variability of the data
    - the level of confidence
    - the detected difference (which is like the level of precision)
    - statistical power (ability to detect a difference if one exists)
    - the decision to use the between- or within-subjects approach

- For comparing a stand-alone benchmark to a historical benchmark or industry standard, the variables that affect sample size are the following:
  - the metric type being used (binary versus continuous)
  - the variability of the data
  - the level of confidence
  - the detected difference (which is like the level of precision)
  - statistical power (ability to detect a difference if one exists)

ANSWERS

Answers to questions on pg. 81 *(Table 6.1)*

- To be 95% confident, you've estimated completion rates to within +/-5%. What sample size should you plan for? **381**

- If you only have the budget to moderate 20 participants, what level of precision can you expect at 90% confidence? **+/- 17%**

- What sample size should you plan for to have a margin of error of no greater than 15% (90% confidence)? **28**

Answers to questions on pg. 84 *(Table 6.2)*

- What sample size would you need to detect a 5% difference between completion rates between two websites with the same participants attempting two tasks on both websites? **246**

- What is the percentage of difference that you can detect if you only have budget and time to moderate 40 participants in a benchmark study? **~25% difference for within-subjects**

- If you want to compare four websites with different participants assigned to each website, how many should you plan on testing to detect an 8% difference?
  481 * 4 = 1,924

Answers to questions on pg. 89 (*Tables 6.3 and 6.4*)

- What sample size would you need to ensure at least 75% of all users can complete a task if 85% of the sample completed the task? **72 from Table 6.3**

- If you want to ensure a product achieves a SUS score above v80 and you plan on testing with 80 participants, what average score would you need to observe? **85** Use Table 6.4 and find the sample size closest to 80, which is 81 in this case, then look at the SUS point difference, which is 5. You would need to observe the average score of 85 versus 80.

- If you want to ensure at least 90% of users can complete a task on their first try, and you expect around 95% of participants in your sample will, what sample size should you plan for? **122 from Table 6.3**

CHAPTER 7:

WRITING THE STUDY SCRIPT

Like building a house, the study script is the blueprint for developing a successful benchmarking study. It's a lot easier to correct mistakes while changing a Word document than later when programming the study or even worse, when you're analyzing your results and realize you've left out critical questions or metrics.

The study script feeds directly from the project booking form (see Chapter 2) or any other initial plans or notes you choose to create. From these documents, you can develop and refine the actual questions and tasks participants will receive. If needed, you can include the instructions for the moderator(s)in this script as well.

 TIP:

> To ensure your study script is addressing all your research questions, consider creating a simple grid that shows which question, task, or metric will address all the questions put forth in the project booking form. See the "Use a Research Grid to Focus Study Decisions" article at measuringu.com/research-grid/ for information on how to do this.

CONTENTS OF THE STUDY SCRIPT

While study plans will differ depending on the needs of the organization and the number of stakeholders, the typical contents of a study script are discussed in the following sections. A full example of a study script we used for a hotel benchmark study can be found in Appendix E. The study script sometimes contains a little meta-information about the study, such as goals and a timeline, but it's primarily the detailed schematic of questions and tasks for participants.

One of the major differences between a moderated and unmoderated study is that participant recruiting happens during the study for tshare many aspects—especially when writing the task scenarios. However, the study scripts for each type of study also have some key differences which are discussed in the following sections.

UNMODERATED STUDY SCRIPTS

We'll walk through the key parts of a typical unmoderated study script and use the hotel comparison website study as an example (see Appendix E for the study script that was used).

- Study information: goals and research questions
- Welcome message and orientation
- Pre-study questions

Study Information, Goals and Research Questions

While the study goals, information, and research questions should be defined in the project booking document (and study plan if you created one), it's good to repeat some of that information in the study script. We often open a study script from prior projects conducted years in the past and one of the first things we need to understand is some of the context for the study.

Welcome Message and Orientation

For unmoderated studies the welcome message is often the first thing participants see when starting a study. A good welcome message contains the following:

- **Context:** Tell participants generally what they'll be doing without revealing too much about the study. For example, you can tell participants they will be asked to complete tasks on one (or multiple) retail websites.

- **Technical details:** Despite the seeming ubiquity of usability testing, for most participants this will be the first time they will have participated in a usability study (either online or in person). For unmoderated studies, provide an introduction to the online platform you are using. For example, we tell our participants that our MUIQ platform uses a browser plug-in when recording screens (this only applies to some studies).

- **Duration**: Give participants a range of how long the study will take to complete. We like to provide a realistic low to high range rather than a single number, for example, 8 to 17 minutes versus 10 minutes. To get an accurate time range, we update it after our soft launch so it is a true estimate based on how long other participants took. The more exacting the estimation of time, such as 8 and 17, versus a more general estimate, such as 10 to 15 minutes, convey to participants that the estimate is more realistic.

- **Statements of confidentiality**: In most cases you should not be collecting personally identifiable information (PII) from participants. Reassure them of that in the welcome message and provide a link to your privacy policy if any PII is collected. An example of our privacy policy is available online at measuringu.com/privacy/.

EXAMPLE WELCOME MESSAGE: COMPARATIVE RETAIL WEBSITE

Welcome! Thank you for participating in this evaluation.

You will now be asked to perform a few tasks on a retail website. After you have read the task and are ready to proceed, click the "Start Task" button. The task instructions will also be shown in a small window on the bottom of your screen so you can refer to them throughout the task. After you feel that you have completed the task successfully or were unable to complete the task, click the "End Task" button.

Please remember that this is an evaluation of a website and not you, so do the best you can to complete the tasks. Some tasks may be harder than others.

Have a piece of paper and pen ready (or some way to copy down information), as you will be asked to write down or remember information during some tasks.

Please do not attend to other work while completing this study. It should take between 14 and 21 minutes to complete.

Technical details

You may wish to include a separate page of technical instructions for the participant, especially if you're requiring them to use a task plug-in or download a mobile app. This can be especially important for mobile benchmark studies, which usually require the downloading of an app to present tasks and record screens. Figure 7.1 shows three examples of the instruction screens for using the Validately Recorder desktop extension, the MUIQ desktop extension, and the MUIQ mobile app.

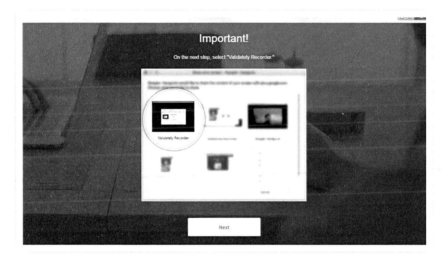

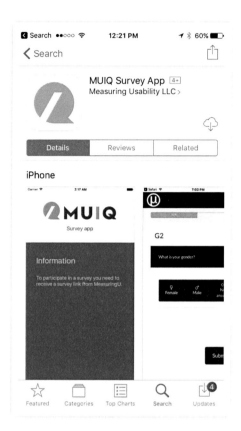

FIGURE 7.I: Examples of browser plug-in extensions for Validately, MUIQ, and the MUIQ mobile app.

PRE-STUDY QUESTIONS

Before presenting tasks (if applicable), the first questions you want to ask your participants will help ensure they're qualified and if so, characterize them for later analysis. Your pre-study questions will allow you to screen out participants who don't match your study criteria and sort and certify those who do qualify.

Demographic and qualitifcation questions

There's often a debate about whether you should include demographic information (which often asks sensitive questions and can lead to participant drop-out) in the beginning or end of the study. While we like the idea of delaying demographic questions to the end, usually key qualification questions (age, occupation, prior experience) will qualify or disqualify participants. We therefore usually begin our pre-study screening with demographic questions and questions about existing attitudes and prior usage.

Screening questions

Prior to collecting any data, you want to make sure you have a pool of the most likely to qualify participants. While panel companies can target general segments of the population (general consumers, students, B2B), many of these people may not be suitable for your study.

It's rare that just any person off the street will be qualified for a benchmark study. When writing screening questions, refer to the booking form or project plan to understand how you defined your users. The goal is to define the type of user you, or your client, have in mind in order to design a concrete, mostly closed-ended set of questions that will produce accurate benchmark data. For example, to gather information so you can assess a participant's suitability for your benchmark study, you can design your questionnaire around the following common screening items:

- Demographics, such as age, gender, income, and job titles
- Prior experience with a website or product
- Roles and company types, such as job responsibilities and types and sizes of companies worked at
- Brand attitudes, meant to screen people who would never use a website, product, or service merely because of a dislike of the brand name
- Authenticity and reliability, meant to gauge a person's honesty and conscientious tendences

Examples of screening and sorting questions

The following section provides examples of both screening and sorting questions. When writing screening and sorting questions, do not use yes or no types of questions. In general, participants tend to agree with these questions, and this type of agreement will not yield the information you need to qualify participants. Also, when possible, prioritize questions intended to screen out participants to minimize the burden on your respondents. For example, if you are screening out people who have used a particular website, make that a single question, and ask it early in the questioning process.

DEMOGRAPHICS EXAMPLE: The following questions are examples of demographic questions tailored to gather the most qualified study participants. For example, the first question is used to screen out participants under 18 or over 65. This requirement is based on the type of client that will most likely use the product or service. The percentages in the brackets indicate the desired quota for each response (e.g., 20% of completed responses should be between 45 and 54). In benchmark studies, it's common to only include people who will most likely use the product being sold on a website, for example.

Question 1:

Please select your age from the choices below:
- Under 18 [SCREEN OUT]
- 18 – 24 [15%]
- 25 – 34 [25%]
- 35 – 44 [25%]
- 45 – 54 [20%]
- 55 – 64 [15%]
- 65+ [SCREEN OUT]

Question 2:

Which of the following best describes your current employment status?

Full time	[ ]	
Part time	[ ]	
Unemployed	[ ]	**Terminate**
Retired	[ ]	**Terminate**

Question 3:

Please indicate your profession:

- Web Developer/Web Designer [SCREEN OUT]
- Student/Retired/Unemployed
- Homemaker
- Market Research/Usability Analyst [SCREEN OUT]
- Teacher
- Engineer
- Doctor
- Sales
- Banking
- Finance
- Other, Please Specify:

> **NOTE:** While you don't have to screen out participants who work in market research or web development, for example, it's often a good idea to screen out people whose jobs are too closely related to the product or service you are benchmarking.

PRIOR EXPERIENCE EXAMPLE: Prior experience with a website or product is one of the strongest predictors of more favorable scoring on both task (completion rates, time, SEQ) and study-level metrics (SUPR-Q, SUS). This information is used to screen out participants, segmenting (cross tabbing) for later analysis, or weighting/controlling for prior experience (see Chapter 11).

Question 1:

In the past 12 months, how many times have you visited the Best Buy website?

- 0 Times
- 1 – 3 Times
- 4 – 6 Times
- 7 – 9 Times
- 10+ Times

Question 2:

Select any of the following services you have prior experience using. (Note: These are presented in random order except for "None of the above.")

Wix.com	[ ]
MailChimp	[ ]
Weebly	[ ]
Constant Contact	[ ] Terminate
GoDaddy	[ ]
iContact	[ ]
Squarespace	[ ]
Campaign Monitor	[ ]
Hootsuite	[ ]
VerticalResponse	[ ]
None of the above	[ ]

NOTE: In some cases, you may *not* want participants who have used a website so you can better gauge the experience of first time users.

ROLES AND COMPANY SIZE EXAMPLE: Deciphering potential participants' professional roles and size of the company they work for can also be a valuable tool to determine their eligibility. For B2B benchmarks, the size of a company is often a good indicator of the type of products and services a participant may be searching for and a good indicator of a participant's qualification. For example, the needs of an IT decision maker at a 1,000+ person company differ from those at a smaller company, say a company with only 25 employees.

Question 1:

Please select the size of your organization:

1 to 50	[ ]
50 to 100	[ ]
100 to 500	[ ] Terminate
500 to 999	[ ] Terminate
1000+	[ ] Terminate

Question 2:

What is your role when it comes to making key banking and finance decisions <u>for your business</u>? **(Select one)**

- I have the lead role in this type of decision-making.
- I share in this type of decision-making but am more involved than others.
- I have a secondary role in this type of decision-making.
- I do not participate in this type of decision-making.

> NOTE: Sometimes it's advantageous to know a potential participant's purchase authority. For B2B studies, you'll often want to ensure that some (or all) of your participants have the authority to make purchase decisions—again, to help with the validity of the findings.

BRAND ATTITUDE EXAMPLE: In some cases, especially for well-known brands, determining potential participants' attitude about a particular brand is very important. Some participants have a strong negative attitude toward brands that may make them unwilling to purchase from that brand or even visit the company's website. Including people who have these negative attitudes in your study will probably skew the results, giving you an inaccurate benchmark. We'll often use a generic brand attitude question like the following to screen out those who rate the lowest favorability. We often ask these same brand attitude questions again at the end of the study (see the "Post-Study Questions" section in this chapter) to measure how the experience hurt or helped participants' attitude toward a brand (see also measuring brand lift in Chapter 11).

Question 1:

How would you describe your attitude toward the following companies?

Target
Walmart
Best Buy
Amazon
[1 – 7, Very Unfavorable – Very Favorable] [SCREEN OUT IF 1]

AUTHENTICITY AND RELIABILITY EXAMPLE: To get some idea about the authenticity of the respondents, you may decide to include questions that can assess the authenticity of the respondent, or at least how much the participant is paying attention and not lying. With so many participants coming from online panels, there is a financial incentive to game the system and get paid, even if it means lying about who you are and what you do. To help detect these disingenuous participants, you can include questions to identify and weed them out.

For example, a participant at one of our UX Boot Camps referred to these as the "Morgan Island" questions (more on this later). He shared some advice he heard from David Harris', author of the book, *The Complete Guide to Writing Questionnaires*, who recommended including a question with fictitious examples. The following is an example of this type of question.

Question I:

In the last six months have you researched or purchased?

A. Sony Dishwasher
B. Morgan Island Vacation Package
C. Neither of the above

In this example, Sony doesn't make a dishwasher and Morgan Island is an island inhabited by rhesus macaque monkeys and trespassing is prohibited under U.S. federal law, making buying a vacation package there unattainable. In a sample study, ~25% of respondents picked either A or B (the fictitious answers).

Question 2:

A merchant account allows businesses to accept credit and debit cards. Which of the following companies, if any, provides your company's merchant account?

A. Our company doesn't have a merchant account
B. PayPal
C. Flagship Merchant Services
D. Merchant Focus
E. Cayan
F. Elavon
G. Paymentech
H: PLC Merchant Solutions
I. I don't know
J. Other (please specify):

> **NOTE:** Another example is from a benchmark study for small businesses that make financial decisions. This example question asked who their current merchant provider is. In this example, PLC Merchant Solutions is a fictitious (but plausible sounding) merchant account.

MODERATED BENCHMARK STUDY SCRIPTS

The moderated study script will look very similar to the unmoderated script. Here are three major differences:

- Notes to the facilitator: As this will be ultimately read by a facilitator, include notes on what the facilitator should and shouldn't do, such as probing after a task, asking follow-up questions, or moving on at a certain point.

- Indications of task success: Indicate how the facilitator should determine task success (e.g., reaching a certain page or completing an action).

- Fewer demographic/intro questions: You'll want to collect as many demographic and background questions (especially the closed-ended types) in your screening document ahead of time and save the precious time with the participant on observing their actions.

The moderated benchmark study script generally has the following structure:

- Study information: goals and research questions
- Welcome message and orientation
- Pre-study questions
- Task scenarios (if applicable)
- Post-task questions
- Post-study questions
- Closing questions

Study Information, Goals, and Research Questions

Similar to the unmoderated study, the moderated study script should contain a brief overview of the study goals, information, and research questions that came from the project booking document (and study plan if you created one). While there is some redundancy in having the study goals in both the study script and booking form or study plan, it's good to have everyone (including the facilitator) reminded of the purpose of the study, as it will help to guide questions and decisions on whether a task or question is appropriate in the context of the study. It's also possible that the study goals have evolved during the process, so including them in this overview to allow for documentation of any changes up to a certain point.

Welcome Message and Orientation

In a moderated benchmark, like a usability study in general, the welcome message needs to let the participant know what to expect. Despite the popularity of usability testing, for most participants this will be their first study. In the welcome message, let them know the expectation about working through tasks as much as possible without help or assistance and provide an overview of what they'll be doing. The following are two examples of welcome messages.

EXAMPLE 1: WELCOME MESSAGE FROM AN ONLINE TICKETING WEBSITE STUDY

> Today, we'll be evaluating the process of using [website name]. Our goal is to gather feedback at each stage of the process on what works well for you and what doesn't. There are no right or wrong answers today.

We are from a third-party research firm, and we will be evaluating the experience, not evaluating you. While you're completing the tasks, we'd like you to think-aloud, tell us your thoughts as you work through the steps to complete a task; let us know what's working and what's not working. Do the best you can to complete the tasks on your own as if I weren't here. If you get stuck and need help, let me know. When you have completed the task, let me know. After each task, there will be a few short questions you will need to answer about the experience.

This session will be recorded. The videos will not be made public; they are used for internal reference only.

We are here if you have questions, and we may ask you a few questions, but in general, we are going to let you work through the tasks without interruption. Do you have any questions before we begin?

EXAMPLE 2: WELCOME MESSAGE FROM A DRAFTING
SOFTWARE STUDY

Thank you for participating in the [product name] benchmark study! You are helping us ensure that [product name] continues to become more efficient and easier to use.

Please work as efficiently and quickly as you can through the following exercises. You don't need to speak out loud and you won't be interrupted. You may use any [product] commands and tools that help you get your work done; there is no "right way" to do any exercise.

You need to tell us when you are starting and stopping each exercise.

When you are ready to begin an exercise (after you're done reading the instructions and have examined any figures), please say:

"I'm starting."

When you finish an exercise, please say:

"I'm done."

It's okay if you don't know how to do part or all of an exercise. When you've gotten as far as you can, say "I'm done" and move on.

At the end of each exercise, you will go to Internet Explorer and describe your experience in a brief survey about that exercise.

Turn to the next page to do a practice exercise.

Pre-Study Questions

Unlike the unmoderated benchmark, the moderated pre-study questions should be more limited. You really want to use the time you have with the participant to observe them attempting tasks and understanding root causes of issues. Ideally, most demographic and pre-study questions should be asked during the screening process, and the answers should be provided to the moderator for reference. However, it's OK to revisit some of the question to both confirm the responses and get the participant in the mindset for the study, such as in the following examples.

1. Have you ever purchased a ticket from a third-party ticket seller before? If yes, answer the following questions:

   a. What was the experience like?

   b. When was the last time you purchased a ticket through a third-party ticket seller?

2. Have you ever sold a ticket through a third-party ticket seller before? If yes, answer the following questions:

   a. What was the experience like?

   b. When was the last time you sold a ticket through a third-party ticket seller?

Task Scenarios

In this section, there are examples of moderated task scenarios. The following examples show the task scenario script we used for a benchmark study for an online ticketing website and for a separate study for accounting software. After each task, we typically ask participants to assess their level of confidence in completing the task successfully and how easy or difficult they found the task (both on 7-point scales). If participants rate the task low in perceived ease, we usually have a probing point for the moderator to ask the participants for their reasons for the low rating.

In an actual study, the post-task questions are asked at the end of every task. To simplify the examples given in this section, the following is the typical format and post-task questions that occur after each task.

POST-TASK METRICS

[MODERATOR TO PRESENT PRINTED SCALES TO PARTICIPANT]

Post-Task Questions:

How confident are you that you completed the task successfully? [1= Not at all confident to 7 =Extremely confident]

How easy or difficult was it for you to complete the task? [1= Extremely difficult to 7 = Extremely easy]

If <5, briefly describe why you chose the number you did.

EXAMPLE 1: ONLINE TICKETING WEBSITE

TASK 1: FIND AN EVENT.

Let's imagine that you want to buy tickets to an event. Remember that we will reimburse you $25 towards the ticket price. Go through the entire process of finding and purchasing the ticket to an event of your choice. Feel free to purchase more than one ticket, since you will be able to keep them.

[MODERATOR TO NOTE POSSIBLE EVENTS]

WED, December 14 – Philadelphia Flyers at Colorado Avalanche – Pepsi Center 8:00 p.m.
MON, December 19 – Dallas Mavericks at Denver Nuggets – Pepsi Center 7:00 p.m.

TASK 2: UPDATE OR ADD ACCOUNT INFORMATION.

Let's imagine that the credit card attached to your account is about to expire. Go through the process of updating your credit card through your StubHub account.

{Note: Moderator can tell them that they can remove the card from their account afterwards if they do not want a card attached to their account.}

EXAMPLE 2: ACCOUNTING SOFTWARE

TASK 1: FIND AND CODE THE INVOICES.

In this exercise you will be focusing on the Accounts Payable (AP) module. To complete this task, you will need the following materials, which have been printed out for you:

- This set of instructions.
- Five (5) initial invoices in printed and electronic form; the electronic copies are in the desktop folder "Invoices".
- A sixth invoice with a clearly identified change action.

Find the set of five (5) initial invoices and enter them into Accounts Payable module. Code these invoices per the instructions on each.

When you feel you have completed the task, let the moderator know by saying "I'm done."

Post-Study Questions

At the end of the moderated benchmark task-based portion, include the study-level questions, which should include a mix of standardized closed-ended questions and open-ended discussion questions to identify root causes of problems in the experience.

As covered in Chapter 5, the most common post-study questionnaires for moderated benchmark studies are the following:

- SUPR-Q for websites
- SUS for software and products

- NPS for all applications and websites
- UMUX-LITE for all applications (especially software)

These questionnaires can be administered orally by a facilitator or electronically by having participants answer questions on separate computer or tablet.

TIP:

Even with only a few items (such as the SUS or SUPR-Q), it can be difficult for participants to recall the scales after each question. We recommend collecting this data electronically or printing the response scale for the participant to see. While it can take longer to ask the participant each question verbally, we've found it provides another opportunity for the facilitator to probe on issues. For example, if a participant provides anything less than a 4 or 5 for an item (e.g., "The software is easy to use"), the facilitator can ask the respondent to explain their response—something that's more difficult to do in an unmoderated benchmark.

Open-Ended Closing Questions

At the end of a study, it's a good time to ask open-ended questions, such as the following examples, to gather important data that may not be reflected in the post-task or post-study questions. This information can give stakeholders a wider view of their product or service.

- What are your overall impressions of installing the antivirus software on your desktop compared to your mobile device?
- What is one thing you would improve about the product?
- What are your overall opinions of [product name]?
- Do you have any questions or comments about anything we did today?

WRITING TASK SCENARIOS

For most benchmark studies, the quality of the findings are often due to the relevance and quality of the task scenarios. You want participants completing representative tasks. Task scenarios for unmoderated studies differ slightly from the more classic moderated approach. The biggest difference and challenge for unmoderated studies is that you don't have a moderator there to verify task success and to clarify task meaning. This makes clearly written task instructions/scenarios even more important for unmoderated studies. You also need some way to verify task success from the output of what the participant does (especially when sample sizes are large, such as greater than 100).

The core idea behind usability testing is having real people trying to accomplish real tasks on software, websites, cell phones, hardware, etc. Identifying what users are trying to do is a key first step. Once you know what tasks you want to test, you'll want to create realistic task scenarios for participants to attempt.

A task is made up of the steps a user has to perform to accomplish a goal. A task scenario describes what the test user is trying to achieve by providing some context and the necessary details to accomplish the goal. Crafting task scenarios is a balance between providing just enough information so participants aren't guessing what they're supposed to do, and not too much information so you can simulate the discovery and nonlinearity of real world application usage. Here are some tips to help you write effective task scenarios:

- **Be specific.** Give participants a reason or purpose for performing the task. Instead of giving generalities like "find a new kitchen appliance," ask them to find a blender for under $75 that has high customer ratings. While participants might start searching with general ideas of what they want, they will quickly narrow their selection based on the given criteria. In the artificial world of usability testing, participants will often encounter problems if the task scenarios are too vague, and they will look to a moderator (if there is one) to guide them.

- **Don't tell the user where to click and what to do.** While providing specific details is important, don't walk the participants through every step. Leading a participant too much will provide biased and less useful results. For example, instead of saying "Click on the small checkbox at the bottom of the screen to add GPS," just say, "Add GPS to your rental car."

- **Use the user's language and not the company's language.** It's a common mistake to mirror the internal structure of a company on a website's navigation. It's also bad practice to ask participants to do things based on internal company jargon or terms. If users don't use the terms used in a scenario, it can lead to false positive test results or outright confusion. Do users really use the term "asset" when referring to their kids' college funds? Will a user know what a product "configurator" is or an "item page" or even the "mega menu?"

- **Have a correct solution.** If you ask a participant to find a rental car location nearest to a hotel address, there should be a correct choice. This makes the task more straightforward for the participant and allows you to more easily know if a task was or wasn't successfully completed. The problem with a "find a product that's right for you" task is that participants are in the state of mind of finding information to solve problems. At the time, there probably isn't a product that's right for them; they're more interested in getting the test done and collecting their honorarium. This can lead to a sense that any product selection is correct and inflate basic metrics like task completion rates.

- **Don't make the tasks dependent (if possible).** It is important to alternate or randomize the presentation order of tasks, as there is a significant learning effect that happens. If your tasks have dependencies (e.g., "create a file in one task then delete the same file in another task"), then if a participant fails one task they will often fail the other. Do your best to avoid dependencies (e.g., have the user delete another file). This isn't always possible if you're testing an installation process, but be cognizant of both the bias and complications introduced by adding dependencies.

- **Provide context but keep the scenario short.** You want to provide some context to get the participant thinking as if they were actually needing to perform the task. But don't go overboard with the details, for example, "You will be attending a conference in Boston in July and need to rent a car" is concise and gives an appropriate level of context for a realistic scenario.

- **Start at a specific URL or location.** Specify where the participant will start the task. For software, it's often the home screen. For websites, it's often the home page. However, depending on the task and study goals, the starting point may be deeper in the product or web page structure.

While you don't want to lead participants and give them step-by-step instructions, you do need to be explicit enough about desired task outcomes. You'll need to provide product names, specific price ranges, and brands. While some people might be concerned that will lead the participant, I rarely see a task-completion rate above 90% in unmoderated benchmark studies. Even with all these details spelled out, participants get lost in the navigation, the checkout procedures, or confused by simple things like terms and overall organizations. These seemingly obvious problems get overlooked when designers and developers are so entrenched building features, they often lose sight of the users' perspective.

It takes some practice to achieve balance—not leading participants on one hand and not making the task too difficult on the other. There are no universally "right" tasks, so don't be afraid to tweak details for different methods (moderated vs. unmoderated) or different goals (findability vs. checkout). It's even fine to read task scenarios out loud instead of having them printed or on the screen (we do this a lot with mobile moderated benchmark studies).

For more information on writing better usability task scenarios, one of the best sources is the classic: *A Practical Guide to Usability Testing* by Joseph Dumas and Janice Redish (1999). Also check out my book *A Practical Guide to Measuring Usability: Quantifying the Usability of Websites & Software* (2010) and, for unmoderated studies, *Beyond the Usability Lab* by Albert, Tullis, and Tedesco (2010).

Determining Tasks Success in an Unmoderated Study

Unmoderated studies are great for collecting data quickly. Many people in our industry have been examining the difference between unmoderated and moderated studies for around a decade now. One of the most noticeable differences between moderated and unmoderated studies is that when a study is unmoderated, as the name implies, you don't have a facilitator with each participant to assess task success and ensure the study is flowing as expected.

There are generally five ways to validate if a task is completed and/or successful in an unmoderated study: question participants, note whether participants reached a specific URL that would indicate success, observe session recordings, view screenshots of the sessions, and rely on self-reported success and/or task completion.

Question participants

After participants attempt a task, ask for information that they would only know if they completed the task. For example, ask about the price or brand of a product. Validation is usually done using a multiple-choice format for quicker scoring.

EXAMPLE OF A RETAIL BENCHMARK QUESTION FOR VALIDATION

Find a blender that has been reviewed by at least 30 people and has at least a 4-star rating. You would like to spend between $37.00 and $40.00 on your blender. Please find this product without using the search box. **Please remember the brand name of the blender, as you will be asked for it later.** [correct answers are in red]

What is the brand of the blender you found?

- Farberware
- Black and Decker
- Oster
- Cuisinart
- Other:

EXAMPLE OF A HOTEL TASK FOR VALIDATION

Imagine you're scheduling a trip to Denver, Colorado and need to book a hotel for your stay. On the following website, find out how much it would cost to book a room (without fees or tax) with one king bed from November 27th to November 29th at the Denver Marriott City Center (use "MEMBER RATE" pricing).

Please write down or remember the cost of the room, as you will be asked for it later. [correct answer is in grey]
How much was the cost of the hotel room (for all three nights)?

a. $588
b. $458
c. $425
d. $547
e. $503
f. Other:

If you provide a multiple-choice option, in most cases we also recommend an "Other" option that allows participants to write in their answer choice. This is especially important if you're using something like price to validate the task's success. Prices have a way of changing by small amounts due to fluctuations of many factors. If we see many of the same prices provided in an "Other" option, we'll review the session recordings and see if we overlooked an option. Even if participants are still wrong, we're able to determine a common cause of the wrong price or product. For example, when we conducted a benchmark study on Enterprise.com there were many of the same incorrect "Other" prices. In this case, the participants had not included the total cost of the rental car, options, and taxes and fees into the price (a major problem identified for the Enterprise website).

Note when participants reach the URLs that indicate success

If there are specific pages that indicate success (such as a product or event detail page), reaching a specific URL can act as an indication of success. This can work especially well when benchmarking with prototypes where there are a more limited number of pages. However, be careful when using validation by URL on a live website. In our experience, there are often a lot of paths and URLs that can still lead a user to a successful location. Our MUIQ platform allows for multiple URL validation.

Observe session recordings

Validate success from observing session recordings. After validation by question and URL, watching session recordings of every participant is the distant third option (assuming your unmoderated solution offers a recording option). For studies with 300 participants and five tasks, that's 1,500 videos to review! This option is typically not something you should rely on.

View screenshots

Looking at the screenshots of participants' work can allow you to see if they completed the work. In a couple benchmarks we've conducted for online apps (email marketing and online storage), we asked participants to take a screenshot after tasks were completed so we could verify if they had completed the task. You'll need a platform that supports image uploads (our MUIQ platform does). This isn't a fail-safe technique, as several participants have had trouble taking screenshots (even with the instructions we provided) and locating the correct screenshot to upload.

Rely on self-reported success and/or task completion

In some situations, you have neither videos, URLs, nor a validation question. This was the case when we conducted a benchmark for online storage companies' desktop and mobile web apps (e.g., Google Drive, Dropbox). Participants had to complete common tasks like uploading files and viewing them on their phone. After each task, we asked participants if they completed the task.

Post-Task Questions

In most cases, post-task questions will be the same for each of the tasks, usually with the exception of validation questions that are specific to each task. As a default, we use the following questions:

- SEQ: Overall this task was? [Scale: 1 = Very Difficult to 7 = Very Easy]
- Open-ended: Briefly describe your experience on the task and why you chose the number you did for the previous question [SEQ].
- Confidence: How confident are you that you completed the tasks successfully? [Scale: 1 = Not at all Confident to 7 = Extremely Confident]

Post-Study Questions

At the end of the study include a mix of closed-ended (usually standardized questions) and open-ended questions. You can find standard questions from the following questionnaires:

- SUPR-Q
- SUS
- NPS
- UMUX-LITE

Preference (if applicable)

If it was a within-subjects comparative study, include a question that asks participants which website they preferred (with "neither" as an option). You can have them select the site and/or ask them about the intensity of their selection. Figure 7.2 and 7.3 are examples of these preference questions.

FIGURE 7.2: Example of a preference question.

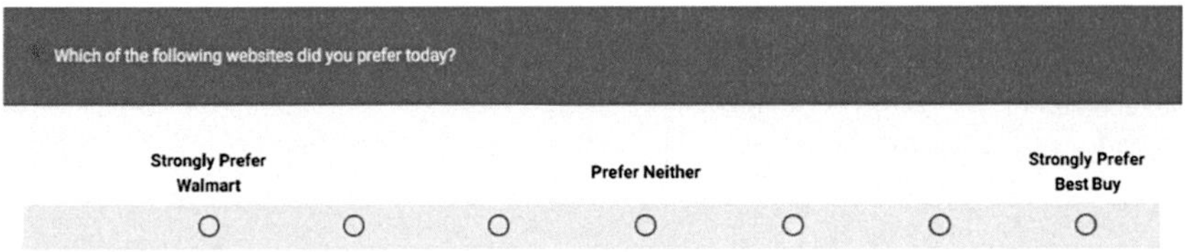

FIGURE 7.3: Example of a preference question with intensity.

For more on analyzing preference data, see Chapter 11.

Detecting cheaters again: Pick this response

Another method for detecting cheaters, or participants who are not genuinely taking your benchmark study seriously, is to include a question that asks participants to select an option; for example, in the middle of a multiple-choice answer list, give them a choice that would not make sense if chosen. These questions are often included in matrix questions, such as in Figure 7.4. (See Chapter 9 for more on participant recruiting.)

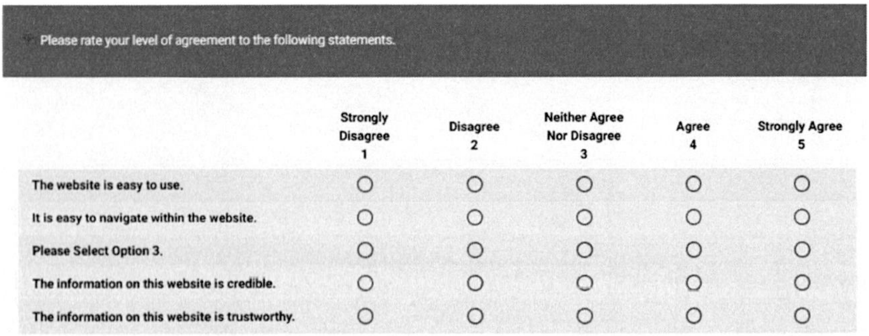

Please rate your level of agreement to the following statements.

	Strongly Disagree 1	Disagree 2	Neither Agree Nor Disagree 3	Agree 4	Strongly Agree 5
The website is easy to use.	O	O	O	O	O
It is easy to navigate within the website.	O	O	O	O	O
Please Select Option 3.	O	O	O	O	O
The information on this website is credible.	O	O	O	O	O
The information on this website is trustworthy.	O	O	O	O	O

FIGURE 7.4: Example authentic/cheater detection question with "Please Select Option 3" item.

Brand attitude (post)

In Chapter 5 we discussed the brand life or drag metric. You will want to ask the same brand favorability question at the end of the benchmark to understand how the experience helped or hurt brand attitudes.

Final comments

At the end of benchmark studies, we like to include opportunities for participants to reflect on the websites, apps, or products tested as well as anything that was or wasn't covered in the study. These are open-ended questions that include examples like the following:

- "If you have any additional comments about the website or product tested today, please include them below."
- "What one thing would you improve on for the website/product you experienced today?"
- "If you would like to participate in a follow-up study for additional compensation, please provide your name and email address below."

CHAPTER SUMMARY AND TAKEAWAY

In this chapter we covered the importance of a good study script as a blueprint for a benchmark study:

- Study scripts contain welcome messages, pre-study questions, tasks (for task-based benchmarks), post-task questions, and final post-study questions with a closing message.
- Moderated benchmark study scripts differ from unmoderated scripts in that they provide notes to the facilitator, indications of task success, and usually fewer demographic and introduction questions.
- For unmoderated benchmarks, you'll need to consider how you will determine task success (e.g., validation by question, URL, or session recording are the most common).
- For unmoderated benchmark studies, you'll likely need to include "cheater questions" to detect participants who might not be providing sufficient effort.

CHAPTER 8:

PREPARING FOR DATA COLLECTION

With a study script written, the next step is to prepare for data collection. For moderated studies, there's less to prepare for other than ensuring your data collection methods are ready (covered later in this chapter). For unmoderated studies, a lot of work goes into preparing the online platforms for participants. This part is often called "programming," where you enter the questions and tasks you developed in the study script stage into your research platform. Granted, your research platform, such as the MeasuringU Intelligent Questioning (MUIQ) platform, does the work, but saying you're "programming" a study just sounds a lot cooler.

UNMODERATED STUDY DATA COLLECTION: PROGRAMMING THE PLATFORM

With the study script completed, you have everything you need to begin programming a study for online unmoderated data collection. The actual technical details and steps will vary depending on the platform you use (and the version of the platform). In the eight years we've been programming unmoderated studies across platforms, while the screen details change, the major steps haven't changed much. We will walk through the steps to program a hotel benchmark study script using our MUIQ platform.

While the MUIQ platform is an advanced research platform that supports over 30 question types and complex branching capabilities, quotas, and randomization, the platform also includes a "Simple Startup" that guides you through the programming process and addresses 80% of the study types we encounter. We designed the Simple Startup around our project booking form format we covered in Chapter 2. The following steps illustrate how to gather data for an unmoderated benchmark study using the MUIQ platform. We use the booking form and study script examples from the hotel comparison study, which are available in Appendix D and Appendix E, as the subject for the following example procedure.

PROCEDURE EXAMPLE: PROGRAMMING THE PLATFORM

1. After starting a new study using the Simple Startup in the MUIQ platform, select the appropriate study type and the study name from the drop-down lists. For this example, we used the "Task-based comparison study" option, which matches the study type given in booking form.

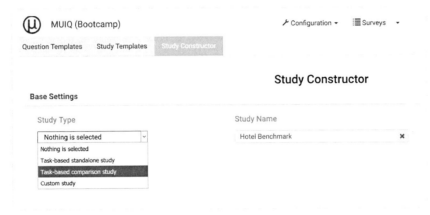

FIGURE 8.1: Starting an example comparison study in the MUIQ research platform.

2. Enter the Welcome Message from the study script, and then create two conditions (here labeled M and B) for the between-subjects testing of the Marriott and Best Western websites (Figure 8.2, see red arrows).

FIGURE 8.2: Entering the welcome message and conditions in the MUIQ research platform.

3. Add the study parameters. For example, the following study parameters have been added (shown in Figure 8.3, see red arrows).

   a) Set the Quota value to 70 (35 will be randomly assigned to one of the two website conditions).

   b) Assign the participants to a condition. In this example, we chose Random and Fully Between participants.

   c) Limit the target platforms. In this example, we limited it to the desktop but allowed participants without the web-extension (which records screens and provides click maps).

FIGURE 8.3: Setting the study parameters in the MUIQ research platform.

4. Add the pre-study questions. For this example, using the study script, I added the demographic questions (many of these questions have been saved as template questions because we use them so often), then I updated the screen out criteria (for example, excluding participants who are under 18). See Figure 8.4.

FIGURE 8.4: Adding the pre-study questions and screen outs in the MUIQ research platform.

5. Continue to add the template questions, for example, BrandAtt (attitude) as shown in Figure 8.5, and then preview the question output (Figure 8.6).

FIGURE 8.5: Adding pre-study questions in the MUIQ research platform.

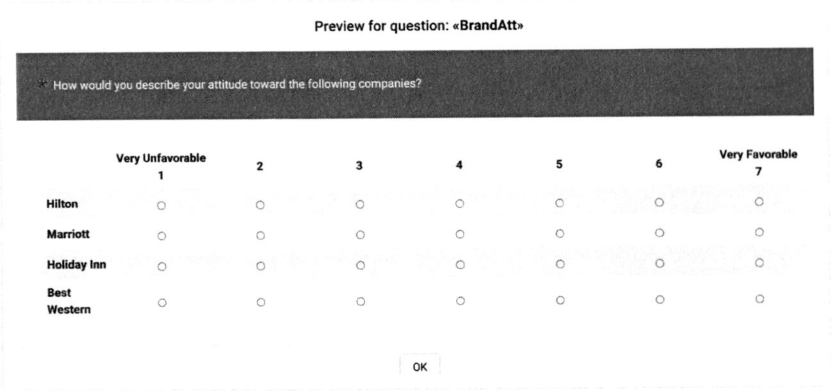

FIGURE 8.6: Previewing the brand attitude question as would be shown to the participant using the MUIQ research platform.

6. Add the tasks. In this example, I added the first task for Marriott. One of the nice features we built into MUIQ is that you can create a task template whereby the same tasks are assigned to each condition and you only have to modify some of the details for each site (like the URL and validation responses). This can be particularly helpful for studies with many tasks. The following steps are shown in Figure 8.7.

a) Give the task a short name.

b) Provide the starting URL (e.g., the Marriott home page).

c) Provide task description. In this example, we wanted to record the screen events.

d) Provide the questions text and the answer options. In this example, we wanted the question to be mandatory and randomized.

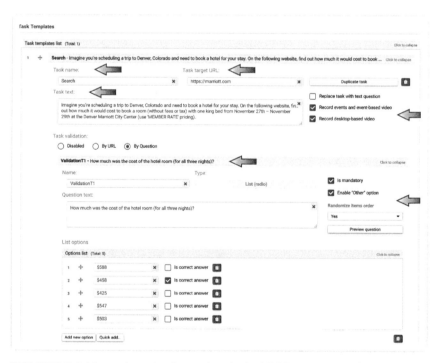

FIGURE 8.7: Adding tasks and task questions in the MUIQ research platform.

7. Add the post-task questions. By default, MUIQ includes the post-task questions we use in most of our unmoderated studies: confidence, ease (SEQ), and a reason for the ratings (open-text). For each task created, the three post-task questions are added (see Figure 8.8).

FIGURE 8.8: Adding post-task questions in the MUIQ research platform.

8. Repeat for the next task. In this example, I created two tasks, but because I used a task template in MUIQ, these two tasks were applied across both website conditions (M and B). MUIQ builds the study like a table of contents in a preview, see Figure 8.9.

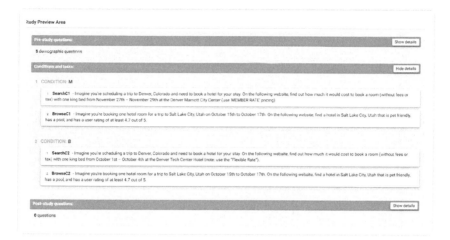

FIGURE 8.9: Study preview area: A real-time table of contents for the study as tasks are added in the MUIQ research platform.

9. Edit details for next condition. With all the details carried over from the tasks I created for Marriott (Condition M), I only need to edit some of the details (task details and verification answers) for the Best Western website tasks in Condition B (see Figure 8.10).

FIGURE 8.10: Study preview area with the task open: Edit the URL and task details for Best Western.

10. Add the post condition questions. In this example, after participants attempt both tasks (in randomized order) on one of the websites, they will answer the 8-item SUPR-Q, which includes the likelihood-to-recommend item used in the Net Promoter Score. I added these questions in the post-condition question section for Marriott and Best Western (see Figure 8.11).

FIGURE 8.11: Post condition SUPR-Q items being added in the MUIQ research platform.

11. Add the post study questions. In this example, I added just one post-study question that all participants got, regardless of which website they were assigned to.

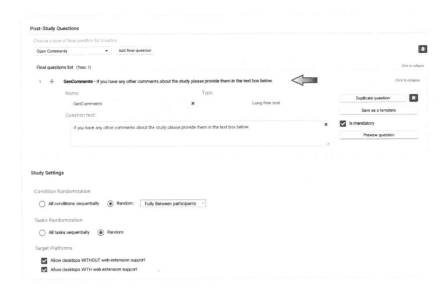

FIGURE 8.12: Post-study open-ended questions being added in the MUIQ research platform.

12. Preview the study structure. Save the study as a template and then select Create study for data collection.

FIGURE 8.13: Study preview prior to creating the study in the MUIQ platform.

Should You Make Responses Mandatory?

As part of the process of programming an unmoderated benchmark, you'll need to decide which questions you make mandatory. Which means if participants don't answer required responses, they can't proceed in the study. There are pros and cons to consider when making responses mandatory.

Cons of mandatory responses

The obstacles you are likely to encounter with required responses can be the following:

- **Frustration and abandonment:** The conventional wisdom is that respondents become frustrated and abandon benchmark studies when they encounter questions that they must answer before proceeding to the next question. The best crafted benchmark study isn't a good one if no one takes it. It might even be worse if people commit to taking a study and abandon it out of frustration. You may have incomplete data and an irritated sample of customers!

- **Non-response bias:** If participants abandon the study because of required responses, this may contribute to response bias, as the people who abandon may be different than those who don't (see Chapter 10 on dealing with missing data).

- **Response bias:** Participants may respond to required questions, but they might lie or randomly pick an answer to get through the survey. There are ways to detect unusual responses, but it's not foolproof.

- **Privacy policies:** When you use participants from certain populations, policies may prevent you from requiring responses. Most institutional review boards (IRBs), for example, have a policy that allows people to opt out from answering any question, including mandatory questions, in benchmark studies.

Pros of mandatory responses

Despite the drawbacks, there are good reasons to require responses:

- **Branching and logic:** One of the best ways to keep a benchmark study short is to only include relevant questions and to not force respondents to answer "N/A" or skip the questions. If a question has logic (skipping several inapplicable questions or tasks) or branches out (depending on how a participant answers previous questions), responses need to be compulsory.

- **Avoiding listwise deletion:** Many of the statistical analyses used to analyze results (such as multiple regression, factor analysis, and cluster analysis) can't handle missing values well. If any response is missing from a respondent, all responses from that respondent are removed from the analysis (called listwise deletion). There are methods for filling in missing values (called imputation, see Chapter 10), but it's not a substitute for real answers, especially if there is systematic bias for people who are not responding. Having someone volunteer their time to answer most of your survey questions to only have their data thrown out may be worse than requiring responses.

- **Reducing overlooked questions:** Not all missing responses are intentional. People make mistakes and overlook questions (especially with matrix questions). Required responses allow respondents to notice this mistake and provide a response. Some platforms (like MUIQ) allow you to request a response without requiring a response, but for most platforms, the only way to remind a participant is to require a response.

Additional thoughts for compensated respondents

The pros and cons of requiring responses apply to surveys where people are asked to volunteer their time. This is a common practice with customer surveys. But in many cases, participants are paid for their time, using national panel providers or Mechanical Turk. Under these circumstances, completing the survey is essentially a job. The more questions you ask, the more you pay to get responses. For paid respondents, not answering questions is like not doing their jobs. However, you still have to consider the effects of people lying or providing erroneous answers.

When participants are not part of a panel but are still compensated or entered into a sweepstakes, you likely have more license to compel responses, but probably not as much as with a paid panel of participants.

Requiring responses increases the burden on the respondent, which in turn may lead to increased abandonment. The actual effect on surveys and benchmark completion rates is unclear, and in some cases, required responses may actually increase the response rate.

When compensating participants, especially with paid panel services, you likely have more license to require responses to most, if not all, questions. Required questions also have the added benefit of reducing survey length by allowing for branching and logic, as well as alerting respondents to questions they may have overlooked.

To improve response rates, reducing the length of the study (number of questions) will likely have a bigger effect on the response rate than the number of required responses. More research is needed to disentangle the effects of survey length and required responses to a variety of survey types.

MODERATED STUDY DATA COLLECTION

For moderated studies, software isn't as needed as it is with unmoderated benchmarks; however, it can help. The setup is similar to a usability test and differs if the study is in person or moderated remotely. Mobile and physical-product benchmark studies also require some different logistics. The following sections highlight the common setups we use for moderated in-person and moderated remote benchmark studies.

Moderated In-Person Benchmark Studies

The in-person or lab-based study setup is very similar to a usability test setup. In-person benchmarks are the go-to method for desktop consumer software (e.g., QuickBooks), business software (e.g., AutoCAD), mobile apps (e.g., Facebook), and websites or web applications that require authentication (e.g., StubHub).

FIGURE 8.14: Picture of the observation room for one of MeasuringU's labs in Denver (looking through the one-way mirror).

The main things you'll need to consider for benchmark data collection are task administration, metric recording, and session/video recordings. For more details on setting up usability labs, see Jeffrey Rubin and Dana Chisnell's book *Handbook of Usability Testing: How to Plan, Design, and Conduct Effective Tests* and *Practical Guide to Usability Testing* (Dumas and Redish, 1999) .

Task administration

The participant needs some way to know what the tasks are. Tasks can be presented to the participant using a print out, displayed electronically using a tablet or a second computer monitor, or displayed dynamically from unmoderated software like the MUIQ.

For simple and short tasks, the facilitator can read tasks to the participant; however, we find this just adds to the memory load of the participant and prefer, when possible, to have tasks displayed or written. When I started benchmarking in the early 2000s, we routinely printed out "participant packets." These packets contained the tasks and instructions the participants needed to complete the study and had a predetermined counterbalanced order. Two of the major disadvantages of using these packets were the task order and handling any changes that needed to occur.

- **Task order:** For most benchmark studies, the order of tasks is randomized to minimize sequence effects (participants improving or degrading performance over time). To do this for a printed package, we had to manually shuffle the tasks, which can be labor intensive and error prone.

- **Changes:** No matter how carefully planned a benchmark is, there will inevitably be changes to the protocol (task wording, questions, or response options). When using printed tasks, this may mean either reprinting many or all of the participant packets.

Metric recording

You're going to need a way to collect task- and study-level metrics and to be sure you have the metrics associated with the right task and participant. Organization is important here, as task order will change and participants may get shuffled. This can be done with using a few additional low-cost tools or using more sophisticated software.

By hand: You can go old school with a stopwatch and printed grid or notebook to handwrite task completion, errors, observations, and answers to post-task and post-study questions (see Figure 8.15). This classic approach still works, but you'll need to plan for the extra time of coding the data from paper to software to aggregate the metrics and insights.

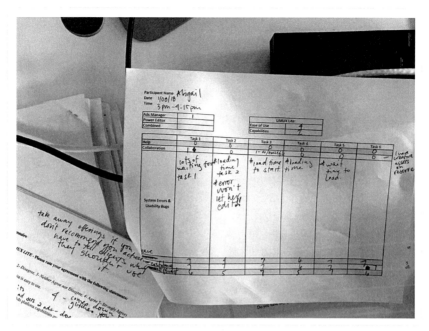

FIGURE 8.15: Notes sheet for collecting post-task and post-study metrics during a moderated benchmark.

Excel-based logger: Our friends David Travis and Todd Zazelenchuk at UserFocus created a simple Microsoft Excel-based logger (userfocus. co.uk/resources/datalogger.html). It tracks task time using a macro and has the essentials for logging events (UI issues), task completion, and some basic post-task metrics.

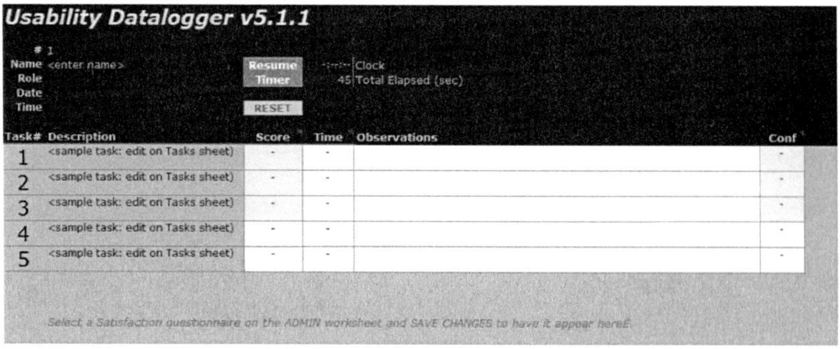

FIGURE 8.16: Screenshot from the Usability Datalogger.

Morae: Morae is Techsmith's extension of Camtasia for usability testing. It has options to record just the screen and to collect time metrics automatically, as well as the option to record both the screens and the participants' faces. We've had some struggles with it in the past with getting task randomization and questions configured properly and didn't use the video and screen logging features (we use the open-source OBS Studio for video recording); however, a lot of researchers continue to have success with Morae.

Custom software: There are enough frameworks to create your own custom software for tracking benchmarking data. In 2008, I developed my own web-based custom logging software that handled the randomization, collected task time, and tracked UI problems in real time. We used it for our studies that validated the keystroke level modeling (KLM) approach and the SEQ.

Unmoderated software: If you have access to an unmoderated platform like MUIQ, UserZoom, or Loop11, you can use this in a moderated session. The software will administer the tasks electronically and let the platform collect the metrics (time) and administer the questions for you. You'll likely want to disable any verification questions if you're assessing task completion from observation. Using this method addresses the randomization issue (if the platform supports it) and allows the facilitator to focus on problem identification and keeping the study moving.

Survey software: You can use free or low-cost survey software, like SurveyMonkey, to administer post-task and post-study questions. These can be displayed on the same machine the participants are using or a tablet. You can use survey software in conjunction with manual metric recording.

Session recording

Having a recording (and maybe also having backup recordings) can make benchmark studies run more effectively. Coordinating the study and recording metrics can be a lot for a facilitator (and even a note-taker). Things go wrong—software can fail, task criteria can change, or mistakes happen—and you may need to go back to recode the metrics. Recordings can be done using software such as Camtasia, Morae, OvoStudios, OBS Studio, or GoToMeeting.

Moderated Remote Benchmark Studies

The major difference between in-person and remote studies is that you will definitely need to have software for remote moderated studies to view the participants' screen, mobile device, and, if feasible, their face. We use GoToMeeting; other options include WebEx, join.me, or TeamViewer. They all have their strengths and weaknesses. Plan for a few minutes of each session for troubleshooting the inevitable technical issues.

Task administration

We've found a few options that work for getting tasks to participants in a remote benchmark:

- **Email the participant packet.** You can email participants an electronic version of the tasks and walk them through the tasks and pages they need during the study.

- **Send them a link to an online web page of the tasks.**

- **Use unmoderated software.** Keep all the tasks and questions together using unmoderated software. This works even if the participant is using desktop software—just have them return to a web browser between tasks.

Metric recording

You can use most of the same options for a remote moderated study as with in-person studies: hand coding, Excel loggers, customer software, or unmoderated software (though Morae doesn't work for these setups).

Session recording

The remote software you use (e.g., GoToMeeting—see Figure 8.17) will record the participant's screen; however, sometimes the recordings don't encode or save so there is a chance you won't have access to the recording later. For this reason, we often record the screen using Camtasia or OBS Studio in addition to the GoToMeeting recordings.

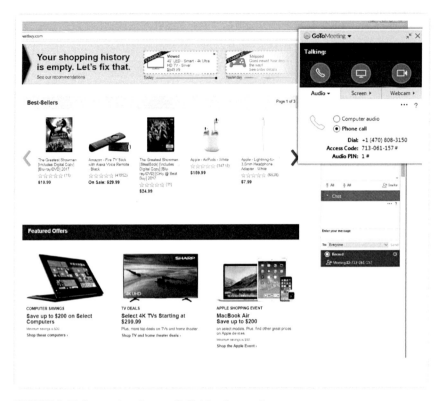

FIGURE 8.17: Screenshot from a GoToMeeting session.

Moderated Remote for Mobile Device Benchmark Studies

While moderated remote benchmarks require some patience and technical troubleshooting, this is especially the case for conducting a remotely moderated benchmark study for mobile devices. You'll still present the tasks the same way as a desktop or website remote benchmark study; however, you'll need some way to view the participant's mobile device. We've found the following three ways to accomplish this:

- **Mirroring:** Have the participant mirror their screen to their computer by using software like QuickTime or Reflector.

- **Webcam or laptop hug:** Have the participant reverse their laptop to use the built-in webcam (see Figure 8.18).

FIGURE 8.18: The laptop hug.

- **External camera and sled:** In rare situations you may need to ship participants a document camera or an observation device, like our MOD 1000, which allows you to see both their mobile devices and gestures (see Figure 8.19). This approach can be quite costly and time consuming if you have more than a couple dozen participants.

 TIP:

When collecting data for your benchmark, keep non-essential people outside the lab. There's evidence that observers and conspicuous monitoring equipment affects both the physiology (heart rate) and in some cases the performance of the participant (e.g., more errors).

FIGURE 8.19: Mobile Observation Device (MOD 1000).

CHAPTER SUMMARY AND TAKEAWAYS

In this chapter we covered preparing for data collection for moderated and unmoderated benchmark studies:

- Unmoderated studies generally require a lot more upfront work to prepare for data collection. Plan time to "program" and iterate changes in an unmoderated platform. These steps include adding
  - Welcome messages
  - Task descriptions
  - Task success criteria
  - Post-task questions
  - Post-study questions
  - Randomization and logic parameters
  - Screen outs and quotas
- For moderated in-person benchmarks, software isn't as critical (although it's very helpful) for data collection and screen recording.
- For moderated remote benchmarks, you will need screen-sharing software that can also record the participant's screen.

CHAPTER 9:
PARTICIPANT RECRUITMENT AND DATA COLLECTION

A benchmark has a key ingredient you can't leave out—the participants! Unfortunately, finding participants isn't always easy. In fact, it's safer to say you should expect it to be the rule and not the exception that it's hard to find qualified participants for a benchmark study. A 2017 study of UX researchers by Ethnio (a UX agency) found out that of all the activities performed—"Recruiting sucks the most."

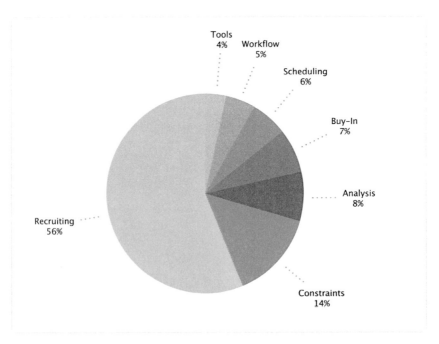

FIGURE 9.1: Recruiting is cited as the biggest "hassle" in UX research. Source: Ethnio, personal communication, December, 12, 2017.

In this chapter I'll provide some guidance on finding participants for both moderated and unmoderated benchmark studies. In particular I'll focus on unmoderated recruiting because it's less familiar to many researchers who are only used to in-person studies, and unmoderated recruiting tends to generate more questions from our clients about how it works.

RECRUITMENT FOR UNMODERATED STUDIES

One of the main advantages of unmoderated benchmark studies is the ability to collect data from a lot of participants quickly. But this means you'll need access to a lot of participants and pay them for their time. The best sources for this are online panels, existing customer lists, and website intercepts.

Use Online Panel Sources

There are dozens of companies that provide access to hundreds to thousands of participants willing to take online surveys for unmoderated benchmark studies. The companies we've worked with the most include the following:

- **Op4G (Opinions 4 Good):** We use Op4G the most. Part of the participant honorarium goes to charity.

- **Toluna:** A huge company with a lot of international reach and specialized profiles.

- **Harris Interactive:** A more expensive panel that maintains probability-based sampling.

- **Amazon's Mechanical Turk:** A good do-it-yourself platform for general consumer profiles.

The general process of working with a company that provides participant panels involves mostly the logistics of connecting their participants to your online data collection tool and ensuring the right participants take the study and get compensated. In general, this involves the following:

- Specifying the profile and sample requirements (e.g., IT decision makers in small to medium businesses)

- Setting up redirect links to your unmoderated platform (this is how the panel tracks who took the study and who was screened out or dropped out, see Figure 9.2 for an example)

- Collecting IDs from participants and confirming with the panel
- Paying or giving points to participants who completed the study

For more information on panel and participant costs, see Chapter 4.

Redirect URLs and study external parameter

☑ Use redirect URLs for the study

External parameter name

IDIN ✖

Use {p} placeholder inside URLs to designate position where actual parameter should be pasted

Redirect URL for study completion

http://myop4g.com/redirect/?a=1&kvi=4648f7e51d4&sid=8845&uid={p}

Redirect URL for study quota

http://myop4g.com/redirect/?a=2&kvi=4648f7e51d4&sid=8845&uid={p}

Redirect URL for study termination

http://myop4g.com/redirect/?a=3&kvi=4648f7e51d4&sid=8845&uid={p}

FIGURE 9.2: Redirect links input fields from MUIQ.

9 things to consider when using online panels

Online panels are the go-to method for collecting data quickly for unmoderated benchmark studies. Despite their wide usage, surprisingly little is known about these panels, such as the characteristics of the panel members or the reliability and accuracy of the data collected from them.

While there isn't much published data on the inner workings of panels, we've conducted our own research and compiled findings from the literature to provide insights for you. You can also ask your panel provider for information on their panels.

1. **Participants belong to multiple panels.**
   There are a lot of choices in online panel providers: Op4G, Toluna, Cint, Research Now, and Harris Interactive to name a few. And there's nothing stopping participants from signing up for more than one panel. In fact, one meta-analysis* found that as many as half of panel participants belong to five or more panels! The implication is that a minority of participants account for a disproportionate amount of the participation. Signing up to multiple panels increases a panel member's chances that he or she gets access to more studies and therefore more rewards.

2. **Multiple panel membership affects attitudes.**

   Belonging to multiple panels isn't necessarily a bad thing. But repeated exposure can have an effect on results. Participants who belong to multiple panels tend to have above average brand awareness and higher stated intent to purchase products (soup or paint in the studies I found). It was also found* that participants who belong to multiple panels and took a lot of surveys in the course of a year tended to be inattentive respondents (completing studies much too quickly and providing only terse responses to open-ended questions).

3. **Length of panel membership also has an effect.**

   One study* found that participants who had been with a panel longer (> 3 years) were less likely to recommend a product (50% vs. 37%). While there are likely a number of reasons for the difference, I suspect it has something to do with study exposure and even desensitization. This desensitization may not be a bad thing; generally, participants tend to overestimate their likelihood to do things (like purchase or recommend). What is somewhat problematic though is not knowing whether your respondents are new to the panel (prone to recommend) or seasoned (somewhat jaded and less likely to recommend).

4. **The average online study lasts around 17 minutes.**

   Study length is a major contributor to dropout. A meta-analysis of 11 panels* found the average study time is 17 minutes, with around half of studies lasting 20 minutes or more, including 13% that were 30 minutes or more. We found that the average time using a panel participant was a bit higher than in our studies, but this average duration can help answer questions about how long is too long relative to the other studies the panel members are taking.

5. **Estimates can vary.**

   It's common to need to estimate the attitude or stated behavior of people in the general population. Samples pulled from online panels are used to estimate the general population (these are called

---

* See *Online Panel Research: A Data Quality Perspective* (2014, Editors: Mario Callegaro et al., Wiley Series in Survey Methodology).

point estimates). Research has shown that point estimates varied, and in some cases varied quite substantially, depending on the panel used and from known external benchmarks. It isn't uncommon for point estimates for metrics, such as intent to purchase and brand awareness, to vary by 15 to 18 percentage points. This discrepancy was seen in a variety of measures, including demographics, stated behaviors (e.g., smoking and newspaper readership), brand awareness, and likelihood to purchase.

6. **UX metrics can vary too, but not as much as expected.**
   The point estimates for common UX benchmark metrics (like the SUPR-Q and NPS—see Chapter 5) varied between panels and for more general demographic and psychographic variables. On average, the differences were between 3% and 10% but in some cases exceeded 20%. This variance was less than we expected given the more ethereal nature of UX metrics.

7. **Changing panels changes estimates.**
   Differences in estimates between panels can, in many cases, exceed real differences in the population. Our recommendation is to not change panels, especially when making comparisons over time, such as the likelihood to recommend a product or brand attitudes. Changing panels is often unavoidable. If you're making comparisons to historical data and you had to change panels, let your reader know to use caution when interpreting the results and provide any information on the differences in panel characteristics (if known).

8. **Probability panels are probably better.**
   Most online panels are called non-probability panels, as they obtain their members using online ads, snowball sampling, river sampling, and direct enrollments; these panels also don't sample proportionally from the general population. Probability panels, in contrast as its name suggests, ensure that every member of a population (often an entire country) has at least some chance of being selected to respond to a study. Probability panel companies have measures in place to ensure some level of representativeness, often for hard-to-reach populations. As expected, probability samples, while rare, tend to (but don't always) perform better than non-probability samples by more closely matching the external benchmarks.

9. **Be wary of panel quality**

It seems each year there is an increasing demand for people to participate in online research, including benchmark studies. This pressure on getting samples can increase the likelihood of participants gaming the system, misrepresenting themselves, or providing poor-quality responses.

We have become increasingly critical of our online panel sources, as we've seen a slow degradation in the quality of responses. This can easily be monitored in unmoderated benchmark studies with session recordings, as we are able to see participants' screens and whether they are providing some effort to attempt tasks. In 2012, we would typically see no more than a 10% discard rate for poor-quality responses. In 2017, that rate was getting closer to 30%, depending on the panel and sample. We've found this unfortunate pattern for both low and high incentive studies. More concerning is that some participants (especially from some poorer quality panels) will go to great lengths to avoid getting screened out of studies (e.g., by incorrectly stating income and age, which are hard to verify).

An unfortunate side effect of this dodgy behavior is artificially high responses for many questions. While more research is needed, we found a case where one client we were working with had initially used one panel which resulted in a large amount of poor data. The data that was retained showed questionable response patterns with most attitudinal questions being rated unusually favorably. We compared their data to a control sample we used from a high-quality panel source to verify the poor quality of their data. It may be difficult to detect such patterns, so be wary of panels that underpay participants or overpromise a sample.

To combat poor panel quality, we've been increasing our efforts to recruit our own participants (as discussed in this chapter), using more direct advertising and reaching out to avoid poor-quality and "professional" participants. See Chapter 10 for more on cleaning data to identify and remove poor-quality responses.

Professional participants

Another problem that can be difficult to avoid is what I call the professional participant. These are people who essentially derive a living (or a sizable amount of money) from taking online surveys and being part of think-aloud services. These participants get rewarded for speaking articulately about websites and design. However, the amount of time they spend taking studies may distort their opinions and behaviors. It's not so bad that I recommend not using these services; just be wary when using sources that may have a lot of professional participants. Consider finding new sources of data to compare the findings.

Access Existing Customers and Prospects

Existing customers who have a relationship with a company and prospects who express an interest in the company or its product are an obvious wellspring for testing.

However, existing customers and prospects aren't a panacea for benchmark testing; they have at least three major drawbacks:

- **Bias:** These participants are likely to have a more favorable attitude and have more familiarity with products and websites. This makes them less than ideal for competitive studies.

- **Not new:** By definition, most of these participants would be considered experienced users in a benchmark study. If you are looking to benchmark the new user experience, these participants wouldn't fit well (unless you are benchmarking a new product).

- **Unfamiliarity with online studies:** Most unmoderated benchmark studies require participants to download a plug-in and are asked to simulate experience with a website or web app. This experience and time commitment can be both new and perplexing for some participants (especially those who are lower-tech) and make many participants drop out of a study. To manage this issue, have detailed instructions and plan to recruit more people. This is the opposite problem of "professional" participants.

The two most common ways to reach these existing customers and prospects is to use direct email and website intercepts.

Direct email

Most organizations maintain a customer list and usually have some sort of ability to communicate with customers using bulk email (for customers who have opted-in). You can invite customers on these email lists to participate in a benchmarking study. Include a short description of what's expected, the honorarium (if any) or sweepstakes (e.g., an iPad), and how long the study may take. To email a lot of participants, don't just add them to a *cc* or *bcc* line in your email. You or your organization will need to use a bulk-email provider to ensure that you don't get blacklisted and your email gets through. See Chapter 4 for some suggestions and costs on sending bulk emails if your company doesn't provide this already.

Website intercepts

Visitors to a company website can be invited to participate in a current or upcoming benchmark study. You can use pop-ups (see the MUIQ example in Figure 9.3) or have opt-in boxes on websites to solicit volunteers to participate in your benchmark. Using this approach, you'll get generally qualified participants because they were on your website on their own accord. Let participants know the time commitment, honorarium, and the dates of the study if it's not immediate. You can also use this approach to pre-screen participants based on demographics, like age and prior experience, then target them for future studies.

FIGURE 9.3: Website intercept example.

Website intercepts aren't a guaranteed way of finding only qualified participants. The people who respond may only be interested in the incentive (if offered). We know of one large consumer electronics website company we worked with that collected participants from an intercept off their home page. They let prospective participants know the honorarium they'd pay for participating in an upcoming study. They collected thousands of emails from people willing to participate but found people were posting the link to coupon and give-away websites, which attracted non-qualified participants. To retain only the qualified participants, additional screening was added after the names were collected.

Some guidance when paying participants

In the never-ending quest to find participants for benchmark studies (and any type of research for that matter), you'll likely confront the question of whether and how much you should offer to pay participants. Here are 13 things to consider when deciding whether an incentive is the way to go for your benchmark study.

1. **Incentives help response rates.**
   Incentives of some form (money, gift cards, iPads, etc.) generally increase response rates to unmoderated benchmark studies. If your study is more time consuming or more difficult, incentives can encourage participants to finish it, and there's some evidence they help with the quality of open-ended responses (see surveymonkey.com/curiosity/academic-research-on-incentives/ for more details). The good news is that incentives alone don't seem to bias participants' responses systematically (e.g., tendencies to agree to statements).

2. **Money is usually better than gifts.**
   Monetary incentives generally increase response rates more than gifts. Prepaid incentives help more than promised incentives, though it's difficult to prepay people for web surveys (unlike sending money in the mail with a hard-copy survey). But money doesn't always help—as mentioned in point #12 below.

3. **Paying can be painful.**
   Mailing out hundreds of $10 checks isn't fun (we've done it), and the process isn't easy with most banks. Mailing physical gifts is even harder because you'll need to collect valid physical addresses. You can use the next best thing to cash: Amazon gift cards and PayPal (at least in the US). Both Amazon and PayPal make it easy for you to pay in bulk, but not everyone has a PayPal account and sometimes you can't use Amazon (e.g., if you're another retailer!). There are also bulk payment providers who can distribute cash for you, but the fee is often as much as the honorarium.

4. **Lotteries may be cheaper and easier.**
   Instead of paying everyone, you can have a lottery, where all participants who completed the study have an equal chance to receive something. The nice thing about a lottery is that you can offer a more substantial incentive (e.g., an iPad or $500) instead of a more modest honorarium (e.g., $10). When you conduct a lottery, you'll need to be sure your participants are aware of their true odds of winning (there are many legality issues) and be sure you have a way of sending the gifts or funds electronically. Also, you must make sure that the item is available and ready to ship, for example, you don't want to offer a new iPad if they're out of stock for months!

5. **Lotteries/sweepstakes are easier but probably not as effective.**
   Lotteries are easier and probably cheaper than paying everyone, but there's some evidence that they aren't as effective as paying everyone. This is likely a natural consequence of how people view incentives. Which would you have: guaranteed money (even a small amount) or a small chance to win a modest amount? A professional survey taker puts his thoughts succinctly:

   "Sweepstakes are for people who can't calculate probability properly—scrape a decent budget together and pay people for their time."

6. **Lotteries have legal issues.**
   You'd think it's simple; you're giving away things! But it's not that easy unfortunately. In many U.S. states (and probably most countries), you really have to be careful on how you conduct your sweepstakes or lottery. In fact, you might have to get some legal help to ensure you're not breaking the law.

7. **Consider other incentives.**
   You don't have to give away buckets of cash or iPads as an incentive. If you have a product or service people like (e.g., store credit) or other discounts or coupons (if it's something you can offer), those options may be an effective incentive. Again, our candid professional survey taker offers his advice:

   "If you're offering a coupon/gift card, it better be good."

8. **Determine the right amount.**

   Higher incentives generally increase response rates, but there is a point of diminishing return. The good news is that while higher incentives improve responses, they don't seem to negatively affect the nature of the responses or the type of people who respond (you just get more people to respond).

   The right amount will depend on your audience (higher for higher-paid professionals) and the length of the study. You may need to experiment with different amounts to see what works.

TIP:

You can do a soft launch (sending an invitation to a small sample) to see what the response rate is likely to be based on your planned incentive.

9. **Budget.**

   You, of course, can only compensate as much as your budget will allow. Even a nominal compensation of $5 adds up quickly if you need more than 1,000 participants for a benchmark. You will likely need to budget for the cost (and time) to get the money to these scores of participants.

   Watch for the following two things when paying participants directly:

   - Be sure you have a survey quota. Some surveys can fill fast, and you don't want to be on the hook for 2,000 payments if you only budgeted for 1,000.

   - If you have to oversample (because of rejecting poor-quality responses), you will likely have to decide whether to compensate all or just the responses you thought were worth retaining.

If you're running a lottery, you'll again want to consider the costs of obtaining the incentive and shipping costs if applicable. And if you're using discount codes, be sure that's factored into your actual sales margin.

10. **Money or gifts can present more legal issues.**

Not everyone can receive money or gifts. Physicians, radiologists, and government employees are among the many participant types who are often not allowed to receive money at all. Also, some industries are not permitted to give money or gifts. For example, there are rules against pharmaceutical companies paying doctors, even nominal gifts, due to the potential conflict of interest.

11. **Appeal to the interest of your participants.**

If the participants feel like their voice will make a difference, you may not need any incentive. This is especially the case if your survey is generally short (think under 10 minutes). For example, if a customer feels like their opinion will help improve a product or service they use, they're more likely to participate in your benchmark study. Or if you have a passionate group of users, (e.g., non-profits), they will likely provide their opinions at much higher rates.

12. **Money may also hurt response rates.**

Not only does compensating hit the bottom line, in some cases, it may negatively affect your response rate. It may seem like offering an incentive is a no-brainer way to get more people to participate. But money is not just like any other type of incentive; people treat it differently.

If your participants are already intrinsically motivated to provide their feedback (e.g., because they believe in your cause or product), offering money can backfire. There's less research on this effect in survey incentives, but it's a well-documented effect in many other contexts.

13. **Don't coerce.**

While it's generally less of a concern for benchmarking studies, there is often a concern about incentives being coercive, especially for certain disadvantaged populations. In the event you are surveying an economically disadvantaged group, be sure your incentive isn't coercing people to feel they *need* to respond in order to get a service, for example.

RECRUITMENT FOR MODERATED STUDIES

Recruitment for moderated benchmark studies uses many of the same sources as unmoderated studies (customer lists, website intercepts, and ads). The major differences are the additional time commitments and logistical considerations needed for people to be in a certain place at a specific time, for example, being at an office location at 9:00 a.m. during the work week or being at your desk ready at a certain time so you can receive instructions for the study. It is generally harder to find people willing to dedicate an hour of time to participate in an in-person or remote benchmark study. You also won't likely have much help from online panels as they do not typically provide support for moderated benchmark studies. Instead you'll need to rely on professional recruiting firms, advertising, and recruiting from customer lists.

Use Professional Recruiting Firms

There are companies around the US and world that recruit for in-person studies; however, many of these companies primarily specialize in recruiting for focus groups and other types of market research. We've worked with Plaza Research and Fieldwork with generally good success when needing to recruit specialized participants, such as architects and software engineers. It can be difficult to get more than 20 or 30 participants, even with the large lists these companies maintain. You may need to supplement this approach with advertising and existing customer lists.

Develop Advertising

You can post ads on Craigslist or Facebook to target qualified participants in one or multiple markets. Getting the ads right and sifting through people who are misrepresenting themselves can take time, but it is often a good option to access people who fit a general consumer profile or to target a specialized population. For more focused recruiting, consider calling non-profits or community organizations and offer to donate some of the honorariums if they help find participants for you.

Create Your Own Panel

We conduct moderated studies (benchmarking and more formative studies) about every week at MeasuringU. Over the last few years, we've recruited thousands of participants using every method described in this chapter. We've maintained a list of participants and their relevant demographic details (including the type of mobile device they have, their occupation, etc.) and which studies they have participated in. This list, which now includes thousands of participants (mostly in the Denver market), allows us to quickly target qualified (and higher quality) participants. If you conduct multiple studies, consider curating your list to act as a panel for moderated and unmoderated research.

Use Customer Lists

As with unmoderated studies, using existing customers is a logical place to find qualified participants for benchmark studies. Our recommendation is to begin creating your own curated list of customers who are willing to participate in moderated and unmoderated studies.

Manage No Show Rates

For moderated benchmark studies (and any in-person study), you should plan for some percentage of participants to not show up. People get busy, forget, or have other things they need to be doing other than participating in your benchmark study. We have several steps in place to keep our no-show rate as low as possible, such as the following:

Email, then call, then call again. Don't just email participants for scheduling; speak to them on the phone to let them know there will be people waiting for them. One day prior to the study, follow up again with a call to speak with the participant (or leave a message). If you are unable to get ahold of them, ask them to send a quick email, return the call, or text.

Communicate that a dedicated time slot has been reserved for them. Despite the popularity of usability testing and benchmarking studies, most people will have never participated in anything like it. Let participants know it is a one-on-one study and time has been reserved just for them. Remind them of the importance of letting you know if they can't attend.

Exploit the consistency bias. In our screening questionnaire, we ask participants to rate how reliable they are and how likely they are to show up for appointments. We don't expect people to rate themselves low, but that's not the point. We are exploiting the consistency principle here. People are more likely to follow through on previously stated actions and behaviors in order to be consistent. Rating yourself as reliable and someone who goes to appointments would be inconsistent with someone who doesn't call or doesn't show up.

Include clear directions. It may seem obvious, but if people can't find your facility or where to park, they may just give up and go home.

Be clear on what to expect. In your email and phone communications with participants, let them know what will be expected of them (e.g., asked to work on accounting software), their time commitment (e.g., 1 hour), and honorarium and how it will be paid (e.g., $100 cash or Visa gift card).

Over-recruit. Even with our best efforts, things happen and people cancel (often no call, no show), even from professional recruiting firms. We've found the best thing to do is anticipate a 10% to 20% no show rate and over-recruit. If you need 20 participants, plan on recruiting 22 to 24.

Over-schedule. Over-recruiting is often not enough to ensure your benchmark study stays on schedule. You may have a couple extra participants ready to participate, but a no call, no show means you'll need to quickly scramble in the hopes of making up for the lost person and time. Having people "float" and always be available can be both costly and difficult. Instead, when we need to stick to a tight schedule, we'll schedule the extra participants ahead of time. This gives us more options. If all the participants show up as planned, you can use these as extra participants or cancel them and pay the participants anyway because you blocked out their time. Of course, if too many participants cancel, budget for a bottle of wine for your recruiter and facilitators!

DATA COLLECTION: PRETESTING AND SOFT LAUNCHING TO PREPARE FOR THE FULL LAUNCH

With your participant source identified, it's time to start collecting data. Before you go into the full launch, you'll want to properly pretest and soft launch your data to limit the amount of issues and to ensure participants can effectively complete the study. The following sections highlight things to consider before fully launching your study.

Prepare for Moderated Benchmark Data Collection

Before launching into the full study, pretest the study particulars to ensure that you are ready. Here is a list of suggestions to review.

Facilitators need to adjust their style in benchmark studies by reducing the amount of intervention and probing to emphasize a consistent collection of metrics. In many large sample moderated benchmark studies, facilitators often "babysit" rather than moderate while participants follow scripts to complete tasks. Because of the large number of participants facilitators manage for this type of study, they often only intervened if problems occur. There's typically only minimal probing or interruptions from facilitators as they will often follow more tightly scripted sessions. For more on different facilitation styles see "The Facilitation Spectrum: From Babysitter to Therapist" at measuringu. com/facilitation-styles/.

Go through the study script. Have the facilitators go through the study script in detail to ensure they understand all the steps. They should pay particular attention to points where they will need to probe participants, and they should know how to score task success correctly for each task.

TIP:

To collect more reliable task-time metrics, we don't recommend facilitators plan to probe or interrupt the participant mid-task. Instead, save questions and probing points for between tasks or after the beginning or end of the study.

Check the technology. If technology always worked as planned, there wouldn't be a need for so many benchmark studies. Murphy's Law definitely applies here, and you'll want to check and double check your tech setup and plan for things to go wrong at the worst time. We have our own separate checklist for technology that includes points for the following:

- **Session recordings:** Be sure the screen recordings, audio, and backup recordings are working.
- **Observer access:** If observers are watching from another room (ideally not in the lab) or remotely, ensure they can see and hear the participant and moderator. We run both GoToMeetings and a live stream of the event.

- **Data recording:** For collecting task-time data, ensure the timing and product/websites are working as expected. This also might include an Excel workbook.
- **Product/website:** Whatever interface is being benchmarked (e.g., account software, web app), ensure the participant's credentials (username/password) work.

TIP:

> Try to reduce the intrusion of monitoring equipment, as there's some evidence this increases stress and error rates.

Practice a dry-run. Facilitators should conduct a dry-run using an internal or "throw-away" participant (e.g., a colleague not involved in the study) to get a sense of how long the study will take and to make sure the technology is working and not interfering with the study.

Plan for a pilot study. If possible, plan for someone to be your "pilot" to run as the first real participant to gauge the effectiveness of the data collection methods. Treat this study as you would any other study, and plan for time after the pilot study to review and adjust study particulars.

Check-in with stakeholders. Address any questions or problems that came up from the pilot participant or technology. This can include any changes in task descriptions, success criteria, pre- and post-study questions, as well as the facilitation style of the moderator.

Now you are ready to fully launch your study!

Prepare for Unmoderated Benchmark Data Collection

For unmoderated benchmarks there are more things that can go wrong. There's no facilitator to assess task success, answer participant questions, or make real-time adjustments. What's more, participants are accessing and completing the study on their terms and there's little time to make changes to the study once it's live. Similar to the pretest for a moderated benchmark study, use the following suggestions to pretest your unmoderated study.

Check study timing. Have some internal participants go through the study to generate a realistic estimate of how long it will take the typical participant to go through the study. If there is a change, update the welcome screens. For example, if it takes 10 minutes for someone familiar with the study to go through, read each question, and attempt each task, assume it will take a typical user between 15 and 20 minutes to complete. Continually revisit the advertised time if you see the median study time is longer or shorter than your initial estimate.

Verify that task success criteria haven't changed. It can be days between when the task script was written and when you move to soft launch. Prices change and product inventory change. Go through the tasks and be sure you can complete each task immediately prior to launching.

Verify the logic and branching. Logic and branching are the terms to describe which participants see which question. For example, financial advisors may "branch" to a different set of questions about their clients, which wouldn't be relevant for general consumers. Some questions may also only be shown if other questions are answered a certain way. For example, if participants indicate they are familiar with a brand, you may ask them to rate their satisfaction with that brand. Go through all the combinations participants can take to make sure your logic and branching work as expected. The more conditions and branches there are, the more time this will take.

Ensure for randomization. For unmoderated benchmark studies, randomization is essential to spread the unwanted effects of learning and fatigue across tasks and competitors evenly. You may need to take the study a few times (and toss out the data) to ensure your randomization scheme is working as intended.

Evaluate required questions. If you need participants to respond to a question, ensure they can't proceed without answering. While you don't want to add undue burden on participants, finding out in your analysis that some questions were skipped can complicate analysis. There are some approaches to working with missing data, but one of the best approaches is to avoid missing data altogether if you can. During pretesting, you may "unrequire" questions to make it easier to go through and check other aspects of the study. Be sure you make them required again by making this one of your later steps.

Test with think aloud services. One of the best uses we've found for services like UserTesting and TryMyUI is having these services' participants go through our benchmark studies—even when we don't intend to use these services for recruiting participants. People from these services are trained and rewarded for thinking aloud, so much so that I've come to call some of them "actors," as they are almost playing the role of a user and make comments typical participants don't, such as making design recommendations. These participants are great for ensuring questions make sense and there aren't any unforeseen issues with the flow of the study.

Prepare to launch—softly! Instead of fully launching your study at the outset, aim to recruit around 10% of your intended number of participants (e.g., 15 out of 150) to test the test. This is often referred to as the "soft" launch, like the soft opening of a restaurant that helps work out any kinks in the system. Instead of checking recipes and service, you check your data, study timing, logic, branching, and session recordings again with actual participants to ensure you're properly collecting the data and from the right people. Pay particular attention to any open-ended questions where participants might be indicating potential problems. Make corrections before proceeding to the full launch.

What happens when an unmoderated study doesn't fill?

Who wants to plan a huge party only to have no one show up for it? You may launch your benchmark study in anticipation of combing through hundreds of responses to find after serval days only a handful of participants have completed the study. Unlike an auction on eBay where all the bids come in at the last minute, the opposite is generally true for unmoderated benchmark studies using online panels or direct email recruiting. You'll usually see the bulk of your sample in the first few days, then the remaining trickle in. The reason is people usually receive an email invitation and respond quickly. The more time that goes by, the more buried the email becomes in people's inboxes.

Here are some common causes of lack of participant engagement and what to do about them.

Reduce the study length. We have found that the length of a study is one of the biggest factors that leads to study drop-out. If you can't find a way to cut out questions, consider assigning a subset of questions or tasks to ensure your study length isn't too onerous. See the following section in this chapter for how long typical online studies last. If yours is on the higher end, this may be your problem.

Add more logic or branching. Does everyone need to answer every question or attempt every task? Look for ways to reduce the burden by removing some questions and directing participants to the most relevant questions and tasks.

Increase or change the incentive. If you can't reduce the study length or burden, try increasing the incentive to attract more participants. Use guidance from your panel if you are using one on the right amount to offer. If you are offering a sweepstakes, you may need to consider direct payment or increase participants' odds of winning.

Assess and/or remove required questions. While you don't want to have missing data in your analysis, be sure required questions really need to be answered. In particular, look at open-ended questions that require participants to type a lot (especially on mobile devices). Remove requirements if possible; though, I recommend doing this after reducing study length, as we've found length has a bigger impact than the number of required questions.

Verify the tech. To record sessions on desktop or mobile devices, participants will need to install a small plug-in for a desktop or download an app for mobile studies. Check that these are working properly and not interfering with the website or web app. For example, in one unmoderated benchmark we noticed the taskbar in MUIQ was slightly blocking a filter on the bottom of a web page. We reconfigured the taskbar to allow it to float on the page. In other cases, the website or app might be malfunctioning or just not accessible to people in certain countries or behind firewalls.

Address concerns. This can be a major barrier for participants (and panel agencies). There is a constant fear of scams and hacking attacks that make headlines and may make your participants less willing to take your study. Consider FAQs and clear privacy policies to assuage concerns.

Change panels. If you are using an online panel, consider looking to other companies. For specialized participants and especially for different countries, some panels just have more participants than others.

Use different recruiting methods. It could be that your participant profile is too difficult to fill for online panels. You may need to look into using your own customer list or posting your own ads to find qualified participants.

Send a reminder. If you are conducting the recruiting, send a reminder email if possible. If working with a panel, they also should be able to remind participants the study is still open. It's often the case that participants assume a study has filled if a few days have passed, a simple reminder may be all you need to fill your benchmark.

How long is the typical online study?

Even when you find the right participants for an unmoderated benchmarking study, there's a limit to how much time people are willing to spend—even for the right incentive. In general, the longer the study, the more people drop out, even those who are paid. There's a balance between packing a study with as many questions as possible while also keeping the study short.

To understand how long a typical benchmark study takes, we started with our data. We conduct dozens of online benchmark studies a year and compiled data from the last three years. This included a mix of benchmark and general unmoderated studies.

We found that 130 unmoderated studies took a median of 14 minutes to complete, with the 25th percentile at 9 minutes and the 75th percentile at 24 minutes. In other words, 75% of the studies we looked at took less than 24 minutes. Participants in online panels will be taking both simple surveys and benchmark studies. A meta-analysis on hundreds of online surveys found an average time of 17 minutes for online studies of all types. Across both sources of data, a "typical" study time is less than 17 minutes and a "long" study is one lasting 30 minutes or longer.

For more information on this research, see "How Long Is the Typical Online Study" at measuringu.com/online-study-time/.

ASSISTING IN MODERATED BENCHMARKS

As with moderating with classic formative usability testing, in moderated benchmark studies there are times when you may need to intervene to help a participant during a task. Here are some considerations to understand regarding assists.

What's an assist? An assist is when a facilitator intervenes to provide help to participants, which often leads to the facilitator completing the task or a portion the task. For example, if a participant is asked to add a hooded sweatshirt to the shopping cart as part of a benchmark task, but is unable to proceed because he or she didn't notice the error message to select a size (the small error message in Figure 9.4), eventually, the facilitator may need to point out the need to select the color and size to proceed to the next step in the task.

FIGURE 9.4: Example problem from a benchmark study where participants were unable to proceed with a task because they didn't notice an error message.

Why assist? If participants become stuck early in a task or study, providing assistance may allow you to uncover any usability issues later in the study that you wouldn't see if you didn't provide assistance, as well as allow you to collect more benchmark metrics from other tasks. The benefits of intervening (additional problems found or more data collected) should outweigh the costs (potentially unrepresentative data for one task because of the intervention). In the hoodie example, more data can be gathered about the shopping cart pages and experience by telling the participant how to proceed.

Don't be afraid to assist. One of the first things facilitators learn is to not coach or lead participants to complete tasks or to turn the session into a demonstration. It can be very difficult to learn not to interfere because people generally want to help others when they struggle. But sometimes intervention is warranted, so you should be prepared to assist if needed. There's not a one-size-fits-all solution to know when to step in; however, there are some common signs to watch for that signal when you might need to jump in.

Know when to assist. Knowing when to wait and when to intervene takes practice. Here are some good indications of when it's time to assist a participant:

- A participant is really struggling. If a participant is repeatedly having trouble or experiencing the same errors, there's no reason to make the experience go on forever. Don't jump on the first sign of struggling though; watch to ensure a participant really can't progress.

- Time is running out. There's a limited amount of time in a study. You should assist a participant when he or she takes too long with one task and won't get to other tasks, screens, or parts of the study.

- There's an imminent disaster. If a participant's continued actions will lead to a problem, such as crashing a system, deleting data, or charging a credit card inadvertently, you'll need to intervene.

- It's not really over. Sometimes participants will think they've completed the task and are ready to move on when in fact they haven't completed the task (or all parts of the task). If this premature task completion happens, you may need to intervene and nudge the participant into considering other options.

Use assists sparingly. While there are times when you need to assist, you should still keep them to a minimum in benchmark studies. If you find you're frequently assisting in a benchmark, consider redesigning your tasks or study. If you or another moderator frequently assist across different studies, then reconsider your facilitation style to see how you can reduce assistance.

Measure assists. Like other benchmark metrics, you should record if you had to assist a participant, noting how many times and for what reason. Tracking the frequency and causes of assists over time can help with diagnosing usability problems or refining your testing protocol (for example, there may be a problem with your study protocol, task instructions, or the software being tested).

Report task completion with and without assists. The major implication for assists in benchmark studies is how to report task data when an assist happens. With a record of assists, you have a choice on how to report completion rates (with assistance or without). Some organizations have policies on which completion rate to report—assisted, unassisted, or both. The unassisted completion rate is by definition lower than the assisted completion rate (when there are assists). Many benchmark studies have high-stakes impacts for companies, and there may be consequences to drops in metrics (for example, if a minimum increase in task completion rate was expected, there can be controversy over whether to report assisted task completion rates).

Know when an intervention is not an assist. Sometimes the facilitator will need to intervene as participants are completing a task but don't necessarily assist them in completing the task. Examples of interventions that are not assists are the following:

- Clarifying task instructions or repeating the task
- Prompting a participant to think aloud
- Helping a participant recover from a software bug, computer crash, or some other technical issue

Understand that not all assists are created equal. In Joseph Dumas and Beth Loring's book, *Moderating Usability Tests: Principles and Practices for Interacting*, they suggest separating the levels of assistance, ranging from the least amount of intervention to the most, to make it easier to report the level that occurred during the intervention.

- Breaking a repeating sequence by asking participants to perhaps read the task again or consider another option.
- Providing a general hint, such as letting participants know the information they need is on a screen they've been to already.
- Providing a specific hint, such as telling participants that the function they need is under a menu item or on the next screen.
- Telling participants what to do, when all else fails, such as telling participants to click a certain button or navigate to an element.

EFFECTS ON TASK TIME WHEN PARTICIPANTS THINK ALOUD

One of the more common questions I get for moderated benchmark studies is whether participants should think aloud while they attempt tasks. Thinking aloud provides rich insight about potential problems with the interface (even if the focus is on metrics), so not collecting think aloud data has the potential to lose a great source of insight. While it might seem like having users think aloud will increase the time on task—the literature is actually mixed (see "Can You Measure Task Time if Users Think Aloud During a Usability Test?" at measuringu.com/thinking-aloud-time/ for more information).

Some studies report no difference, some show longer task times for thinking aloud, and others report faster task times for thinking aloud. It has been hypothesized that the reason users can perform faster while they think aloud is because this vocalization allows them to think more clearly through their approach for completing the task.

My advice is generally to allow participants to think aloud but not to prod them and definitely not to interrupt them to probe. Some users will express their thoughts as they complete tasks, and others are silent. When I see a problem that I want to know more about, I wait until after the task is complete and ask the user to elaborate more on what they did and why. This is called retrospective probing. I find this retrospective approach gets me the biggest bang for my user buck (or euro). Be sure you use the same approach when you make comparisons year over year to ensure consistency in your data collection. The relative comparison in times will usually be more valuable than the stand-alone time.

CHAPTER SUMMARY AND TAKEAWAYS

In this chapter we discussed that benchmarking has two key ingredients that can't be left out—the participants and the data:

- Participant recruiting is consistently listed as one of the most challenging aspects of benchmark testing (and all UX research).

- To find participants for unmoderated benchmarks, you can use one of many online panel companies, direct emails to customers, or website intercepts.

- When using online panels, be wary about the quality of the panels and how they obtain and pay participants and check the quality of responses. Also, know that most panel participants belong to multiple panels.

- Incentives generally help response rates (and are required for using panels). Paying participants is more effective than gifts or lotteries/sweepstakes.

- To find participants for moderated benchmarks, you can use professional recruiting firms, advertise, email your customers, or create your own panel from previous studies.

- Plan to pretest then soft-launch your moderated and unmoderated benchmark studies to prevent problems. This will ensure that participants can work through the study, and you can collect the data you need.

- For moderated benchmarks, you'll need to carefully weigh the pros and cons of assisting participants when they struggle during tasks.

- When collecting task-time in moderated benchmark studies, it's generally OK to have participants think aloud but it's also OK if they don't. However, you'll want to avoid interrupting task performance with reminders to think aloud.

CHAPTER 10:
ANALYZING AND DISPLAYING YOUR DATA

In this chapter we'll cover the steps and methods you need to know to identify poor-quality responses, what to do with missing data, and the best ways to summarize study- and task-level metrics. Spending time upfront removing poor-quality responses and handling missing data should save a lot of the time and headaches from having to rerun your analyses.

Before getting into the analysis of your data, you're going to need to clean it. Cleaning doesn't involve a disinfectant, and it doesn't mean removing responses that aren't favorable. Cleaning is a major step for unmoderated studies but less so for moderated studies where participants are observed by a facilitator (so there's little room for cheating).

CLEANING DATA IN UNMODERATED BENCHMARK STUDIES

In our experience, around 10% of participants (often ranging from 3% to 20%) "cheat" in surveys and unmoderated UX studies, and their data needs to be tossed out or "cleaned." These responses are usually a combination of cheaters, speeders, respondents misrepresenting themselves, or participants just not putting forth effort—all of which threatens the validity of the studies' findings.

 TIP:

> To clean your data, you can export it to Excel (most unmoderated platforms should have an export to Excel or CSV to examine individual responses). Some platforms may also allow you to exclude or filter participants online, but be sure you can see the timings and responses by participant.

There's no simple rule for excluding participants in a benchmarking study. Instead we use a combination of the following methods to flag poor-quality respondents, progressing from the more to the less obvious indicators. This process helps ensure we're obtaining higher quality results and valid findings from our benchmark studies.

Most Obvious and Easiest Detection Methods

First, you'll want to start with the easiest methods to eliminate poor-quality responses. These methods help you remove the most obvious of the poor-quality responses. Notice that if one response falls into this category, you don't automatically throw it out; however, if a response falls into two or more categories (or combined with an advanced method), you should think twice about including it.

Poor verbatim responses: A participant who has multiple verbatim responses that consist of gibberish ("asdf ksjfh") or terse, repetitive responses ("good" or "idk") is often an indicator that he or she is not taking the study seriously and may be speeding through rather than answering thoughtfully. Answers to the open-ended questions should be one of the first and easiest ways to identify a poor-quality respondent. See Figure 10.1 for some examples of this issue.

While multiple poor responses are usually grounds for removal, a single gibberish or nonsense response is not necessarily a big problem, provided the other verbatim responses are answered thoughtfully. For example, we've found in some cases it could have been from requiring a respondent to answer a question he or she was unable to answer meaningfully.

Irrelevant responses: Occasionally, respondents will provide responses that do not match the question asked but are not gibberish. These could be lines that were copied and pasted from other places, or even the question itself could have been copied and pasted into the answer. At first glance these responses look legitimate (because they are long and contain common words you'd expect in surveys), but on close examination they may be indications of participants gaming the study. Unfortunately, there are even cases of automated "bots" providing random plausible responses to open-ended questions and answering closed-ended questions. (It also happens with scientific research.) As with poor responses, multiple nonsense responses are a bigger concern than a single suspicious response.

Cheater questions: If a "cheater question" was included (e.g., "Select 3 for this response") and the participant answered it wrong, it is cause for additional examination. One wrong answer can simply be a mistake, so use caution when deciding to include or exclude participants based on this criterion. We've found that incorrectly answering a single cheater question may exclude too many participants. (Those who made mistakes when responding or were perhaps only distracted temporarily.)

Speeders: A participant who completes the study too quickly is a cause for concern. For example, if a participant takes two minutes to finish a 50-question survey, it is highly unlikely that he or she is providing genuine, thoughtful responses. It's more common for participants to speed through questions, pages, or tasks (if running an unmoderated study) than through the entire study. Here are two suggestions when deciding how fast is too fast: First, be sure not to be too strict in defining your "too fast threshold." We have been quite surprised how quickly some people can answer survey questions and complete tasks. Second, where possible, look at the speed of individual tasks, pages, or questions as opposed to the time it takes to complete the entire study. These more granular measures of time we've found are more sensitive to detecting speeders.

While it would seem flagging speeding participants for removal is an easy first step, earlier research and our own data has found it's not necessarily a good indicator of poor- and high-quality responses in and of itself. The same goes for very slow participants; taking a very long time may just be an indication of a participant getting distracted while taking survey and not necessarily indicative of poor quality. The primary exception being when you need to collect time-on-task in online usability studies and task times are unrealistically long, they need to be removed. The good news is with speeders, even if you don't remove all of them, we've found little difference between speeder and non-speeder data, which is similar to earlier research that suggests speed alone isn't a good indicator of poor-quality responses.

Less Obvious and More Difficult Detection Methods

Like hackers who learn to evade anti-spam detectors or speeding motorists who know where the speed traps are, some panel participants have found increasingly more sophisticated ways to game the system (receive an honorarium without conscientiously responding). This is especially concerning when a small number of participants may disproportionally account for participation across multiple panels.

Inconsistent responses: Some questions in a study tap into a similar concept but are phrased with a positive or negative tone. The SUS is a good example of a questionnaire that uses this alternating tone. It doesn't make much sense for a participant to strongly agree to the statement, "The website is easy to use" and strongly agree to the statement "I found the website very cumbersome to use." This is an indication of an inconsistent response. Be careful when using this technique. We've found people can make a legitimate effort to complete a study but still make the mistake of forgetting to disagree to negatively toned statements when they have positively agreed to the positive statements. If you're using this approach, consider evaluating multiple inconsistent responses for a safer approach.

Missing data: When compensating participants, we'll often make many, if not all, questions in our studies mandatory. When not all questions are required and participants neglect to answer many of them, this non-response is another symptom of poor-quality responses. Just as concerning with non-response though, is how your data might be biased if participants are systematically not responding to some questions. You should consider examining whether the missing data is random or more systematically biased.

Pattern detection: Participants who respond using conspicuous patterns, such as straight lining (all 5s or all 3s) or alternating from 5s to 1s on rating scales, also indicate a bot or a disingenuous respondent. But again, be careful—if participants had a good experience on a website, it's not unsurprising for them to rate the experience as exceptional, on say 8 or 10 items. There's more concern if you see straight lining or patterns for 20 or 30 questions in a row.

Session recordings: If the study is task-based with screen-recordings, then you can observe what participants are doing while completing the study. For example, you may observe no activity happening on the screen during a task, or users who are distracted by Facebook, or in some cases we've seen participants haphazardly clicking as if to fool this fraud detection, similar to dodging speed traps.

Disqualifying questions: For many studies, we look for participants with particular characteristics. If a participant somehow is admitted into a study by answering a screening question a certain way, but then reveals in the open-ended answers they are not qualified, they are excluded (e.g., a participant needs to have a particular credit card, but in an open-ended question reveals that he or she doesn't have any credit cards). This can also be done in combination with a cheater question if, for example, participants state they are familiar with fictitious brands or have bought products that don't exist.

Applying These Methods to Clean Your Data

We use the above methods to informally score each candidate for quality of response. Deciding on how strict we follow the criteria for each method depends on the needs of the study.

Respondents who fail multiple checks are the first to be flagged for removal. For example, respondents who provided gibberish responses, incorrectly answered cheater questions, and completed the study very fast are the first to be removed. A participant who answered a cheater question wrong but provided helpful responses to the open-ended questions is often worth retaining.

I also highly recommend not permanently deleting respondents from your dataset. Instead, flag them as poor quality in a way that allows you to unflag them in the future. We've found that in some cases we were too strict in applying our criteria and removed too many people and then needed to add them back into the results.

Keep in mind that you're measuring people, not robots, and people get tired, bored, and distracted but still want to provide genuine input. Some level of poor-quality responses is inevitable, even from paid respondents, but the goal is to winnow out those who don't seem to provide enough effort from those who perhaps got a little distracted. If you find a lot of poor-quality respondents in your data, be sure you make your studies easy to complete, use the right panel, and provide a reasonable honorarium (see Chapter 9 for more information on these points).

FN	FO	FP	FQ
SearchPref. V	SearchCmmt. When searching for information on financia	SearchTools. Briefly describe what search to	AddlComment
Products disp	ggfhfghgfhgf	ggfhfghgfhgf	ggfhfghgfhgfh
Funds display	Graphics	Search box/bar	0
Products disp	yes	yes	yes
Funds display	yeah	yes	none
Products disp	good	likely	good
Funds display	all the information you provide to me in the short and me	all the information you provide to me in the s	none
Products disp	what they're offering and how secured they're as well..im	google of course and others platform	none.its good
Funds display	sad and stuff	sad and stuff	sad and stuff
Products disp	this is very good I liked so much	this is very good I liked so much	this is very goo
Funds display	What is the minimum investment.	The filters	The Blackrock
Products disp	Measuring U survey	Measuring U survey	Measuring U su
I have no pref	None	None	0
Funds display	all visible research m ub akk ckasses	filters are best	0
I prefer them	performance	priceperformancename	none
Funds display	The year end percentages on yields.	equity and return search tools	0
Funds display	Dates	I used google search engine	None

FIGURE 10.1: Example output from a benchmark study with the more egregious offenders highlighted in red and less obvious ones in yellow. Both were removed for analysis.

DEALING WITH MISSING OR INCOMPLETE DATA

Despite the best planning, you'll inevitably have to deal with missing data in your benchmark studies. This is especially the case for unmoderated studies. Missing data typically comes from participants not answering questions or completing tasks (either intentionally or unintentionally).

The first step in addressing missing data is identifying the type of missing data. There are three types of missing data:

- **Missing completely at random:** There is no pattern in the missing data for any variable. This is the least problematic type of missing data.

- **Missing at random:** There is a pattern in the missing data but not for your primary dependent variables, such as likelihood to recommend or SUS scores.

- **Missing not at random:** There is a pattern in the missing data that affect your primary dependent variables. For example, it could be that lower-income participants would be less likely to respond in a survey and thus affect your conclusions about income and the likelihood to recommend. Missing not at random is your worst-case scenario. Proceed with caution.

Missing data is like a medical concern; ignoring it doesn't make it go away. Ideally your data is missing at random and one of these approaches will help you make the most of the data you have. Here is a list of solutions to help you manage missing data:

- **Listwise deletion:** Delete all data from any participant with missing values. If your sample is large enough, then you can likely drop data without substantial loss of statistical power. Be sure that the values are missing at random and that you are not inadvertently removing a class of participants.

- **Recover the values:** You can sometimes contact the participants and ask them to fill out the missing values. For in-person studies, we've found having an additional check for missing values before the participant leaves helps.

- **Imputation:** Imputation is replacing missing values with substitute values. The following methods use some form of imputation:

  - Educated guessing: It sounds arbitrary and isn't a preferred course of action, but you can often infer a missing value. For related questions, for example like those often presented in a matrix like in Figure 10.2, if the participant responds with all 4s, assume that the missing value is a 4.

Please rate your level of agreement to the following statements about the Chipotle website.

	Strongly Disagree 1	2	3	4	Strongly Agree 5
The Chipotle website has a clean and simple presentation.	○	○	○	◉	○
The Chipotle website is easy to use.	○	○	○	◉	○
I find the Chipotle website to be attractive.	○	○	○	◉	○
The Chipotle website is trustworthy.	○	○	○	◉	○
It is easy to navigate within the Chipotle website.	○	○	○	○	○
The Chipotle website's capabilities meet my requirements.	○	○	○	◉	○
The information on the Chipotle website is credible.	○	○	○	◉	○
I will likely return to the Chipotle website in the future.	○	○	○	◉	○

FIGURE 10.2: Example of participant responses with a missing value. It's likely the participant would have selected a 4 for the missing value.

- Average imputation: Use the average value of the responses from the other participants to fill in the missing value. If the average of the 30 responses on the question is a 4.1, use 4.1 as the imputed value. This choice is not always recommended because it can artificially reduce the variability of your data, but in some cases, it makes sense.

- Common-point imputation: For a rating scale, this involves using the middle point or most commonly chosen value. For example, on a 5-point scale, substitute a 3, the midpoint, or a 4, the most common value (in many cases). This is a bit more structured than guessing, but it's still among the riskier options. Use caution unless you have good reason and data to support using the common-point value.

- Regression substitution: You can use multiple-regression analysis to estimate a missing value. We use this technique to deal with missing SUS scores. Regression substitution predicts the missing value from the other values. In the case of missing SUS data, we had enough data to create stable regression equations and predict the missing values automatically in the calculator.

- Multiple imputation: The most sophisticated and, currently, most popular approach is to take the regression idea further and take advantage of correlations between responses. With multiple imputation, software creates plausible values based on the correlations for the missing data and then averages the simulated datasets by incorporating random errors in your predictions. It is one of a number of examples where computers continue to change the statistical landscape. Most statistical packages like SPSS come with a multiple-imputation feature.

 TIP:

You may need to revisit this list after your initial round of analysis to see how numbers may or may not change when addressing missing data.

ANALYZING DATA AND PREPARING FOR PRESENTATION

With the data gathered, it's time to analyze your data to understand the user experience. To analyze the data, you can use the following common platforms.

Platforms for Analyzing Data

Research/survey platforms web apps: Most data collection platforms (including MUIQ, UserZoom, and Loop11) contain their own basic graphing and data summarization tools. These are typically only sufficient for providing basic descriptive statistics around your demographic, study, and task metrics, and they have less support for statistical comparisons or providing confidence intervals (MUIQ supports both). If you're using them, be sure you can filter out any participants you removed.

Excel: Excel is the go-to program we use for summarizing study-level and task-level metrics. It's not great for conducting advanced analysis (like regression or ANOVA), but for 90% of benchmarking graphs and analysis, Excel does the trick. To learn some essential Excel skills, see measuringu.com/excel-1/ and measuringu.com/excel-2/. A free benchmarking Excel package is available for download on the MeasuringU website: measuringu.com/benchmarkbook/

StatsUsabilityPack: I created this usability statistics package using Excel that does just about everything you'd need to do to apply statistics to benchmark data (and just about any UX data). There is a companion book that also shows you step-by-step instructions on how to conduct the most frequent analyses, appropriately called *Excel & R Companion to the 2nd Edition of Quantifying the User Experience* (Lewis and Sauro, 2016). Both are available online measuringu.com/product/expandedstats/ and measuringu.com/book/excel-r-companion-to-quantifying-the-user-experience/.

SPSS: Many graduate students in the behavioral sciences are familiar with the Statistical Package for the Social Sciences (SPSS) software. The software has since expanded into other markets and has everything you need to conduct basic and advanced statistical analysis. The major drawback is it comes at a huge price tag. We've also found its graphs are more cumbersome to create.

R: The free R statistical package is an alternative to SPSS that many graduate programs are adopting. It's open source and has lots of free add-on packages that can accomplish more than even SPSS can. The major drawback is it is command-line based, so you'll need to get comfortable with its syntax language. The free R-studio helps with some of the core commands, but there is still a bit of a learning curve with R. We have several common procedures built into R that can be downloaded. (See *Excel & R Companion to the 2nd Edition of Quantifying the User Experience* for more information.)

Minitab: Minitab is a statistical package that's less expensive than SPSS and has more of an engineering focus compared to SPSS's behavioral science focus. It's a package I learned a long time ago and is still a go-to for me to conduct quick statistical calculations and graphs.

Data Analysis

In this section, I go through the analysis of a raw output data gathered in the MUIQ platform by using Excel to analyze the data. This example uses data collected from the unmoderated hotel benchmark study. You can download and view the dataset, PowerPoint template, and calculator at measuringu.com/benchmarkbook/. As a reminder, this sample dataset came from a between-subjects study where participants were randomly assigned to complete two tasks on either the Marriott or Best Western websites. See Appendix E for the study script and task scenarios. You can start with study-level metrics or task metrics (for task-based benchmarks)—it's your preference. For task-based benchmarks, I usually like to start with the task metrics.

For this section, I use unmoderated comparative benchmark data for most of the examples. However, the calculator and output would be the same if the data was from a moderated benchmark study (the sample size would just be smaller). Where appropriate, I'll call out differences between the moderated and unmoderated analysis approaches.

Provide the participant data

With a clean dataset ready to analyze, you can start with providing some essential descriptions of the study's participants. This involves summarizing demographics (e.g., age, gender, income) and psychographics (e.g., prior experience, brand attitudes).

Most demographic variables are best summarized using frequency distributions and means, such as illustrated in Figure 10.3 and 10.4 for prior experience from a moderated computer drafting software benchmark study.

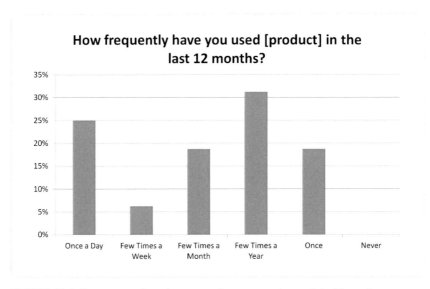

FIGURE 10.3: Frequency of product usage frowm a moderated drafting software benchmark study.

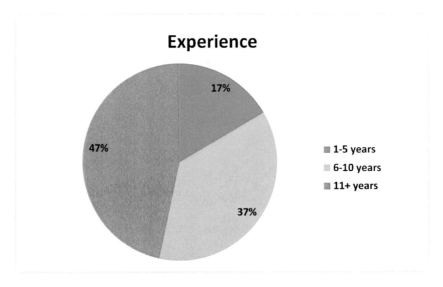

FIGURE 10.4: Tenure of usage from a moderated drafting software benchmark study.

We'll cover additional ideas on displaying demographics in moderated and unmoderated benchmark studies in Chapter 12 on reporting your results.

Analyze task data

When analyzing task-level data for benchmarks, start with the completion rate. This is the fundamental task metric for usability and UX benchmark studies. If few participants are completing tasks, you should expect lower metrics throughout. You'll also need to complete task-completion rates to complete task times.

TIP:

> You may need to do some recoding depending on your unmoderated platform. In UserZoom, for example, the data is outputted as codes (1 – 4) for task completion, indicating task success to different types of failure (timeout, abandon, or failure), and rating scale data often starts from 0 even though it displays as a 1.

Task completion rates

To report task completion rates, you'll need to have your data converted into 1s (for task success) and 0s for task failure. If a participant abandoned a task or there was a timeout on a task (leading to failure), code both as 0s. You can report abandonment and timeouts separately as other metrics if needed.

Verify the task success criteria

To prepare your raw task completion output for analysis, first verify the task success criteria. Even if you get 1s and 0s as the output from your tool, check that the task success criteria didn't change or doesn't need updating. For example, if you set a price or date as the validation question, be sure those prices and dates are still valid, as inventory and pricing change all the time.

You can also examine the "Other" options as validation questions to see if the same value is repeated. These options can be a good indication that another value should be considered a task success. For example, in the first task for the Marriott website, participants were asked how much it would cost to book a room for two nights at a particular hotel. The correct answer was $448 for two nights ($224 per night). In examining the

"Other" options, several participants provided the value of $224—which was the price for one night, not both nights (see Figure 10.5). While this was technically not the right answer, it did indicate that the participant had found the right room rate and got the essence of the task correct. In this case we felt it was worthy of task success and coded these responses, which were flagged as failures, as successes (1s). We then applied the same criteria to the Best Western website. You can see this in columns O and P in the hotel sample output file (Figure 10.5).

N How much wa	O How much wa	P Success(m1)	Q How confiden	R How easy or
Other	448	1	6	3
Other	448	1	7	5
Other	224	1	1	2
662		0	7	7
Other	224	1	7	7
662		0	4	4
Other	The hotel was	1	7	7
Other	672	0	7	7
Other	448	1	6	5
Other	261	0	3	3
458		1	5	4

FIGURE 10.5: Some of the "Other" options were coded as task success.

Calculate the completion rates
The next steps can be achieved by hand or by using the downloadable benchmark calculator available online at measuringu.com/benchmark-book/. The MeasuringU benchmark calculator is used in the following procedure to demonstrate how to accurately calculate the completion rates for a benchmark study.

1. Select the "Completion Rates" link from the main tab of the calculator (Figure 10.6).

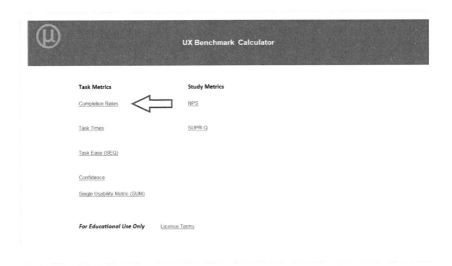

UX Benchmark Calculator

Task Metrics	Study Metrics
Completion Rates	NPS
Task Times	SUPR-Q
Task Ease (SEQ)	
Confidence	
Single Usability Metric (SUM)	

For Educational Use Only   License Terms

FIGURE 10.6: UX Benchmark Calculator home screen.

2. **Compute the completion rates.** With the values verified and coded as 1s and 0s for all tasks, compute the percentage of participants who completed the task. You have two options to do this using the UX Benchmark Calculator.

a) Option A: Paste the raw 1s and 0s from your output into the columns labeled Task 1, Task, 2, Task 1, Task 2 (see Figure 10.7A1). This will autofill the values in the X (completed tasks) and N (attempted tasks) columns (see Figure 10.7A2).

b) Option B: You can do this by hand first by adding up all the 1s and counting the total number of participants who completed the task. Divide the sum of the 1s by the count values for each task. Type the total of the completed tasks in the X column and the total of the attempted tasks in the N column. Note: If you type values in the X and N columns, it will overwrite the formulas in these columns that sum the 1s and count the 0s—save a copy of the calculator before doing this or download a new copy to preserve the formulas.

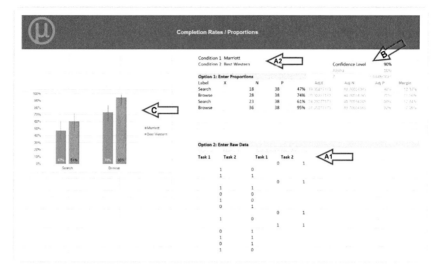

FIGURE 10.7: Completion rate calculation in the UX Benchmark Calculator with sample data.

3. **Calculate confidence intervals.** The confidence level can be adjusted up (to 95%) or down (e.g., 85%) by adjusting the value, see Figure 10.7B (see Chapter 11 for more information on how confident you need to be). See Chapter 3 in *Quantifying the User Experience, 2nd Edition* (Sauro and Lewis, 2016) for a detailed explanation on computing and interpreting the confidence intervals for completion rates.

4. **Graph the completion rates and their corresponding confidence intervals.** The graphs are automatically updated when using our Benchmark Calculator, see Figure 10.7C. The labels on the graph can be adjusted by changing the labels in the Condition 1 and Condition 2 cells, see Figure 10.7A2. The error bars on the graph are computed in the spreadsheet. For more information, see the sidebar "Adding Error Bars to Graphs in Excel".

5. **Perform a statistical test (advanced and optional).** The statistical test to perform for this type of data is the N-1 two-proportion test (see Chapter 11). The p-value for the Search task
   is $p = .25$ and for the Browse task is $p = .01$. This shows no
   statistical significance for Search but a statistically significant
   difference for the Browse task (this significance is also seen
   with the non-overlap in the confidence intervals on Browse and
   overlap with Search).

 TIP:

See Chapter 11 for more information on interpreting p-values and deciding which statistical test to conduct. Don't worry, you don't have to
memorize a lot of statistics. You can safely use the confidence interval
overlap method as described in the sidebar in this chapter—it will be
sufficient for most comparisons.

6. **Interpret the data.** In interpreting the data, Best Western had
   higher task completion rates for both tasks and statistically
   higher for the Browse task.

USING CONFIDENCE INTERVALS WITH BENCHMARK DATA

This benchmark study (like virtually all benchmark studies and surveys) samples only a small portion of the population. The completion rates will fluctuate each time we sample again, and each sample we take differs by some small amount from the actual completion rate (if we were able to measure all possible people who would use these interfaces). Confidence intervals provide the most plausible range of the unknown population completion rate or average score (for rating scale data or times). It's like saying we are 95% confident in the method of computing confidence intervals, but not for any given interval. Any given interval we compute from sample data may or may not contain the population average. Even though 95% of samples will contain the population average, we just don't know if the one sample we took is one of the 5% that doesn't.

You can use the overlap in confidence intervals as a quick way to check for statistical significance. If the intervals do not overlap, then you can be at least 95% confident there is a difference (for 95% confidence intervals). If there is a large overlap, then the difference is not significant (at the $p < .05$ level). The intervals can actually overlap and still be statistically significant, so when there is some overlap, it's best to conduct the two-sample t-test and find the p-value. The three graphs in Figure 10.8 illustrate this.

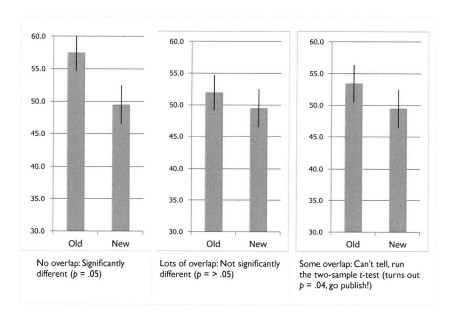

No overlap: Significantly different (p = .05)	Lots of overlap: Not significantly different (p = > .05)	Some overlap: Can't tell, run the two-sample t-test (turns out p = .04, go publish!)

FIGURE 10.8: Using the overlap (or non-overlap) in the confidence intervals to determine statistical significance.

Moderated completion rate example of output
To illustrate how to present your data to stakeholders, see Figure 10.9 and 10.10. These figures show the completion rates and confidence intervals from a moderated stand-alone benchmark for accounting software with 20 participants (Figure 10.9) and a year-over-year benchmark for computer-assisted drafting software with 30 participants in each year (Figure 10.10). Even though they come from a moderated study, both of them have raw data that looks just like the sample data from the hotel benchmark study (1s and 0s).

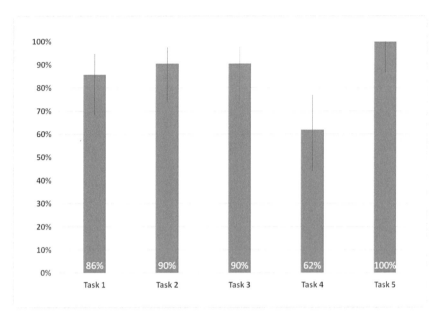

FIGURE 10.9: Task completion rates and 90% confidence intervals for five tasks (names intentionally removed).

All tasks in the accounting benchmark study had a relatively high task-completion rate (>60%) but Task 4's lower rate is worth investigating (Figure 10.9). In the drafting software benchmark, some tasks showed statistical improvements in completion rates (e.g., T3, T14, and T15 in particular) and some tasks showed nominal decreases (e.g., T1, T7, and T12).

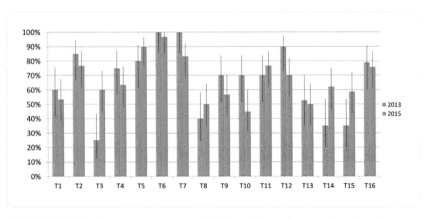

FIGURE 10.10: Task completion rates and 90% confidence intervals for 16 tasks (names intentionally removed) for a computer-assisted drafting software application for a comparison benchmark from 2013 to 2015.

Post-task ease

Next, we'll compute the average scores and confidence intervals for post-task ease ratings from the Single Ease Question (SEQ). The raw values are in the sample spreadsheet (Column R) in Figure 10.11. The procedure that follows this figure gives an example of how to compute the scores and confidence intervals using the UX Benchmark Calculator.

NOTE: You may need to recode the output. You again may need to do some recoding depending on your unmoderated platform. In UserZoom, for example, the data is often coded as 0 to 6 even though the responses might have been displayed as 1 to 7.

N	O	P	Q	R
How much w:	How much w:	Success(m1)	How confider	How easy or
Other	448	1	6	3
Other	448	1	7	5
Other	224	1	1	2
	662	0	7	7
Other	224	1	7	7
	662	0	4	4
Other	The hotel was	1	7	7
Other	672	0	7	7
Other	448	1	6	5
Other	261	0	3	3
	458	1	5	4

FIGURE 10.11: Colum R contains the post-task SEQ: How easy or difficult was the task to complete?

1. Select the "Task Ease (SEQ)" link from the main tab of the calculator.

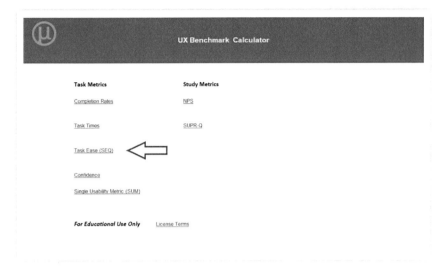

FIGURE 10.12: Selecting the "Task Ease (SEQ)" link from the UX Benchmark Calculator home screen.

2. **Compute the averages.** As with the completion rate data, you can use the summary data or raw data.

   a) Option A: Paste the raw values (1s to 7s) from your output into the columns labeled Task 1, Task, 2, Task 1, Task 2, see Figure 10.13A1. This will autofill the values in the M, SD, and n columns, see Figure 10.13A2.

   b) Option B: If you have the mean, standard deviation, and total number of participants that completed the task, type these values in the M, SD and n cells, respectively for each task. Note: Typing in these summary values will override the formulas in these cells. Save a copy of the calculator before doing this or download a new copy to preserve the formulas.

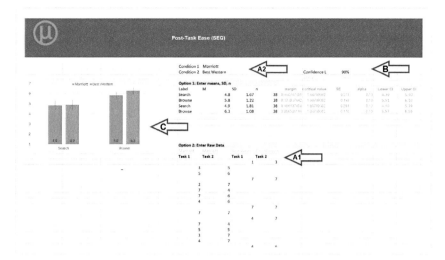

FIGURE 10.13: Post-task ease (SEQ) calculations using the UX Benchmark Calculator and sample data.

3. **Calculate confidence intervals.** The confidence intervals are calculated automatically from the mean, standard deviation, sample size, and level of confidence. You can adjust the level of confidence up (to 95%) or down (to say, 85%) by adjusting the value, see Figure 10.13B.

4. **Graph the average ratings and their corresponding confidence intervals.** These graphs are automatically updated when using our Benchmark Calculator, see Figure 10.13C. The error bars on the graph are computed in the spreadsheet. See the "Adding Error Bars to Graphs in Excel" sidebar in this chapter. The labels on the graph can be adjusted by changing the labels in the Condition 1 and Condition 2 cells, see Figure 10.13A2.

5. **Perform a statistical test (advanced and optional).** The statistical test to perform for this type of data is the two-sample t-test (see the "Conducting Statistical Tests and Interpreting P-Values" section in Chapter 11). The p-value for the Search task is $p = .89$ and for the Browse task, it's $p = .12$, indicating no statistical significance (also seen with the overlap in the confidence interval).

6. **Interpret the data.** As shown in Figure 10.13, when comparing the two conditions for perceived ease of use, there's not much differentiation between the Search task, but there is more of a differentiation for the Browse tasks, although not quite at the 90% level of confidence.

Task ease examples of output

See the following figures that illustrate how you can display results of post-task ease ratings (using the same 7-point SEQ) and confidence intervals from the moderated stand-alone benchmark. The examples are from an accounting software benchmark and a cross-device benchmark for a retail website.

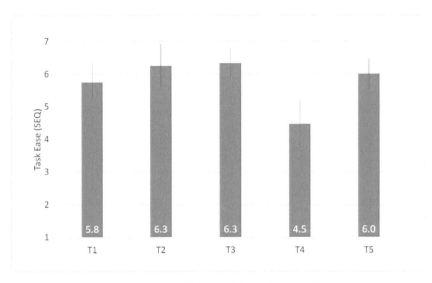

FIGURE 10.14: Task ease ratings and 90% confidence intervals for five tasks (names intentionally removed).

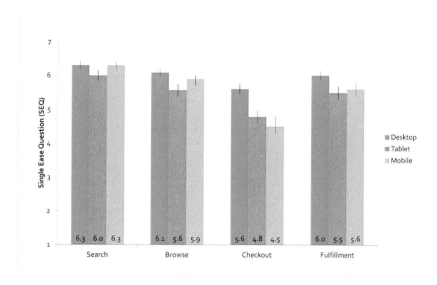

FIGURE 10.15: Task ease ratings and 90% confidence intervals for four retail tasks across device type (desktop, tablet, and mobile web).

Task time

For task time data, we'll need the task completion rate data, which we had previously computed. In our example, the raw task times are in the sample spreadsheet towards the end of the sheet starting with column BG (see Figure 10.16). The times for participants who were successful are within each time column labeled "Success." For example, column BH has the task times (in seconds) for only participants who completed the Marriott search tasks successfully.

BG	BH	BI	BJ	BK	BL
Group time: MSearc	Msearch Success	Group time: MBrow	MBrowse Success	Group time: BSearc	BW Search Success
				145	
383	383	326			
157	157	135	135		
				122	
164	164	127	127		
68		120			
133	133	318			
204		279	279		
				158	
272	272	164			
				144	144
244		434	434		
197	197	424	424		
268		240	240		
70	70	47			
				221	
80	80	124	124		
385	385	490	490		
				196	196
400		500	500		
159	159	316	316		
118	118	73			
				308	308
				149	
				201	201
				228	228
				268	268
196		114			
				89	
				171	171
				423	423
172		129	129		

FIGURE 10.16: Task time data for all tasks and successfully completed tasks in the sample worksheet.

The following procedure uses the UX Benchmark Calculator and the example study, the hotel benchmark, to illustrate how to compute the task times for benchmarks.

1. Select the "Task Times" link from the main tab of the calculator (Figure 10.17).

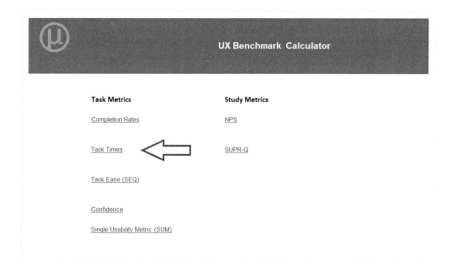

FIGURE 10.17: Selecting the "Task Times" link from the UX Benchmark Calculator home screen.

2. **Compute the average task completion time.** Paste the raw task times for successfully completed tasks into the columns labeled Search, Browse, Search, Browse, see Figure 10.18A. Unlike the completion rate and task ease data, you need the raw task time data to compute the average and confidence intervals. The reason for this is that the recommended method for computing confidence intervals and average time uses a log transformation on a participant's individual values. See Chapter 3 in *Quantifying the User Experience, 2nd Edition* (Sauro and Lewis, 2016) for the background of using the log transformation for confidence intervals and for selecting the best "average" time.

TIP:

You can repeat this exercise for all task times (not just times from successfully completed tasks) but be sure to describe the type of task time (e.g., task completion or total time on task).

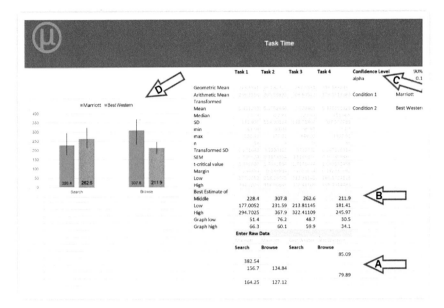

FIGURE 10.18: Task time calculations using the UX Benchmark Calculator and sample data.

3. **Compute the average time.** The recommended average time (the "Best Estimate of the Middle") is shown in Figure 10.18B, the yellow-highlighted row.

4. **Calculate confidence intervals.** The confidence intervals are calculated automatically from the log transformed values and the level of confidence. You can adjust the level of confidence up (to 95%) or down (to say, 85%) by adjusting the value, see Figure 10.18C.

5. **Graph the average task completion times and their corresponding confidence intervals.** These graphs are automatically updated when using our Benchmark Calculator, see Figure 10.18D. The error bars on the graph are computed in the spreadsheet. The labels on the graph can be adjusted by changing the labels in the Condition 1 and Condition 2 cells (Figure 10.18C).

6. **Perform a statistical test (advanced and optional).** The statistical test to perform for this type of data is the two-sample t-test (see Chapter 11). In our example, the p-value for the Search task is $p = .46$ and for the Browse task $p = .65$, indicating no statistical significance. The non-overlap in the confidence intervals also indicates it's not statistically significant, although it is very close for the Browse Task 2. The difference between the generally large p-value of .65 but confidence intervals that look a lot closer is because the statistical test is performed on the arithmetic means, and the confidence intervals are built around the best estimate of the middle (the geometric mean or median). See *Quantifying the User Experience, 2nd Edition* Chapter 5 for more on the details of this approach.

7. **Interpret the data.** As shown in Figure 10.18, there's more of a mixed pattern with the task times. It took users nominally longer to complete the Search task on the Best Western website (orange bars). However, the data for the Browse task for the Best Western website showed that it was nominally faster for successful participations over Marriott. If this were your data, depending on the consequences of the study, this may be enough evidence to conclude that the times are different enough (despite the non-significance) to justify treating them as different until more data (or a future study) show otherwise. If you were hoping to make public statements (e.g., in marketing materials) that one hotel's website was easier to search or browse through, it would be hard to back that statement up with the data; there was simply not sufficient evidence in this study to warrant a statement such as this, and the tasks should be treated as roughly equal.

Moderated task time example output
The following figures show an example of how to present your task times and confidence interval data to stakeholders. The figures show data from a moderated stand-alone benchmark for accounting software (Figure 10.19) and a year-over-year benchmark for computer-assisted drafting software (Figure 10.20).

Task times can be harder to interpret in stand-alone studies, and the example in Figure 10.19 is no exception. The first task was quite involved, as participants had to create several invoices, which led to the 21-minute average task time. These times, however, become important baselines for comparing against in future tests. It will allow the product teams to know if the design changes led to faster times—which is what we see in the next example (Figure 10.20).

Figure 10.20 shows task times in the year-to-year comparative benchmark. The data demonstrate the general trend with the tasks— most took slightly longer to complete, which was explained by new feature enhancements.

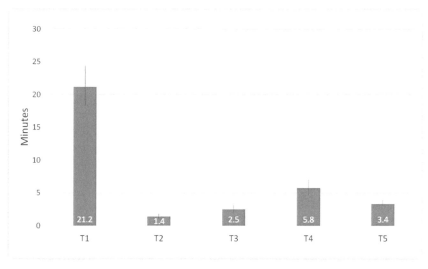

FIGURE 10.19: Task completion times and 90% confidence intervals for five tasks (names intentionally removed) from an accounting software benchmark.

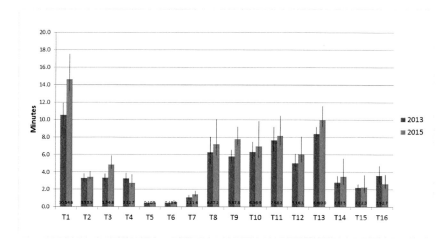

FIGURE 10.20: Task completion time and 90% confidence intervals for 16 tasks (names intentionally removed) for a computer-assisted drafting software comparison benchmark from 2013 to 2015.

Confidence

Next, we'll compute the average scores and confidence intervals for the post-task confidence ratings. The raw values start in the sample spreadsheet (Column Q) for the first task, see Figure 10.21.

> NOTE: You again may need to do some recoding depending on your unmoderated platform. For example, with UserZoom, the data is often coded as 0 to 6, even though the responses are displayed as 1 to 7.

N	O	Success(m1)	How confiden	How easy or
How much wi	How much wi			
Other	448	1	6	3
Other	448	1	7	5
Other	224	1	1	2
	662	0	7	7
Other	224	1	7	7
	662	0	4	4
Other	The hotel was	1	7	7
Other	672	0	7	7
Other	448	1	6	5
Other	261	0	3	3
	458	1	5	4

FIGURE 10.21: Column Q contains the post-task confidence question.

The following procedure uses the UX Benchmark Calculator and the example study, the hotel benchmark, to illustrate how to compute confidence for benchmarks.

1. Select the "Confidence" link from the main tab of the calculator (Figure 10.22).

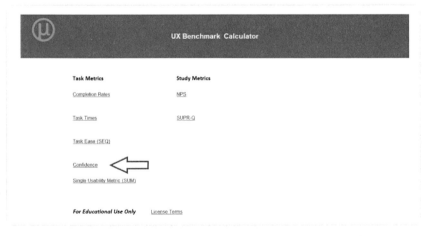

FIGURE 10.22: Selecting the "Confidence" link from the UX Benchmark Calculator home screen.

2. **Compute the averages.** As with the task ease data, you can use the summary data or raw data.

a) Option A: Paste the raw values (1s to 7s) from your output into the columns labeled Task 1, Task, 2, Task 1, Task 2, see Figure 10.23A1. This will autofill the values in the M, SD, and n columns (see Figure 10.23A2).

b) Option B: If you have the mean, standard deviation, and total number of participants that completed the task, type these values in the M, SD, and n cells, respectively for each task. Note: Typing in these summary values will override the formulas in these cells. Save a copy of the calculator before doing this or download a new copy to preserve the formulas.

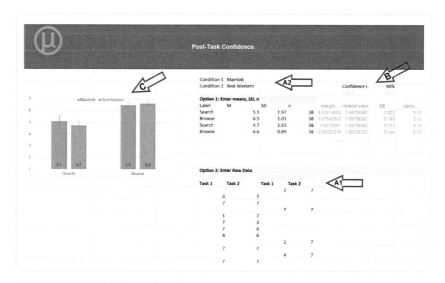

FIGURE 10.23: Confidence calculations with sample data in the UX Benchmark Calculator.

3. **Calculate confidence intervals.** In this example, the confidence intervals are calculated automatically from the mean, standard deviation, sample size, and level of confidence. You can adjust the level of confidence up (to 95%) or down (to say, 85%) by adjusting the value, see Figure 10.23B.

TIP:

Participants' self-reported confidence ratings are different than the confidence intervals. The former is from rating scale data and the latter speaks to our estimate of the average value from those rating scales. But post-task confidence ratings themselves have confidence intervals, making statements about our confidence and the participants' confidence quite cumbersome—but try not to confuse the two!

4. **Graph the average ratings and their corresponding confidence intervals.** These graphs automatically updated when using the Benchmark Calculator (as shown in Figure 10.23C). The error bars on the graph are computed in the spreadsheet.

5. **Perform a statistical test (advanced and optional).** The statistical test to perform for this type of data is the two-sample t-test (see Chapter 11). The p-value for the Search task is $p = .37$ and for the Browse task $p = .65$, indicating no statistical significance (also seen with the overlapping confidence intervals).

6. **Interpret the data.** In this example, there isn't much differentiation between post-task confidence. Participants were clearly more confident on the Browse task relative to the Search task, but there is little difference between websites.

Competitive retail comparison example output
Figure 10.24 is another example of how data can be presented to clients. In this case, this bar graph represents post-task confidence from a five-site competitive retail benchmark. While all reported confidence scores were relatively high (above 5 out of 7), participants were generally less confident on the Browse task on Website C.

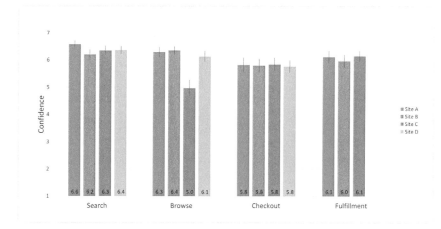

FIGURE 10.24: Example of post-task confidence for a comparative benchmark in the online retail industry for four websites (A to D on four tasks (Search, Browse, Checkout, Fulfillment).

Summarize the data to a Single Usability Metric

In one of the first benchmarking studies I helped work on for Intuit's QuickBooks in 2002, we summarized the task metrics (we had a lot more post-task ratings), but the multiple task metrics made it harder to digest and communicate to executives. We wondered how we could describe the task user experience succinctly when some completion rates were higher, some task-ease ratings lower, and sometimes higher—all for the same tasks. Our solution was the Single Usability Metric (SUM). The SUM essentially converts all the metrics to the same percentage scale and then averages the score. This solution allowed us to give a concise account of users' experiences for a particular task. The SUM gave our client (and future clients) a metric that was easy to understand. For more on the background of SUM, see "A Method to Standardize Usability Metrics into a Single Score" Sauro and Kindlund (2005).

Continuing with our example, the next step is to compute the average scores and confidence intervals for the post-task confidence ratings. As with the other steps in the analyzation process, the raw values are in the sample spreadsheet.

The good news is that if you are using the UX Benchmark Calculator and you have entered the other task metrics, the SUM is automatically calculated. There are some settings to be aware of that I'll review in the following procedure.

1. To view the SUM score for all tasks, select the "Single Usability Metric" link from the main tab of the calculator (Figure 10.25).

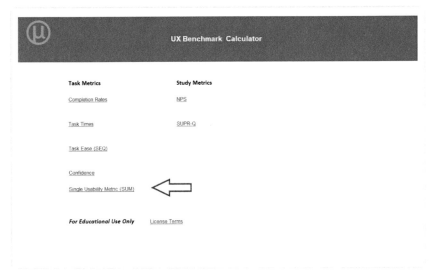

FIGURE 10.25: Selecting the "Single Usability Metric (SUM)" link from the UX Benchmark Calculator home screen.

The SUM values are computed on four separate tabs, one for each task (SUM T1 through SUM T4 in the workbook, as shown in Figure 10.26). The SUM tab pulls the SUM score and confidence intervals for all tasks, so no data entry is needed other than changing the labels (in this use the Marriott and Best Western condition names and the task names I've been using throughout this chapter).

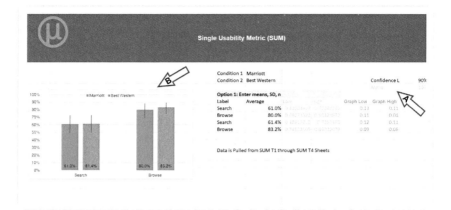

FIGURE 10.26: Single Usability Metric (SUM) calculations with sample data in the UX Benchmark Calculator.

2. **Calculate confidence intervals.** The confidence intervals are calculated automatically from the average of the confidence intervals for each of the three component metrics (completion, time, and ease). You can adjust the level of confidence up (to 95%) or down by adjusting the value, see Figure 10.26A. This change will affect the confidence level for all tasks.

3. **Graph the average SUM score and their corresponding confidence intervals.** These graphs are automatically updated when using the Benchmark calculator (Figure 10.26B).

4. The calculations are shown in Figure 10.27. The following areas that may need configuration are shown in the figure as well:

   - Confidence Level: This is set on the SUM tab and can be overwritten by task if needed.

   - Time Percentile: The time percentile (in this case 75%) indicates that the 75th percentile of task times should be the basis for a computed time specification. See Sauro and Kindlund (2005) for more on using this approach for computing time specs.

- Error Opp: If you are using errors, you need to specify the number of opportunities for errors per task (Error Opportunities). In this example, the value is ignored because there is no error data. See my book *A Practical Guide to Measuring Usability* (2010) for more on specifying error opportunities.

- Sat Spec and Conf. Spec: These values are predetermined levels based on historical data for the 7-point SEQ and the 7-point confidence scale. Values of 5.1 and 5.5 are approximately average historical values. See "10 Things To Know about the Single Ease Question (SEQ) for more on this value available at measuringu.com/seq10/.

- Time Spec: This value is auto-derived by taking the 75th percentile time of participants who completed the task. It can be overwritten, too, for example, by entering the median time of a best-in-class competitor value or a known benchmark.

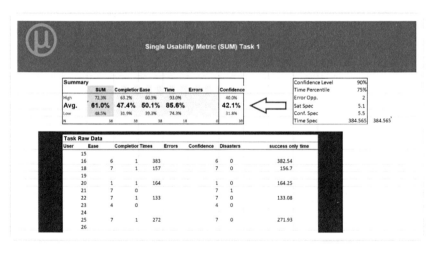

FIGURE 10.27: Single Usability Metric (SUM) raw value calculator for Task 1 using the UX Benchmark Calculator.

5. **Interpret the data.** The SUM scores quantitatively did what we have been doing mentally—higher ratings on some measures are offset by lower ratings on the other. The result is only a slight nominal bump for Best Western for the Browse task, but both show generally similar experiences when averaged together this way.

Moderated SUM example output

The following figures illustrate the SUM scores for the accounting software benchmark and for a benchmark comparing a retail website's desktop, mobile, and tablet experiences (a cross-device benchmark). Showing clients these graphical representations allow for an easier understanding of multiple metrics aggregated into one score.

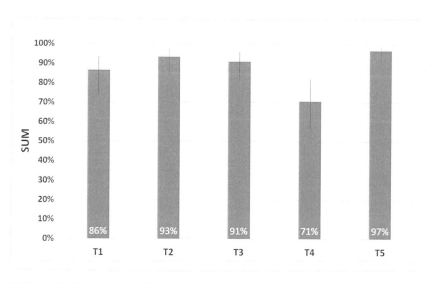

FIGURE 10.28: Single Usability Metric (SUM) scores for five tasks for a moderated benchmark for accounting software.

Figure 10.29 shows the SUM scores for the same retail website but on three platforms (desktop, tablet, and mobile). We can see that for mobile devices, the checkout experiences are noticeably (and statistically) poorer than for the desktop and to some extent the tablet.

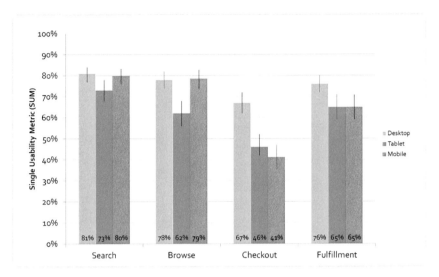

FIGURE 10.29: SUM scores for a retail website benchmark on three platforms (desktop, tablet, and mobile).

Figure 10.30 below shows the SUM scores for three years on the same automotive website. After some increase in the task experience in 2012, most tasks had worse experiences after some new features were introduced in 2014.

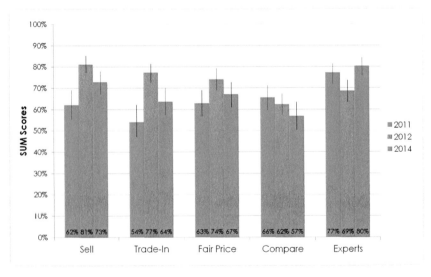

FIGURE 10.30: SUM Scores for three years of benchmarking data on an automotive website.

Additional task metrics

Here are some additional task-level metrics that supplement the core task metrics covered so far.

Disasters

As introduced in Chapter 5, disasters are when participants both fail a task but rate it highest in confidence (a rating of 7 on a 7-point scale). This can be computed for each task in Excel by counting participants that failed and rated the highest in confidence. As shown in Figure 10.31, for example, the disaster rates from the hotel benchmark data show Marriott's Search task had noticeably more of these unwanted experiences relative to the other task experiences. These experiences (disasters) are likely worth investigating. See Chapter 11 for understanding the "why" behind the metrics.

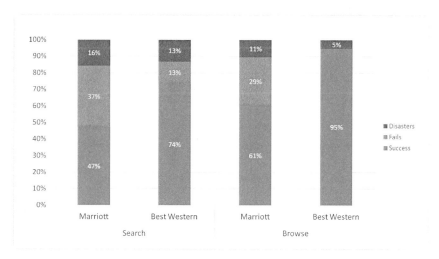

FIGURE 10.31: Disaster rates across the hotel website tasks.

Another example that is one of the most useful illustrations of disasters comes from another benchmark study I worked on for a third-party automotive information website. One of the tasks in the benchmark was for participants to rate the fair market value of their car (an appraisal). Unfortunately, many participants got the incorrect appraised value but were highly confident they were correct (28% were disasters), as shown in Figure 10.32.

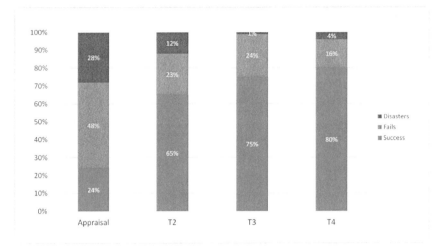

FIGURE 10.32: Example of a high disaster rate from a benchmark study for an automotive website—28% of participants incorrectly appraised the value of a car but were highly confident in the appraisal's veracity.

WHERE ARE THE ERRORS?

When I helped analyze the QuickBooks benchmark data in 2003, we used errors as one of our key metrics and eventually included it in the SUM calculation. One of the concerns at the time was the amount of time and effort it takes to log and code errors for analysis; it takes a lot of time to meticulously identify the errors participants make and usually requires reviewing hours of video. Since then, of the hundreds of benchmarking studies I have helped conduct or analyze, we've used error data only a handful of times. Instead we've found product teams are more interested in identifying the usability problems and less interested in the mistakes. This is especially the case because those participant mistakes show up as longer task times, lower task completion rates, and lower task-ease ratings. When errors are recorded, we find they are more commonly collected in smaller scale formative (rather than summative/benchmark) evaluations. However, you may find that noting errors are a good outcome measure (especially for certain high-frequency tasks), so don't be afraid to measure and benchmark against them. Just be prepared for the amount of time it will take. For more on measuring and reporting errors, see the Metrics chapter of *A Practical Guide to Measuring Usability*.

There are additional task-level metrics that we don't cover in this chapter but sometimes appear in benchmark studies as covered in Chapter 5. These include the following:

- **Assists:** noting how often participants need assistance to complete tasks
- **Task-specific satisfaction questions:** for example, asking if a participant is satisfied with a product detail page
- **Deviations:** noting if a participant deviates from an optimal path to complete a task
- **Clicks:** monitoring the click-count (Although task time is usually a better measure of efficiency, clicks can provide some concrete examples of engagement.)
- **Page depth:** noting the total number of pages viewed (as a measure of content exposure)

Study Level Metrics

Retrospective and task-based benchmarks will have study-level metrics to compute. Using the example in this chapter, for the sample study, we collected data using the SUPR-Q, NPS, and brand attitudes, which I review in the following sections before covering additional post-study metrics.

SUPR-Q

The SUPR-Q (Standardized User Experience Percentile Rank-Questionnaire) is a standardized measure of the website user experience. It contains a rolling database of 150 websites, which allows raw scores from a benchmark to be both standardized and compared to this group as a percentile rank. More information on licensing the SUPR-Q for benchmarking studies is available at measuringu.com/product/suprq/. Even without the standardized license, the SUPR-Q is a valuable tool for comparing websites in a benchmark study across the constructs of usability, appearance, trust, and loyalty. The raw values start in the sample spreadsheet (Column AO), see Figure 10.33.

AN	AO	AP	AQ	AR	AS	AT	AU	AV	AW	AX
Please descri	How likely are	Please rate y	Please rate y	Please rate y	Please rate y	Please rate y	Please rate y	Please rate y	How likely are	Please rate y
It was simple									6	3
	5	4	4	5	5	4	4	2		
	8	4	4	5	5	2	4	4		
I followed the task and found the place easily.									10	5
	6	3	4	4	4	4	4	4		
	7	4	4	3	4	3	4	4		
	10	5	5	5	5	5	5	5		
	6	3	3	4	4	4	3	3		
It was easy to search, and add in the special parameters by clicking the checkmarks									10	5
	10	5	5	5	5	4	5	5		
It was easy to navigate the page to list the amenities that I needed.									10	5
	9	5	5	5	5	5	4	5		
	8	4	4	5	4	3	4	5		
	8	3	3	4	4	2	4	3		
	8	3	5	5	4	2	5	3		
i just had to click the obvious boxes									8	4
	10	5	5	5	5	5	5	5		
	8	5	5	4	4	4	5	5		
The website was simple and easy to use. I loved the interface because after I added the dates and location I was quickly, with									9	5
	9	4	4	4	4	4	4	4		
	0	1	1	3	3	1	1	1		
	8	4	4	4	4	3	4	3		
I was unsure as to what to capture. I captured the prices of one of the hotels but didn't pay attention to which hotel it was. It r									7	4
provided a filter to choose pet friendly hotels									9	4
Being able to check/click the amenities made it super easy. Review numbers were also displayed next to the hotel name.									9	5
it was simple although my first try I couldn't get it to load any hotels									8	4

FIGURE 10.33: The SUPR-Q data for both websites are in the sample spreadsheet starting in column AO.

1. Select the "SUPR-Q" link from the main tab of the calculator (Figure 10.34).

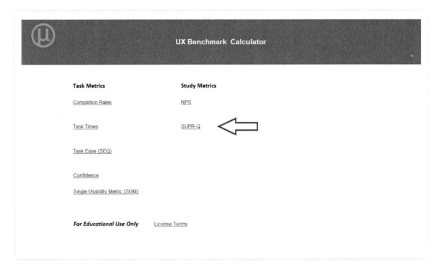

FIGURE 10.34: Selecting the "SUPR-Q" link from the UX Benchmark Calculator home screen.

2. **Copy the raw values from your spreadsheet and then paste the values into the sections under the "Paste Sample 1 Here" and so on**, as shown in 10.35A. Note: Order matters here. Ensure you are pasting the right items from your raw data to the correct corresponding item in the calculator. The 11-point likelihood-to-recommend item is the first in the example spreadsheet and the fifth (Q5) in the calculator. Double check that your raw values range from 1s to 5s for 7 of the items (Q1-Q4; Q6-8) and 0s to 10s for item Q5.

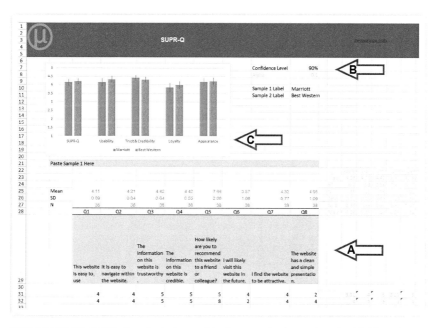

FIGURE 10.35: SUPR-Q calculations with the sample data using the UX Benchmark Calculator.

3. **Calculate confidence intervals.** In this example, the confidence intervals are calculated automatically from the raw values for the 8 items for both samples and the confidence level. You can adjust the level of confidence by adjusting the value, see Figure 10.35B.

4. Graph the average ratings for the overall SUPR-Q score—the four components of usability, trust, loyalty, and appearance—and their corresponding confidence intervals. These graphs are automatically updated when using the Benchmark Calculator, as shown in Figure 10.35C.

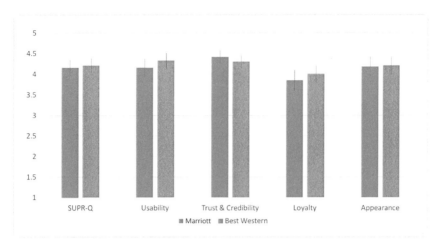

FIGURE 10.36: Graph output of the SUPR-Q.

5. **Perform a statistical test (advanced and optional).** The statistical test to perform for this type of data is the two-sample *t*-test (see Chapter 11) on each factor. You could also conduct an ANOVA, but you'll still likely want to compare each factor separately (see Chapter 10 in *Quantifying the User Experience 2nd Edition*). The *p*-value for the difference between SUPR-Q scores is $p = .69$, indicating no statistical significance (also shown as the overlap in the confidence interval).

6. **Interpret the data.** Across most dimensions of the SUPR-Q, the Best Western website was rated higher as can be seen in Figure 10.36. This is continuing the theme we saw with the task-based metrics. With a larger sample size, some of these differences would likely become statistically significant.

Net Promoter Score (NPS)

The popular NPS is computed by consolidating the 11-points of the likelihood-to-recommend (LTR) item into 3-points of promoters (9s and 10s), passives (7s and 8s), and detractors (0s to 6s). This LTR item is also used in the computation of the SUPR-Q score as part of the loyalty factor (see the previous section on SUPR-Q).

AN	AO	AP	AQ	AR	AS	AT	AU	AV	AW	AX
Please descri	How likely ar	Please rate y	Please rate y	Please rate y	Please rate y	Please rate y	Please rate y	Please rate y	How likely ar	Please rate y
It was simple									6	3
	5	4	4	5	5	4	4	2		
	8	4	4	5	5	2	4	4		
I followed the task and found the place easily.									10	5
	5	3	4	4	4	4	4	4		
	7	4	4	3	4	3	4	4		
	10	5	5	5	5	5	5	5		
	6	3	3	4	4	4	3	3		
It was easy to search, and add in the special parameters by clicking the checkmarks									10	5
	10	5	5	5	5	4	5	5		
It was easy to navigate the page to list the amenities that I needed.									10	5
	9	5	5	5	5	5	4	5		
	8	4	4	5	4	3	4	5		
	8	3	3	4	4	2	4	3		
	8	3	5	5	4	2	5	3		
i just had to click the obvious boxes									8	4
	10	5	5	5	5	5	5	5		
	8	5	5	4	4	4	5	5		
The website was simple and easy to use. I loved the interface because after I added the dates and location I was quickly, with									9	5
	9	4	4	4	4	4	4	4		
	0	1	1	3	3	1	1	1		
	8	4	4	4	4	3	4	3		
I was unsure as to what to capture. I captured the prices of one of the hotels but didn't pay attention to which hotel it was. It r									7	4
provided a filter to choose pet friendly hotels									9	4
Being able to check/click the amenities made it super easy. Review numbers were also displayed next to the hotel name.									9	5
it was simple although my first try I couldn't get it to load any hotels									8	4

FIGURE 10.37: The likelihood-to-recommend item is in column AO and AW for both websites.

1. Select the "NPS" link from the main tab of the calculator (Figure 10.38).

FIGURE 10.38: Selecting the "NPS" link from the UX Benchmark Calculator home screen.

2. **Copy the raw values from your output, and then paste into the "Sample 1" and "Sample 2" columns, as shown in Figure 10.39A.** Change the label values for the samples (I have them labeled Marriott and Best Western). Values should be from 0 to 10.

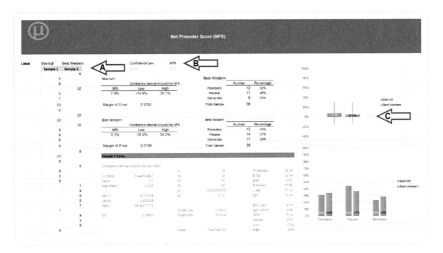

FIGURE 10.39: Net Promoter Score (NPS) calculations with the sample data using the UX Benchmark Calculator.

3. **Calculate confidence intervals.** The confidence intervals are calculated using the difference between paired proportions (calculations are in the calculator). You can adjust the level of confidence by adjusting the value (Figure 10.39B).

4. **Graph the Net Promoter Scores with confidence intervals.** These graphs are shown in the top graph (10.39C and Figure 10.40). The second graph in Figure 10.39 shows the percentage of promoters, passives, and detractors by website.

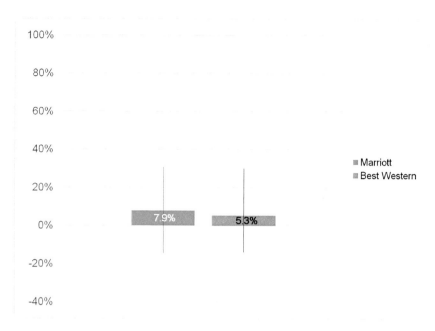

100%

80%

60%

40%

■ Marriott
■ Best Western

20%

0%   7.9%   5.3%

-20%

-40%

FIGURE 10.40: Net Promoter Scores (NPS) for Marriott and Best Western showing very little difference.

5. **Perform a statistical test (advanced and optional).** The Net Promoter Score is a more complicated measure to compare statistically. The reasons for this is that rating scale data is converted to paired binary data. The "right" statistical procedure is still the subject of ongoing research. For now, there are a couple approaches. You can conduct a two-sample t-test on the raw responses (the 0s to 10s), just as we did for SEQ and confidence data. Using this approach, the p-value is $p = .94$, indicating no statistical significance (also shown as a large overlap in the confidence intervals).

Another approach is the chi-square test, which would look for differences between *any* three of the segments (promoters, passives, and detractors). Future research is needed to determine the "best" statistical test for comparing Net Promoter Scores. For now, I recommend comparing the LTR means. For more discussion on this topic see "Reducing the Noise in Your Net Promoter Analysis" available at measuringu.com/nps-noise/.

6. **Interpret the data.** The Net Promoter Scores for both web-sites are virtually identical. For website benchmarks with a mix of existing and new users that participate in the study, we typically see an average value of around 0%. That's an equal number of promoters and detractors, and we see slightly more promoters here for both websites. The large overlap in the error bars indicate little evidence for statistical significance and that it is plausible that the true NPS for both hotels is 0.

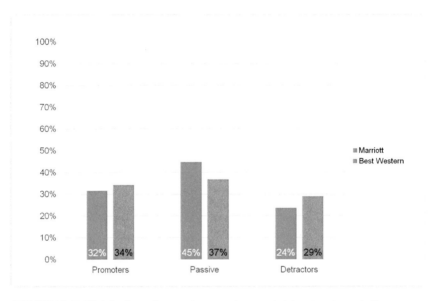

FIGURE 10.41: Distribution of promoters, passives, and detractors by website.

System Usability Scale (SUS)

The SUS, despite its age (30+ years), remains a popular post-study measure. We recommend the SUPR-Q over the SUS for websites (see the "The SUPR-Q measures more than usability" section in Chapter 5), but for software and hardware products, the SUS and UMUX-LITE (see the next section) are recommended for their succinctness and external benchmarks.

While the SUS wasn't used in the hotel benchmark sample data, the following are some examples of how to effectively present the SUS data. The examples are from a moderated benchmark study for accounting software (Figure 10.42) and from a retrospective benchmark study of consumer and business software (Figure 10.43). See "The System Usability Scale (SUS)" section in Chapter 5 for a reminder on how to manually score SUS responses, or for a comprehensive reference, see *A Practical Guide to the System Usability Scale (SUS)* (Sauro, 2011).

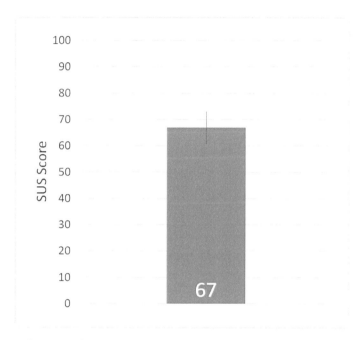

FIGURE 10.42: SUS score from the moderated accounting software benchmark.

The SUS score for the accounting software benchmark at 67 puts it at around the industry standard average score of 68 and gives it a grade of a C (average). See Table 5.1 in Chapter 5 for percentile ranks and grades. In our year-over-year retrospective benchmark, SUS scores fluctuated for the products, some nominally up (e.g., WebEx, AutoCAD), with most nominally down (e.g., QuickBooks).

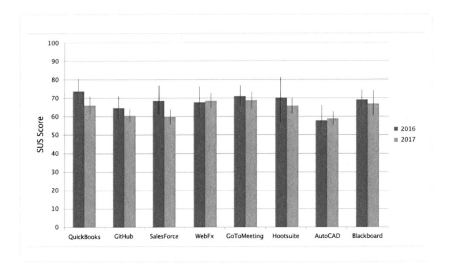

FIGURE 10.43: A selection of year-over-year SUS scores from MeasuringU's annual consumer software bencvmark report.

Another example of the SUS in an unmoderated benchmark of an automotive website is shown in Figure 10.44. The SUS was presented twice in the study, after two groups of tasks that focused on different functionality of the website. The latter three tasks focused on more advanced (and less used functionality) and consequently received lower SUS scores.

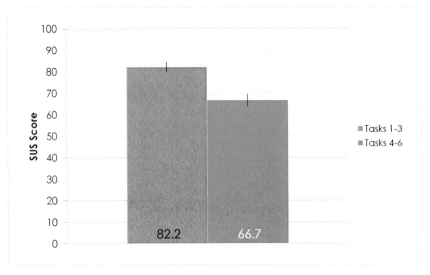

FIGURE 10.44: SUS scores for an automotive website benchmark collected twice in the same study.

UMUX-LITE

The Usability Metric for User Experience-LITE is just two items (see Chapter 5) and can approximate SUS as well as provide its own measure of perceived ease and usefulness. The UMUX-LITE can be presented as a mean from both items ("I think the software is easy to use" and "The software's capabilities meet my requirements") or separately. I refer to them as the ease and usefulness items respectively. The UMUX-LITE mean score can also be used as a proxy for estimating a SUS score with above 85% accuracy—not bad for only two items compared to 10! See "Measuring Usability: From the SUS to the UMUX-LITE" available at measuringu.com/umux-lite/ for more on using the UMUX-LITE, including using it to estimate SUS scores.

The UMUX-LITE is one of our key metrics in our consumer and business software retrospective benchmark reports. Figure 10.45 shows the average scores for Google Docs and Microsoft Word. MS Word is edging out Google Docs in both perceived ease and usefulness—but not by much (considering the former is free and the latter represents a significant income stream for Microsoft).

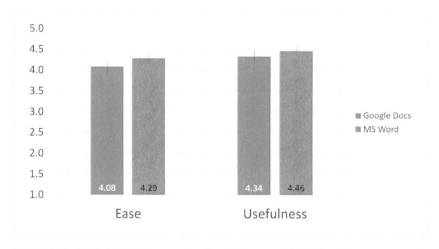

FIGURE 10.45: UMUX-LITE means for Google Docs and MS Word from our annual consumer software retrospective benchmark.

There's a lot more you can do with benchmark data, and we'll cover more techniques in the next chapter.

CHAPTER SUMMARY AND TAKEAWAYS

In this chapter, we covered how to analyze data, what metrics to use, how to clean data and account for missing data, and gave some examples of how the data should be displayed:

- Plan to clean data from unmoderated benchmarks, especially when collected from online panels.

- Use multiple methods to clean, including identifying poor-quality responses, open-ended responses, "speeders," and "cheaters."

- Try to account for missing data. Look for a pattern to non-responses and attempt to "impute" the missing values.

- Decide if you need external software, which is highly likely, to analyze data. Though, unmoderated platforms usually have basic analysis capabilities.

- Explore external packages to analyze benchmark data, including free or low-cost solutions (e.g., Excel, StatsUsabilityPakExpanded, R) to more expensive and extensive packages (e.g., SPSS and Minitab).

- Use the free downloadable benchmark calculator to compute task and study-level metrics (downloadable at measuringu.com/benchmarkbook/). This calculator also provides graphs for presenting to stakeholders.

CHAPTER 11:
ADVANCED ANALYSIS

In this chapter we'll cover more advanced analyses that include analyzing preference data, interpreting p-values, cross tabbing, and digging into the visualizations and data often collected by unmoderated platforms. While I refer to this as advanced analysis, it doesn't mean it's always optional. Often the most insightful findings come from the steps outlined in this chapter. So don't just skip this one!

ANALYZING PREFERENCE DATA

Understanding which experience participants prefer is often one of the more interesting (and consequential) outputs of a benchmark study. Preference data can be collected in a within-subjects benchmark study (same participants experiencing multiple websites). For example, in a within-subjects benchmark for three financial websites, both consumers and financial advisors attempted tasks on three sites and were asked which site they preferred using. Figure 11.1 shows there wasn't much difference in preference for consumers, but financials advisors statistically preferred Site C. There are also some between-subjects studies (different participants on different websites) where participants can be asked which product or website they prefer (even if they didn't directly experience them during the study). For example, participants may be asked to compare the website they are evaluating to a very well-known website, such as Amazon.

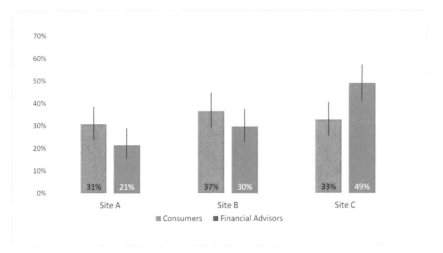

FIGURE 11.1: Preference data for three financial websites in a within-subjects comparative benchmark for consumer and financial advisors.

NOTE: There are a few ways to test for statistical significance with preference data. One approach is to examine the non-overlap in the confidence intervals as we've done in this example. Other approaches include comparing preference selections to chance and conducting a chi-square test. For more information on analyzing preference data, see "How to Statistically Test Preference Data" available at measuringu.com/preference-data/.

UNDERSTANDING BRAND LIFT AND DRAG

We often want to know the effect the website experience had on participants' attitudes toward a brand. This is often referred to as brand lift or brand drag (see Chapter 5). For example, in the Enterprise and Budget rental car competitive benchmark study, participants were asked to rate their attitudes toward each of the two rental car brands prior to and after renting a car through each website. We used a 7-point scale from 1 = very unfavorable to 7 = very favorable. As shown in Figure 11.2, the brand favorability rating for Budget increased 12% on average—from 4.7 to 5.3. The brand favorability rating for Enterprise decreased 15% on average—from 5.3 to 4.5.

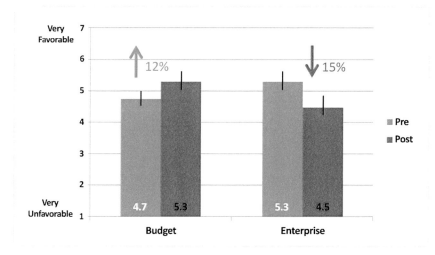

FIGURE 11.2: Brand favorability before and after renting a car through the website. Budget lift was 12% and -15% for Enterprise.

The negative drag for Enterprise suggests that the website experience hurts customers' attitudes toward the brand. Because attitudes tend to affect actions, it's likely that continued degradation of the attitude toward the brand will result in reduced business. As it happens, other study data revealed the likely causes of Enterprise's negative drag was that customers couldn't add-on options (GPS, car seat) without difficulty, and they couldn't find the final rental price of the car at all (because it wasn't shown!).

As another example, Figure 11.3 shows the brand favorability ratings for four popular retail companies before and after participants spent 20 minutes attempting tasks on their respective websites. In this example we can see both the relative brand favorability (highest for Site D) and that all websites had a slight brand drag with the scores dipping slightly (about .1 of a point). To assess the changes for statistical significance, use the paired t-test for each site (see the "Conducting Statistical Tests and Interpreting P-Values" section later in this chapter).

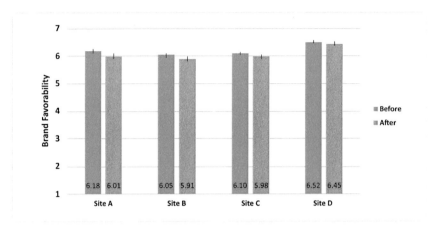

FIGURE 11.3: Brand favorability (1= very unfavorable and 7 = very favorable) for four retail brands.

EXAMINING VARIABLES—CROSS TABBING

Cross tabbing is the process of examining more than one variable in the same table or chart. It can be a simple yet powerful way to understand how different segments of the benchmark data differ. It can be done with continuous outcome variables (e.g., rating scales or time) or binary variables (e.g., completion, customer segment, or task). For example, Figure 11.4 shows how the attitude toward how useful product filters were on three websites differed by task and participant profile (consumer vs. financial advisor).

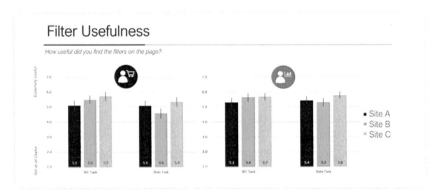

FIGURE 11.4: Cross tabbing task by website by participant type (consumer vs. financial advisor).

The cross-tabbing analysis in Figure 11.4 suggests that the consumers generally found the filters less useful than the financial advisors on both tasks, and filters were least useful for consumers for the "Date Task."

Figure 11.5 shows a cross tab of the Net Promoter Score by site experience for four websites in a comparative retail website benchmark study. Focusing on Site 4, we can see that participants with less experience (visiting 1 to 3 times) generally had lower Net Promoter Scores.

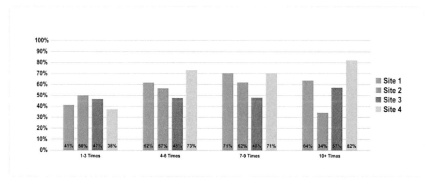

FIGURE 11.5: Cross tabbing Net Promoter Score by website by experience on the website (from 1 to 3 times to 10+ times in the last year).

Collapsing Variables

One technique to help for both cross tabbing and for a better understanding of patterns in your data is to collapses the variables. Collapsing variables is just another way of saying combining variables, often into two groups (which is called dichotomizing), so you can more easily cross tab and run statistical comparisons between the lower and higher ends of an independent variable. While it's good to have a lot of fidelity in a response option, collapsing variables is a good option for analyzing certain aspects of data. For example, I recommend asking participants about their prior experience with a website or product at the beginning of a benchmark study, as we did with the sample hotel benchmark data. Table 11.1 shows the frequency of experience reported by the 76 participants for the hotel benchmark study.

	Marriott		Best Western	
0 Times	15	20%	36	47%
1-3 Times	41	54%	33	43%
4-6 Times	16	21%	5	7%
7-9 Times	2	3%	2	3%
10+ Times	2	3%	0	0%

TABLE 11.1: Distribution of prior experience with the Marriott and Best Western websites from the sample benchmark study.

You can collapse these levels into no experience and at least some experience as shown in Table 11.2.

	Marriott		Best Western	
No experience	15	20%	36	47%
At least some experience	61	80%	40	53%

TABLE 11.2: Collapsed categories of prior experience with the Marriott and Best Western websites.

This new collapsed variable can be used in your analysis and in cross tabs. For example, I took the newly dichotomized experience variable (No Experience vs. Some Experience) and compared participants' stated likelihood to return to the website after the experience of using it. You can see the mean differences in scores by website in Figure 11.6.

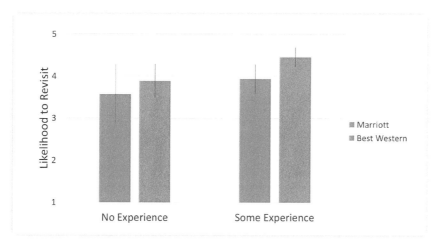

FIGURE 11.6: Stated likelihood to revisit the website by dichotomized prior experience for the Marriott and Best Western websites.

This cross-tabbing analysis allows us to see that while prior experience has an impact on likelihood to revisit a website (as we'd expect), participants for the Best Western website who have some experience had statistically higher scores than participants with the same level of experience for the Marriott website.

 TIP:

> When collapsing variables, you'll need to set the break points to yield a reasonably balanced group—you typically don't want 95% of your responses with a high experience and 5% with a low experience.

CONTROLLING FOR PRIOR EXPERIENCE

Rarely is a customer population made up of a homogenous group of customers who share the same attributes. Consequently, our benchmark samples contain a mix of participants who may or may not reflect the composition of the customer population.

There are a number of variables that affect how customers think and behave toward products and services. One of the most common variables that impacts our measurements is prior experience. More than gender, age, income, and occupation, prior experience with products, software, and websites has a major impact on customer attitudes and behavior.

We see this extensively in UX benchmarks. In general, the more experience participants have had, the better their performance on tasks and the more positive their attitudes toward the product or service being benchmarked will be. The idea is you don't want to just be measuring a participant's prior experience, especially when that disproportionately affects one site over another in a competitive benchmark.

One way to control for prior experience in benchmark studies is to match the experience level of the sample with the expected experience level of the population. If you believe, for example, that 60% of website visitors use the site weekly and the other 40% use it less, you can recruit participants to match that composition. You can then compute confidence intervals and run statistical comparisons (between, say, two design alternatives) and draw conclusions as to which design users perform better on or prefer. This is what I did in the previous section for collapsing experience levels. Most of our MeasuringU clients choose this method—matching the sample to the population—because, when you explain it to stakeholders, it makes sense to them.

However, you can't always weight your sample to match the population because it may be difficult to find people that match your population to participate in a benchmark. For example, your data shows that 30% of your mobile website users have not accessed your website in the last year. Getting the 30% of your mobile website users may not be possible. When you need to determine which website is preferred, you don't want the decision to be based on the improper composition of your sample.

With unbalanced samples, two approaches can mitigate and control for the effects of prior experience on your outcome measures: a weighted t-test and a Type I ANOVA. The analysis of variance (ANOVA) is the statistical procedure used to compare more than two means at once. More importantly, it enables you to see the effects of multiple variables simultaneously. The ANOVA is more computationally intensive than the t-test and usually requires specialized software, such as SPSS, R, or Minitab, to conduct. Enlisting the assistance of a statistician for the setup and analysis of ANOVA results is generally very helpful. See the "Additional Statistical Analyses" section in this chapter for more information on using ANOVA.

About the Weighted T-Test

A relatively simple method for handling weighted data is the aptly named weighted *t*-test. This is a variation of the *t*-test I described earlier in this chapter. The *t*-test works for large and small sample sizes and uneven group sizes, and it's resilient to non-normal data. (We cover it extensively in Chapter 5 of *Quantifying the User Experience 2nd Edition*). While the *t*-test is a "workhorse" of statistical analysis, it only considers one variable when determining statistical significance. This means that you can't compare participants' attitudes on two websites *and* factor in their prior experience (say, low experience and high experience).

However, the weighted version of the *t*-test does factor in a second variable. It adjusts the means and standard deviations based on how much to weight each respondent. For example, participants that should account for 60% of the population and have scores that are weighted at 60%, even if they make up only 20% of your sample. You can see the computation notes in "Weighted Comparison of Means" (1998) by J. Martin Bland and Sally Kerry available online at bmj.com/content/316/7125/129.

Using the Weighted T-Test

Here's how the weighted *t*-test works. For a study of an online retail website, we wanted to see which website was statistically preferred on a number of dimensions, including confidence and ease. For this example, we had 857 qualified participants who were randomly assigned to Website A or Website B. We used a 10-point confidence scale.

The mean, standard deviation, and sample size for both groups for a confidence question are shown in Table 11.3.

	Mean	SD	N
Website A	8.58	1.74	429
Website B	8.37	1.92	428

TABLE 11.3: Unweighted mean confidence scores for two websites (on 10-point scales).

Even though Website A had a nominally higher mean score (8.58 vs. 8.37), using a standard t-test to compare the means, we found no significant difference at the alpha = .05 level of significance ($p = 0.095$). See the "What Does Statistically Significant Mean?" section in this chapter for interpreting statistical significance for p-values.

However, we know that prior experience has a major impact on attitudes toward interfaces, and packed within both samples are four groups of participants, each with progressively more experience with the website.

Not only did the sample contain a heterogeneous subgroup of experience, it was not proportionally representative of the population's experience breakdown. Table 11.4 shows the breakdown of the sample in Website A and Website B compared to the makeup of the user population.

Experience level	Website A	Website B	Population
1	2%	3%	2%
2	12%	10%	9%
3	44%	47%	39%
4	42%	41%	50%

TABLE 11.4: Experience level for the participants assigned to Website A and B compared to the population composition (1 = least experienced and 4 = most experienced).

The biggest difference is seen with people with the most experience (4 in the table). While this group makes up half of the population, it only comprises between 41% and 42% of the sample in Websites A and B.

These groups also have differing opinions about the designs they were exposed to. Table 11.5 shows that one of the biggest differences in attitudes was for the most experienced participants (Experience level 4), which rated Website A .39 points higher than B. What's more, the least experienced participants preferred Website B over A.

Experience level	Website A	Website B	Difference	Population
1	8.42	8.67	-0.25	0.02
2	8.85	8.82	0.03	0.09
3	8.56	8.44	0.12	0.39
4	8.53	8.14	0.39	0.5

TABLE 11.5: The mean responses to a confidence question (higher is better), the difference in means by experience level (1 to 4), and the population composition of that experience level.

The weighted *t*-test creates a composite mean and standard deviation to proportionally account for the subgroup size (computational notes available online at bmj.com/content/316/7125/129). The updated means and standard deviations are shown in Table 11.6 with the original data.

	Weighted		Non-Weighted	
	Mean	SD	Mean	SD
Website A	8.56	1.68	8.58	1.74
Website B	8.29	1.94	8.37	1.92

TABLE 11.6: Experience level for the sample of customers assigned to Website A and B, compared to the population composition.

The results of the weighted *t*-test generate a *p*-value of .03, which is statistically significant at the alpha = .05 level of significance. You won't always see differences in significance values between the weighted and unweighted approaches; it depends both on how disproportionate your sample is and on how much the lower-weighted groups differ from the higher-weighted groups.

With these results, we can conclude both that Website A had higher ratings and that the rating difference wasn't attributable to incorrectly proportioned sample sizes. You can also use the approach for any mediating variable in a benchmark study (such as geography, gender, or occupation) and not just for prior experience.

TIP:

> You should have a good reason and actual data to support using weights. Don't just weight your data to achieve statistical significance. While many variables in your sample will differ from the population, many won't have a large enough effect (if any effect at all) to justify weighting.

UNDERSTANDING THE "WHY" BEHIND THE METRICS

While the primary goal of benchmark studies is to collect metrics to describe the user experience, it doesn't mean you shouldn't understand what's driving higher or lower numbers on task- or study-level metrics. Understanding the "why" behind the numbers is the essential next step to diagnose and ultimately fix problems with the experience. The following sections discuss the approaches we use in benchmark studies to understand the "why."

Verbatim Analysis

In unmoderated and moderated benchmark studies, there are (and should be) open-ended comments for participants to provide. These comments are a good place to start understanding the why. If a participant provides a low-likelihood-to-recommend score (a detractor), an open-ended question immediately following this closed-ended question, online or in person, can examine his or her reasons for providing a low score.

You can evaluate responses systematically by sorting and coding them. However, even a quick reading of a subset of what participants are saying will give you some idea about what's driving high or low scores. For example, participants in the business software benchmarking study we conducted reflected on their experience with common B2B software programs and provided their likelihood-to-recommend (which drives the Net Promoter Score). We asked participants to briefly explain their ratings, which can be particularly helpful for low scoring responses. One respondent gave a Learning Management System (LMS) software program a score of 5 on an 11-point scale (a detractor) and said:

> "Although [name of software] allows you to connect with students on a more personal level than email… it still has a large amount of issues present. The layout of [name of software] is horrid, and users should have an option to collapse the menu found on the left-hand side of the screen. Although it's an adequate LMS program, it isn't better than [another LMS software]."

There's a lot of great feedback packed into that one comment. It doesn't mean the product developers should immediately start updating the software, but it does mean it's likely worthy of further investigation.

For detailed steps on the process of sorting and coding verbatim comments, see "How to Code & Analyze Verbatim Comments" available at measuringu.com/code-verbatim/.

Log Files and Click Streams

Looking at where users click, how long they spend on a page, and how many pages they visit can give you some idea as to why tasks might be taking too long or reasons for low task completion rates (all key metrics discussed in Chapter 5).

Log files also allow you to quickly see whether participants are getting diverted to the wrong page, either unintentionally (through following a link) or intentionally (browsing Facebook while attempting a task). (The latter case would be a good reason to exclude the participant's responses.)

For an unmoderated benchmark we conducted on the Budget website, we had a hard time understanding why one participant's task time was so long (a key measure of efficiency)—as seen in Figure 11.7. An examination of the log files and clicks revealed the user was actually intercepted with a separate website survey.

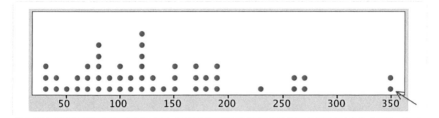

FIGURE 11.7: Distribution of task times from the Budget benchmark study. An analysis of log files revealed one of the long task times came from a participant being intercepted by another survey.

Visualizations of Click Behavior

In an unmoderated benchmark study of websites, knowing where people click can tell you a lot about reasons for task failures and longer task times. In general, the first click is highly indicative of task success.

Most unmoderated platforms include some type of data visualization on where and how people click on websites or web apps. The following sections provide more information about popular data visualization methods, such as heat maps and click maps.

Heat maps

Knowing where participants click, even down to the pixel location, helps identify how well calls to action (or task instructions) are working and how participants' actions differ by screen size and device type. The heat map in Figure 11.8 shows the actions a participant took during an Audible website study while using a desktop computer. Participants in this unmoderated benchmark study were asked to find a book they were interested in. You can see the smattering of clicks around the search function (blue) and then around the main banner background (called the hero image).

FIGURE 11.8: Example heat map data from MUIQ for a benchmark of Audible.

In another example, the heat map in Figure 11.9 is from a benchmark of the restaurant reservation website OpenTable. There is a heavy concentration of clicks on the main calls to action (the search box for reservation times, location, cuisine, and the Find a Table button) and a lack of clicks below the fold (not shown).

FIGURE 11.9: Example heat map data from MUIQ for a benchmark of OpenTable.

Click maps

While heat maps show where people click, overlapping elements (like mega menus) on web pages can make it difficult to know which element on the page was clicked. In some studies, we've spent a lot of time trying to figure out whether people clicked hero banners or background images from heat maps (like in the previous Audible example). The different resolutions of the different devices participants use to view a web page make the location of elements on a page less consistent, as well.

Our solution to this problem is the click map that records the exact element that was clicked and the percentage of participants who clicked it. You can see in the click map from the Audible website study in Figure 11.10 that participants in the study clicked elements from the mega-menu (e.g., Browse Audible, Sci-Fi, and Teens) and not on the hero image. With the click maps, it is much easier to understand where participants are making their first click, which is highly indicative of task success.

FIGURE 11.10:
Example of click
map data from
MUIQ for a bench-
mark of the Audible
website.

As another example, the click map in Figure 11.11 is based on the OpenTable heat map.

FIGURE 11.11: Example of click map data from MUIQ for a benchmark of the OpenTable website

We can see the majority of participants (67%) interacted with the Location, Restaurant, or Cuisine search box and Find a Table button (79%). But again, the click map provides more clarity than the heat map. For example, we can now see that only 8% changed the search location to Denver (the light blue box floating on the background image) using the "Choose Your Location" drop-down menu at the top of the page. This suggests the drop-down element is not the primary method for changing locations when finding reservations. It means other parts of the experience need to support location changing (which is likely why the search box also supports a location search).

Tree maps

Having a log file show every URL a participant visits is very valuable to understand individual browsing patterns. But it's also very time consuming to comb through—another example of having a lot of data but not as much meaning. The MUIQ platform provides a way to visualize these log files and paths users take through a website using a tool we call a tree map. The tree map in Figure 11.12 shows the paths users took on the Audible website (a zoomed in view of the values are shown in figure 11.15).

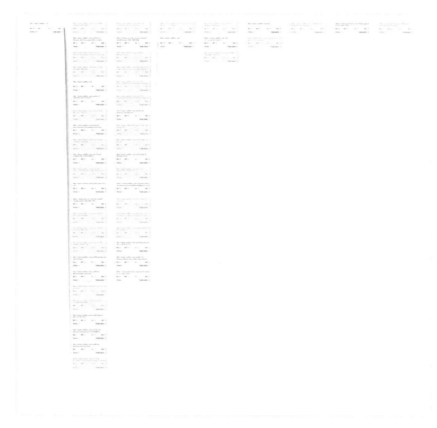

FIGURE 11.12: Example tree-map data from the MUIQ platform for a benchmark of Audible (yellow boxes show when a search term was used by participants; white boxes signify that the search term was not used).

To support more insight from this display, we have the ability to search for URL strings, which can be helpful in identifying how often certain pages were visited. The yellow highlighted boxes show the places where a search results page was displayed on the Audible website (which was around half of the time). It shows how pivotal a role the search function plays in the browsing experience for audio books.

Linear tree maps

The tree map shows us all unique combinations of pages (and aggregations of pages). But we often want to know the most common paths users take, and that can be harder to derive from the tree map alone. For this reason, we derived what we call the linear tree map that aggregates the most common paths for the first few clicks (typically 1 to 5 clicks). The linear tree map in Figure 11.13 shows the most common paths users took for the first three clicks on the Audible website and helps answer one of the most common questions we get asked: What paths are users taking on our website?

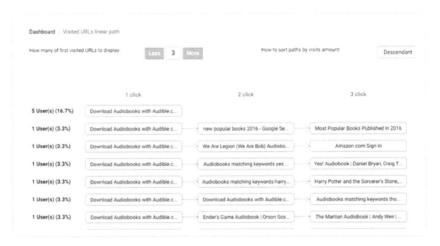

FIGURE 11.13: Example linear tree map data from the MUIQ platform for a benchmark of the Audible website

Videos and Session Recordings

While a picture can speak a thousand words (click maps and heat maps), a recording of what participants are doing can tell at least 10,000 words. For unmoderated benchmark studies, not being with a participant makes it difficult to assess task completion and understand why other metrics might be higher or lower.

One of the best features to help understand the why behind the numbers is to have a video of what participants were doing while attempting tasks. Session recordings like that from the MUIQ research platform provides this capability. While it's unreasonable to always need to review hundreds or thousands of videos (something you'll get with a 5-task study that has 150 participants), strategically selecting a few videos to understand the root cause is often sufficient and revealing.

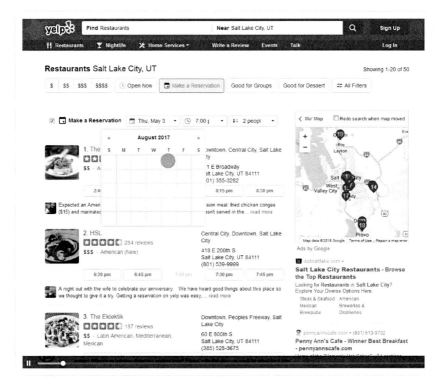

FIGURE 11.14: Screenshot of a participant's session recording from MUIQ from a benchmark study of the OpenTable website.

For example, the screenshot in Figure 11.14 is from a session recording from MUIQ taken during a benchmarking study we ran on the Yelp website as part of our SUPR-Q data collection. While Yelp has been a popular website for restaurant reviews, they've been expanding their reservation system to compete with websites like OpenTable.

We asked participants in an unmoderated study to find a Thai restaurant in Salt Lake City. Only 49% completed the task successfully. To understand why half couldn't, we examined some of the session videos and found a few users struggling with the filters. Here is a summary of a 30 second video from a 2.5-minute session video. A video clip of this example is available at measuringu.com/why-numbers/.

1. The participant searches for "Thai food" restaurants in Salt Lake City and selects the "Takes Reservations" filter. The problem is this option shows all restaurants that accept reservations in general and not just ones that accept reservations via the Yelp reservations website.

2. The participant then (correctly) selects the "Make a Reservation" option but doesn't realize selecting this option erases his original search criteria. Now all restaurants in Salt Lake City that accept Yelp reservations (not just Thai restaurants) are shown.

3. The participant then searches for "Thai food" again, which in turn removes the "Make a Reservation" option—back to square one.

4. Finally, the participant selects the "Make a Reservation" option again, which again erases his original "Thai Food" search and the participant ends the task (likely frustrated by the experience as indicated by his low post-task SEQ rating).

The end result of using this method is we now have both a measure of the experience (a low completion rate) and what to fix to improve it (the filtering interactions).

5 Metrics to Diagnose Website Problems for Online Studies

To understand the problems that occur on a website, nothing quite beats watching users. The process provides a wealth of information both about what users can or can't do and what might be causing problems in an interface. The major drawback to watching users live or recordings of sessions is that it takes a lot of focused time. The typical sample size in moderated studies of 5 to 20 participants isn't too much of a time commitment. But with unmoderated studies, the ability to collect data from hundreds of participants quickly means even a few tasks per study requires watching thousands of videos.

While there won't be a replacement for watching session recordings and coding them (something our research team does regularly), we're always looking for more systematically and quicker ways to identify patterns in behavior.

We've found that a few metrics automatically collected in unmoderated studies are good for diagnosing potential problems with websites. The MUIQ research platform collects these metrics for every page visited and summarizes them by page. These metrics are available for each web page using the tree maps. Figure 11.15 shows a magnified image of the tree map from Figure 11.12. Each "branch" of the tree provides information for different key metrics: scrolling or lack thereof (SC), rapid or repeat clicking (RP), click latency (DL), clicking on non-clickable elements (NC), and task exits. Other software such as Google Analytics may also provide some of these metrics. Here are the five metrics in more detail.

FIGURE 11.15: Key metrics summarized on each page of an unmoderated study (in this example from a Marriott benchmark study).

1. **Scrolling or lack thereof (SC)**
   Not all essential elements (content, products) can be shown on one page or "above the fold." Scrolling is usually inevitable and increasingly so with the design trend of long or infinite scrolling pages.

   But scrolling doesn't always happen. Tracking the percentage of users who click a key call-to-action (CTA) or find information that is lower on a page can reveal a lot about how effective the design and content are, as well as who may or may not be digesting it.

2. **Rapid or repeat clicking (RP)**
   A related issue to clicking non-clickable elements is when participants double- or triple-click elements. This can be a symptom of latency (pages not responding) or even carryovers from desktop behavior where double-clicking is a common action. What's more, rapid clicking can be an indication of participant frustration. Some

have called this "rage clicking" where website users become frustrated and start clicking indiscriminately (and often on non-clickable elements). You can see a video that illustrates this behavior that this metric summarizes at measuringu.com/website-problem-metrics/.

3. **Click latency (DL)**
   The opposite of rapid clicking is long delays between clicks. While long delays don't always mean a problem exists, it can be another symptom of users potentially struggling to navigate within pages, possibly on non-clickable elements or taking time to make decisions on a page.

4. **Clicking on non-clickable elements (NC)**
   In the early days of the web, websites were littered with "click here" links, in part to help users know, well, where to click. While we've come a long way since then (for the most part), some websites and pages still suffer from an affordance problem—people not knowing what elements are clickable. It can be images, links, headings, or the page background that gets clicked or overlooked. Tracking how many non-clickable elements were clicked shows when participants don't know where to click.

5. **Task exits**
   Knowing how many participants land on certain pages and the paths they take is helpful by itself (this is the "Visits" metric in Figure 11.15). But often knowing where participants exit or give up on a task is much more telling of a user's experience. The "Task exits" metric reveals where participants end their experience—for better or for worse—and again provides an idea about where the page navigation isn't meeting expectations.

Moderated Follow-Ups—for Unmoderated Benchmarks

In a moderated benchmark, you have the benefit of being able to both see interactions and ask participants to vocalize reasons for their actions. In an unmoderated benchmark, you don't have this ability. But one of the most effective ways to understand why people behave or act the way they do in unmoderated studies is to ask them. While what people do and what they say isn't always the same, it often is and can usually answer a lot of questions about why the metrics are the way they are.

We've had a lot of success getting at the why by simply asking participants in benchmark studies whether they're willing to participate in a follow-up study. In the moderated follow-ups (usually conducted remotely), we ask participants to revisit the unmoderated study to have them get back into the mindset they were in while they were answering questions or attempting tasks.

This process allows participants to more easily explain and articulate their thoughts by leveraging the power of thinking aloud. The obvious disadvantage with this approach is that it takes time to run the sessions, adds time to the study because you're adding a step, which consequently adds cost. But time permitting, we find it's a small price to pay for the rich understanding of the why behind the numbers.

CONDUCTING STATISTICAL TESTS AND INTERPRETING *P*-VALUES

Throughout Chapter 10 we used the confidence interval overlap in the graphs as an approximate way of detecting statistical significance. As mentioned in the sidebar "Using Confidence Intervals with Benchmark Data" in Chapter 10, when the error bars don't overlap, we can conclude statistical significance (at the level of confidence of the error bars—usually 90% or 95%).

However, this approach isn't something we can always rely on, and we often need more precise methods. For example, the error bars can actually overlap by up to 25% for differences that are statistically significant. This is why it's important to conduct statistical tests to generate a *p*-value. A detailed discussion of what statistical significance means can be found later in this chapter in the section "What does Statistically Significant Mean?"

The actual statistical test to use depends on generally two things:

- The type of data: continuous or discrete binary
- If the data was collected from a within- or between-subjects study

Fortunately, most comparisons in a benchmark analysis can be done using only two statistical tests depending on whether the study is between- or within-subjects.

Between-Subjects

- Two-sample *t*-test: task times and rating scale data
- Two-proportion test: completion rates

Within-Subjects

- Paired *t*-test: task times and rating scale data
- McNemar Exact test: completion rates

The exact procedure for setting up these comparisons will differ depending on your stats package (e.g., SPSS, R, or the StatsUsabilityPakExpanded). In the following sections, I provide examples of interpreting this output from the StatsUsabilityPakExpanded and SPSS using the example studies from Chapter 10. For the formulas and background, see Chapter 5 in *Quantifying the User Experience, 2nd Edition* as well as detailed step-by-step interpretation for using R or Excel in the *Excel & R Companion to Quantifying the User Experience*.

Between-Subjects Comparisons

The two-sample *t*-test and the two-proportion test are the statistical tests used when comparing different participants in different groups.

The two-sample *t*-test

Multi-point rating scale data like the SUS, SEQ, and SUPR-Q and task-time data can be treated as continuous data. Continuous data can be subdivided into smaller meaningful units. For example, we can have a task that takes a minute, half minute, 10 seconds, and so forth. For rating scale data, while typically displayed as discrete units (e.g., participants pick a number from 1 to 7), the mean itself can be treated continuously. For a more technical discussion on this approach, see Chapter 9 on Enduring Controversies in Statistics in *Quantifying the User Experience, 2nd Edition*.

Using our hotel study as an example, we put the raw data for the search tasks into the StatsUsabilityPakExpanded calculator. The output, or comparison data, is shown in Figure 11.16 (StatsUsabilityPakExpanded) and Figure 11.17 (SPSS). Both generated a *p*-value of .412 (see the red arrows in the figures). While we observed a lower ease rating for Best Western (.37 points lower), this difference is not statistically significant (at the p < .05 level of significance).

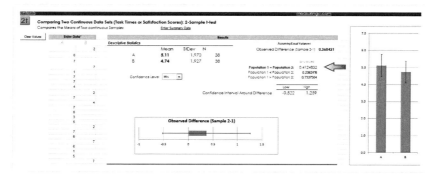

FIGURE 11.16: Output from StatsUsabilityPakExapanded.

→ **T-Test**

Group Statistics

	T2	N	Mean	Std. Deviation	Std. Error Mean
R2	MSearch	38	5.11	1.970	.320
	BSearch	38	4.74	1.927	.313

Independent Samples Test

		Levene's Test for Equality of Variances		t-test for Equality of Means						
									95% Confidence Interval of the Difference	
		F	Sig.	t	df	Sig. (2-tailed)	Mean Difference	Std. Error Difference	Lower	Upper
R2	Equal variances assumed	.001	.982	.824	74	.412	.368	.447	-.522	1.259
	Equal variances not assumed			.824	73.964	.412	.368	.447	-.522	1.259

FIGURE 11.17: Two-sample t output from SPSS (From Analyze ->Compare Means ->Independent Samples *t*-test Menu in SPSS 23).

The N-1 two-proportion test

Task completion rate data is coded as binary: A value of 1 indicates task success and a 0 indicates task failure. The recommended statistical procedure for comparing two between-subjects proportions for any sample size is called the N-1 two-proportion test. It's a derivation of the chi-square test that works well for small samples (it used N-1 degrees of freedom, which is where it gets its clumsy name). While it's not a default test in SPSS, Minitab, or R, it is available as part of the StatsUsabilityPakExpanded.

Using the completion rates from our hotel study, the browse task for Marriott (28 successful tasks out of 38) and for Best Western (36 successful tasks out of 38) generated a difference of 21 percentage points and a corresponding *p*-value of .0124 (red arrow in Figure 11.18). This is statistically significant at the typical alpha threshold of .05.

FIGURE 11.18: Output of the N-1 two-proportion test from the StatsUsabilityPak-Expanded.

Within-Subjects Comparisons

The paired *t*-test and the McNemar Exact test are the statistical tests used when comparing the same participants in both groups. To give an example how to use these tests, I am using data from a benchmark study of three financial services websites. Participants in the study attempted two tasks on the three websites.

Paired *t*-test

The paired *t*-test compares rating scale data and task-time data when the participants are used for both comparisons. Figure 11.19 and 11.20 show the difference in task times between two of the websites for one task were statistically significant.

The average time to complete the tasks was lower on website JS compared to JM. Be sure your data is set up "paired" so the same participant's data is on the same row. The calculations use the difference between each participant's time to compute the *p*-value.

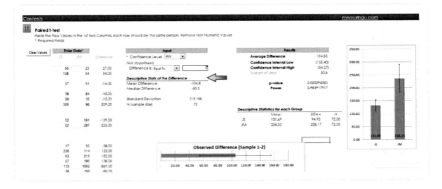

FIGURE 11.19: Paired *t*-test on task-time data for a financial services website benchmark from the StatsUsabilityPakExpanded calculator.

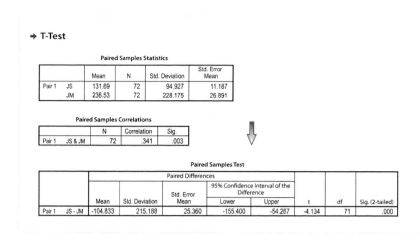

→ T-Test

Paired Samples Statistics

		Mean	N	Std. Deviation	Std. Error Mean
Pair 1	JS	131.69	72	94.927	11.187
	JM	236.53	72	228.175	26.891

Paired Samples Correlations

		N	Correlation	Sig.
Pair 1	JS & JM	72	.341	.003

Paired Samples Test

		Paired Differences					t	df	Sig. (2-tailed)
		Mean	Std. Deviation	Std. Error Mean	95% Confidence Interval of the Difference				
					Lower	Upper			
Pair 1	JS - JM	-104.833	215.188	25.360	-155.400	-54.267	-4.134	71	.000

FIGURE 11.20: Paired *t*-test output from SPSS (From Analyze ->Compare Means ->Paired Samples *t*-test menu in SPSS 23).

McNemar Exact test

The McNemar Exact test is the analog to the N-1 two-proportion test for within-subjects completion rates. Again, be sure your data is aligned so each row has the same participant's data. Using the same task from the financial benchmark study in the paired *t*-test, the large differences in completion rates—71% vs. 31%—are also statistically significant (*p* < .001). Unfortunately, I'm not familiar with computing the McNemar Exact test in SPSS.

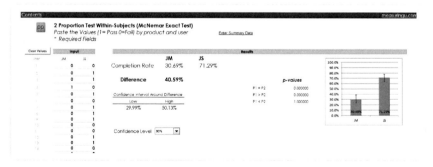

FIGURE 11.21: McNemar Exact test.

What Does Statistically Significant Mean?

Statistically significant. It's a phrase that's packed with both meaning— and syllables. It's hard to say and harder to understand. Yet it's one of the most common phrases heard when dealing with quantitative methods.

While the phrase statistically significant represents the result of a rational exercise with numbers, it has a way of evoking as much emotion: bewilderment, resentment, confusion and even arrogance (for those in the know). To help demystify this phrase, I've unpacked the following most important concepts to help you with interpreting *p*-values when making comparisons in benchmark studies.

When it's not due to chance. In principle, a statistically significant result (usually a difference) is a result that's not attributed to chance. More technically, it means that if the null hypothesis is true (which means there really is no difference), there's a low probability of getting a result that is large or larger than what you observed.

Statisticians get really picky about the definition of statistical significance and use confusing jargon to build a complicated definition. While it's important to be clear on what statistical significance means technically, it's just as important to be clear on what it means practically.

Consider these two important factors:

- **Sampling error:** There's always a chance that the differences we observe when measuring a sample of users is just the result of random noise, chance fluctuations, or happenstance.

- **Probability:** There's never certainty. Statistics is about probability; you cannot buy 100% certainty. Statistics is about managing risk. Can we live with a 10% likelihood that our decision is wrong? A 5% likelihood? 33%? The answer depends on context: What does it cost to increase the probability of making the right choice, and what is the consequence (or potential consequence) of making the wrong choice? Most publications suggest a cutoff of 5%—it's okay to be fooled by randomness 1 time out of 20. That's a reasonably high standard, and it may match your circumstances. It could just as easily be overkill, or it could expose you to far more risk than you can afford.

What it means in practice. Let's look at a scenario from a benchmarking study with 100 participants (50 attempting a task on each website). Here are the completion rates:

- 25 out of 50 participants (50%) completed the task on website A
- 35 out of 50 different participants (70%) completed the same task on website B

Can we reliably attribute the 20-percentage-point difference in completion rates to the effectiveness of one website over the other, or is this random noise?

How do we get statistical significance? The test we use to detect statistical difference depends on our metric type and on whether we're comparing the same users (within-subjects) or different users (between-subjects) on the designs as covered earlier in this chapter. To compare two completion rates as we're doing here, we use the N-1 two-proportion test (between-subjects). Figure 11.22 shows a screenshot of the results using the StatsUsabilityPakExpanded for comparing two proportions.

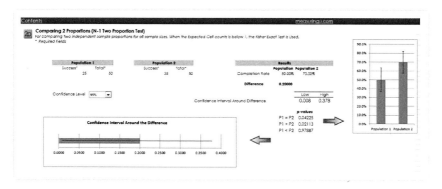

FIGURE 11.22: Points in the N-1 two-proportion calculator to obtain statistical significance.

To determine whether the observed difference is statistically significant, we look at two outputs of the statistical test (see earlier in this chapter on which statistical tests to use for benchmarking studies).

- **P-value:** The primary output of statistical tests is the *p*-value (probability value). It indicates the probability of observing the difference if no difference exists. Using the example shown in Figure 11.22, the *p*-value is 0.042, which indicates that we'd expect to see a meaningless (random) difference of 20% or more only about 42 times in 1,000. If we are comfortable with that level of chance (something we must consider before running the test), then we declare the observed difference to be statistically significant. In most cases, this would be declared a statistically significant result.

- **Confidence interval (CI) around difference:** A confidence interval around a difference that does not cross zero also indicates statistical significance. Using Figure 11.22 as an example, "the graph shows the 95% confidence interval around the difference between the proportions outputted from the stats package. The observed difference was 20% (70% minus 50%), but we can expect that the difference itself will fluctuate if this study was replicated. The CI around the difference tells us that it will most likely fluctuate between about .08% and 38% in favor of the second website. But because the difference is greater than 0%, we can conclude that the difference is statistically significant (not due to chance). If the interval crossed zero—if it went, for example, from -2% to 35%—we could not be 95% confident that the difference is nonzero, or even, in fact, that it favors the second website.

What it doesn't mean. Statistical significance does not mean practical significance. The word "significance" in everyday usage connotes consequence and noteworthiness. Just because you get a low *p*-value and conclude a difference is statistically significant, doesn't mean the difference will automatically be important. It's an unfortunate consequence of the words Sir Ronald Fisher selected when describing this method of statistical testing.

To declare practical significance, we need to determine whether the size of the difference is meaningful. In our conversion example, one landing page is generating more than twice as many conversions as the other.

This is a relatively large difference for A/B testing, so in most cases, this statistical difference has practical significance as well. The lower boundary of the confidence interval around the difference also leads us to expect at *least* a 1% improvement. Whether that's enough to have a practical (or a meaningful) impact on sales or website experience depends on the context.

Additional Statistical Analyses

To answer most user-research questions, fundamental statistical techniques like confidence intervals and the statistical tests of the two-sample *t*-test, paired *t*-test, two-proportion test, and the McNemar Exact tests will do the trick. But to answer some questions for a benchmark analysis most effectively, you need to use more advanced techniques. There are three techniques that we often use in benchmark studies to answer more specific research questions: regression analysis, ANOVA, and logistic regression. Each of these techniques requires specialized software (e.g., SPSS, Minitab, R) and training to learn how to set up and interpret the results. But even if you aren't ready to execute these techniques yourself, you can still learn what they are, when to use them, and some things to look out for.

Regression analysis

When you want to understand what combination of variables best predicts a continuous outcome variable like customer satisfaction, likelihood to recommend, time on task, SUPR-Q, SUS, or brand attitudes toward usability—use a regression analysis. This technique also goes by the name of key-drivers analysis because you're able to determine which independent variables have the biggest impact on your dependent (outcome) variable.

You can use both continuous and discrete variables (dummy coded) as independent (predictor) variables. For example, in our benchmark study of airline and aggregator websites, we conducted a key-driver analysis to understand what features of airline websites impacted the SUPR-Q and how much. We did this first across all websites and then for each airline. Slides from that report are shown in Figures 11.23 and 11.24.

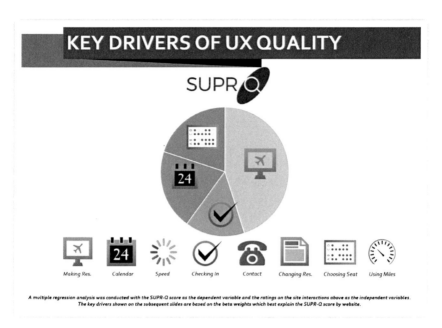

FIGURE 11.23: Example output (after graphic design) of a key-drivers analysis of airline websites.

We found that making a reservation, checking-in, the usability of the calendar, and choosing a seat on the airline website were the statistically significant key drivers (see Figure 11.23).

FIGURE 11.24: Example output (after graphic design) of a key-drivers analysis of four airline websites.

We found the key drivers differed by airline. For example, the ease by which a participant could choose a seat was a big positive driver, and the ability to change a reservation was a negative driver of SUPR-Q scores—but only for Delta's website.

 TIP:

> Be sure a linear relationship exists between your variables by graphing them. You also don't want the independent variables to correlate highly with each other (usually r > .8)—a condition called multicollinearity, which renders the regression equation unreliable. See Chapter 11 in *Quantifying the User Experience 2nd Edition* for more on regression analysis.

ANOVA

An analysis of variance (ANOVA) tells you whether the means from more than two groups have a significant difference, such as the SUPR-Q scores across five websites. The more familiar *t*-test is a special case of the ANOVA when there are only two groups to compare.

What makes an ANOVA powerful though is it allows you to look at multiple variables at a time *and* understand what combination results in the largest difference. This is called the interaction effect.

For example, you may want to know which of the four websites has the fastest task time for filling out a form. Is that form on one page or split across two pages? That's one variable (the form design) with two levels (form A and form B). This research question can be answered using a *t*-test. But if you want to understand how another variable, say the device type (mobile vs. desktop), affects form completion time, you would use an ANOVA. It allows you to ensure that the form design that's fastest to complete on a desktop computer isn't time-consuming on a mobile device.

If you think this sounds similar to regression analysis, you'd be right. The ANOVA is just a regression analysis with discrete independent variables. Both techniques are part of a larger technique called general linear modeling (GLM). See Chapter 10 in *Quantifying the User Experience 2nd Edition* for more on using ANOVA.

TIP:

> When you compare many groups, you increase the chance of finding a difference from chance alone (called alpha inflation). You should plan to use a multiple comparison technique, such as a Bonferroni correction or my preference, the Benjamini–Hochberg procedure, to differentiate the signal from the noise. Often when you're comparing groups, you really only care about comparisons with your product or website, which reduces the number of comparisons and consequently alpha inflation.

Logistic regression

It's often the case that dependent variables are discrete and not continuous. For example, you may be primarily interested in purchase rates (purchase vs. not purchase) or conversion rates (recommend or didn't recommend)—both are discrete binary. In such cases, a regular regression analysis won't work. Instead, you'd use a different but related technique called logistic regression analysis, which converts the data using a logit transformation. In logistic regression, you still want to know what combination of independent variables best predicts the outcome, as in regular regression. The only difference is the outcome variable is discrete (usually binary). For example, you may want to understand how attitudes toward a brand (favorable or unfavorable) and customer tenure (new vs. existing) affects the likelihood to recommend a product.

TIP:

> While logistic regression doesn't have the same linearity assumptions as regular regression, you still need to look for highly correlated independent variables (multicollinearity), to have a large sample size, and must interpret log-odd ratios, which is more challenging.

How Confident Do You Need to Be?

The typical level of confidence we work with in benchmark studies is the 90% level. This means our methods of computing confidence intervals will contain the actual unknown completion rate or average score for 90 out of 100 samples we take.

The confidence level is related to the *p*-value obtained when conducting statistical comparisons (see the "Conducting Statistical Tests and Interpreting *P*-Values" section in this chapter). For most of our applied research, we flag differences as "statistically significant" if its *p*-value is less than 0.10 (or 10%) and especially when the *p*-value is less than .05 (or 5%).

The confidence level and the *p*-value that determines the threshold for statistical significance are values we set ahead of time, using what we call the alpha level. If we choose an alpha level of 0.05, for example, then a *p*-value smaller than 0.05 is considered statistically significant, and our confidence level (1–alpha) is 0.95.

Although we most often set alpha to 0.05, it can take any value from just above 0 (e.g., 0.00001) to just below 1 (e.g., 0.99999). I'm often asked about the best level of confidence to use. The answer is that it depends on the consequences of being wrong. To help put that into context, the following are different thresholds commonly used to determine the confidence level (and *p*-values) in different situations; you can use these examples to determine what is appropriate for your situation.

Pharmaceutical confidence level—99%+: When a bad decision can lead to injury or death—say, when you're evaluating clinical trials and drug interactions—you want a high level of confidence in your intervals and a high standard for declaring statistical significance. Of course, higher levels of confidence come with higher costs; testing in the pharmaceutical environment often involves sample sizes with thousands of participants.

Publication confidence level—95%+: When your reputation is on the line, like peer-reviewed journals and high-level political polls, a confidence level of 95% is typically required (and corresponding *p*-value of less than 0.05). When you choose to break with the 0.05 norm, plan to defend your choice. And, if publication is one of your goals, it's going to be difficult to publish your research if your *p*-values exceed .05.

Industrial confidence level—90%+: When you are trying to understand if a product or service is providing a good (or great, or not so great, etc.) user experience, we often use a 90% confidence level. For example, when we complete an analysis for a client, we often are analyzing both survey data and usability benchmarks, so we need a 90% confidence level to ensure that a two-sided statement equates to 95% confidence for a one-sided statement (e.g., at least 75% of users can complete a task). In many environments, dipping below 90% takes your stakeholders out of their comfort zone. See Chapter 4 in our book *Quantifying the User*

Experience, 2nd Edition for more discussion on one- and two-sided confidence intervals and Chapter 9 on associated controversies in measurement and statistics.

Exploratory confidence level—80%+: When you need only reasonable evidence—when, for example, you're looking at product prototypes, early-stage designs, or the general sentiments from customers—the 80% level of confidence is often sufficient. When your sample sizes are smaller, confidence intervals widen and you rarely get statistically significant results with high confidence. Also, when you relax your alpha to 0.20, you'll be fooled more often by chance variation. However, when the consequences of being wrong are not dire, though, then this may be a sufficient level to choose.

Casino confidence level—51+%: When there's little or no downside to being wrong, and if you have to pick among poor alternatives, a 51% confidence level is at least better than flipping a coin. As they say: What happens in Vegas, stays in Vegas—and that's the case with your money too. In a casino, the longer you play the less likely you're going home a winner. Games of chance are rigged to give the house a small edge. However, if your business is on the line, we don't recommend declaring statistical significance with *p*-values of 0.49—unless your business happens to be high-stakes poker.

While you may want to go for high confidence in every situation to minimize the risk of being wrong, the price to pay for high confidence is large sample sizes. With high confidence and smaller sample sizes, you increase the chances of another problem in statistics (false negatives), that is, not declaring statistical significance when there actually is a difference.

CHAPTER SUMMARY AND TAKEAWAY

This chapter covered more advanced—but often essential—analyses:

- Analyze preference data using confidence intervals (or other methods) to understand which experience is preferred.
- Examine a brand's lift or drag by comparing brand attitude data before and after tasks in a study.

- Examine potential differences between groups by cross tabbing variables. You can more easily cross tab and run statistical comparisons by collapsing variables, often into two groups— called dichotomizing.

- Control for participant prior experience, which is often a strong predictor of UX metrics, by using a weighted t-test or reporting out on different (often collapsed) levels of experience.

- Understand the "why" behind your numbers. Examine verbatim comments, log files, click behavior visualizations (like heat maps and click maps), and session recordings.

- Assess statistical significance by using a p-value (precise) or overlaps in confidence intervals (approximate).

- Determine if you need to include additional statistical analyses, which include multiple regression analysis (e.g., "What are the biggest 'drivers' of the Net Promoter Score?") and the ANOVA (e.g., "Is there a difference between any of the four groups?").

- Know that a statistically significant difference is a result that's not attributed to chance (in principal). More technically, it means that if there really is no difference, there's a low probability of getting a very small p-value by chance.

- Determine the level of confidence you need (e.g., 80%, 90%, 95%, or 99%). This depends on how precise you need to be and the consequences of being wrong. We recommend a 90% level of confidence for most benchmark studies and a p-value of less than .10 or .05.

- Decide which statistical test fits your needs. While there are a lot of statistical tests, most comparisons you'll need to make in a benchmark analysis can be done using only two statistical tests depending on whether the study is between-subjects (two-sample t-test or N-1 two-proportion test) or within-subjects (paired-t test or McNemar Exact test).

CHAPTER 12:
REPORTING YOUR RESULTS

Now that you've analyzed and summarized and researched the reasons behind the numbers, it's time to report. Reporting structures differ depending on the audience and objectives. We've worked on very detailed reports with hundreds of slides to more compact ones with only 5 to 10 key findings slides. You'll ultimately need to ensure your report matches the needs, and you may need multiple reports and revisions. The following sections detail a format that we find works well for most benchmark studies.

ANATOMY OF A BENCHMARK REPORT

In our benchmark reports we typically start broad, first with context and background on the study and the methodologies used. We then go more specific, providing a balance between metrics and explanations throughout.

Our typical presentation program that we use is PowerPoint (still called a slide deck) and in some cases Google Slides (especially when our client is Google!). We only write more text-heavy Microsoft Word-based reports for an academic audience. The following sections in this section are based on our typical presentation format and provide a structure for your presentation.

Title Slide and Name
Include a descriptive title and picture on the title slide. Many organizations have their own standard title slide and format. Figure 12.1 shows an example that comes from the hotel industry benchmark study we conducted in 2017.

FIGURE 12.1: Example title slide from a UX benchmark report for hotel websites.

Executive Summary

Your benchmark report is likely to contain a lot of data and slides. Most of our benchmark reports are at least 30 to 50 slides. The executive summary is a place to bring it all together. When appropriate, we like to include the following:

- Which product or website was preferred and had the higher scores (if a competitive study).

- Task-level highlights (e.g., differences in completion rates or times and by competitor if applicable). If it is a stand-alone study, any poor or high scores often merit attention. One way to justify saying a score is poor or high is by reference to tools like the SUPR-Q percentile ranks or the SUS grading scales (as referenced in Chapter 5).

- Insights into reasons for high or low scores on the websites or products being evaluated.

- Any other important research questions (e.g., impacts of product filters, advertising, or trustworthiness).

Figure 12.2 shows an example executive summary from the hotel benchmark industry study.

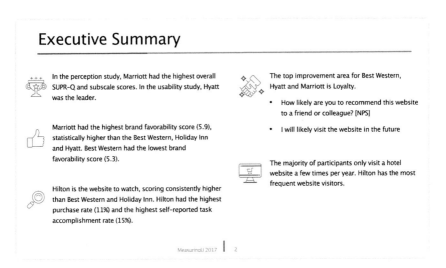

FIGURE 12.2: Example executive summary slide from a UX benchmark report for hotel websites.

Study and Methodology Overview
We like to include one to three slides that provide an overview of some of the main factors covered in the booking document (Chapter 2).

- Study methodology (e.g., moderated in-person/remote or unmoderated)
- Study dates (because websites and products change a lot!)
- Sample size(s) for all products
- Platform(s) desktop, mobile, etc.

Study Overview

STUDY DESIGN

Online Unmoderated
Usability Test

SAMPLE SIZE

76 Participants
Mix of Gender, Education,
Income, Age

DATES OF STUDY

Aug 14 – 15, 2017

MeasuringU 2017 | 42

FIGURE 12.3: Example study overview slide from a UX benchmark report for hotel websites.

Study Methodology

A total of 199 participants completed an online task-based survey assessing the perceptions and preferences of filter capabilities on three asset management websites. Each participant conducted two tasks on each website. The websites were presented in a random order.

Testing Dates
September 28 – October 6

101
Consumers

98
Financial Advisors

Website A   Website C

Website B

MeasuringU 2017 | 2

FIGURE 12.4: Example study methodology slide from a comparative UX benchmark report on financial websites.

Participant Summary

You will likely have many demographic variables. We don't like to present them all at the beginning of the deck (unless it is critical to see all). Instead we select a subset, usually a mix of the more important variables. For example, for a mobile application benchmark study, we included the sample size, age, and gender breakdown by website all in one slide so stakeholders could more easily see the comparisons.

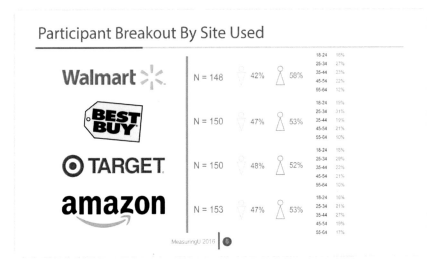

FIGURE 12.5: Example participant summary slide from a UX benchmark report for retail websites.

Figure 12.6 shows another example from the hotel benchmark study that combined a retrospective benchmark with a task-based benchmark (we called it "Usability").

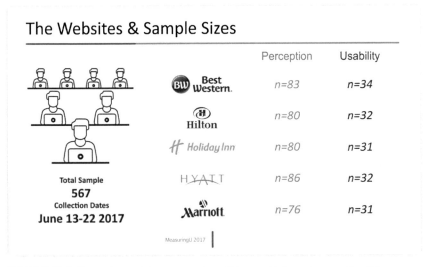

FIGURE 12.6: Example participant overview slide combining retrospective "Perception" and task-based "Usability" data for a hotel benchmark.

For moderated benchmark studies, we like to include a grid of the participants and usually one or two key pieces of information, such as product or industry experience. See Figure 12.7 for an example.

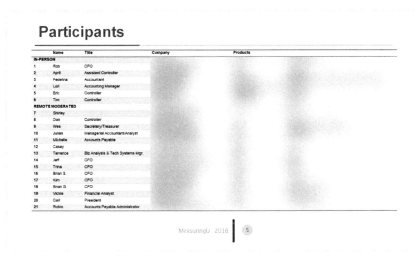

FIGURE 12.7: Participant overview for a moderated benchmark. It includes company name, products used, and prior experience (details intentionally obscured).

Tasks
For task-based benchmarks, provide the tasks as the participants saw them.

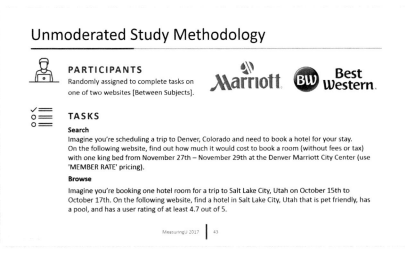

FIGURE 12.8: Example methodology and task slide from a UX benchmark report for hotel websites.

Task Metrics

If a benchmark study includes tasks, we typically include one slide for each task metric collected. You may decide to start with study-level metrics (and would if it is retrospective), so consider these guidelines suggestions, rather than rules. The figures in this chapter give examples of different task metrics and how we presented them to our clients.

- **Start with completion rates.** Completion rates are the fundamental task metric. If participants have a hard time completing tasks, it provides color for the subsequent metrics. We usually follow with task-level ease and task completion time.

- **Include call-outs.** Whenever a metric looks unusual, low, or notable in some way (because it's higher than a competitor), we like to include some explanation for it on the slide and usually provide more detail in the subsequent sections. Figure 12.9, 12.10, and 12.11 show examples of appropriate use of call-outs to highlight and explain concerning metrics.

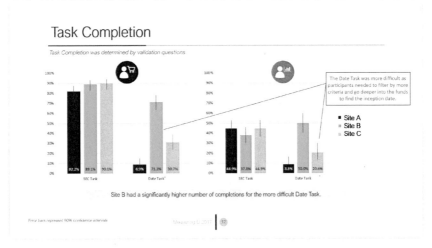

FIGURE 12.9: Task completion rates for three financial websites by two participant types (names redacted).

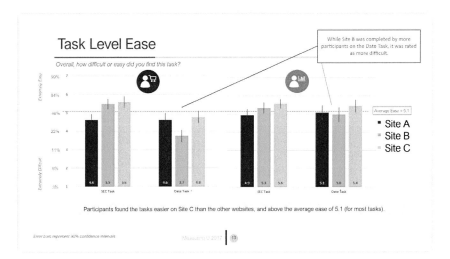

FIGURE 12.10: Task ease (SEQ) for three financial websites (names redacted).

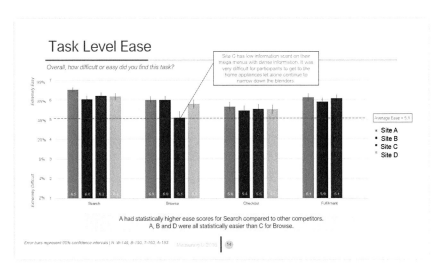

FIGURE 12.11: Task level ease for four retail websites (names redacted).

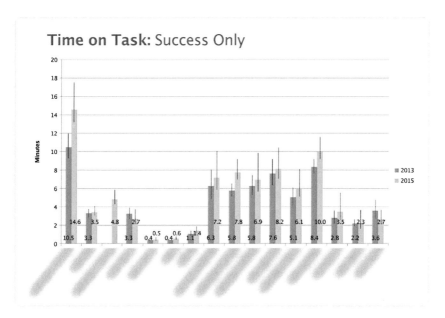

FIGURE 12.12: Task time for a moderated software benchmark comparing task times for the 2013 and 2015 benchmarks (task names intentionally obscured).

We often include cross tabbing data for the task level in this section. Figure 12.13 shows an example of this technique using the SUM by experience metric for an unmoderated benchmark study.

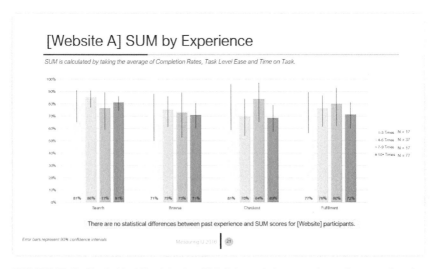

FIGURE 12.13: Single Usability Metrics (SUM) by website experience for a retail website across four tasks (names changed).

Study Metrics

The study level metrics provide the broader overview of the experience as shown in the following figures.

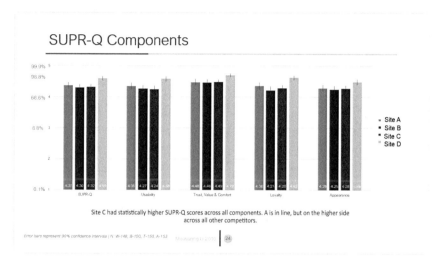

FIGURE 12.14: SUPR-Q scores for a comparative retail website benchmark with raw means and percentile ranks (names changed).

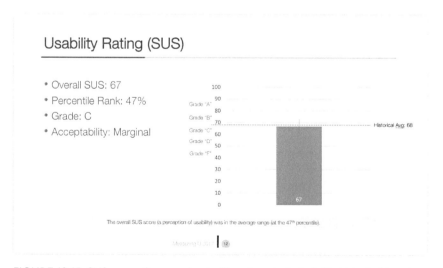

FIGURE 12.15: SUS scores for a moderated benchmark study (with historical benchmarks, grades and percentile ranks referenced).

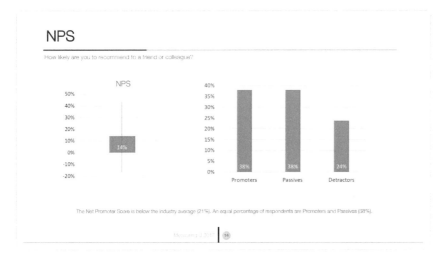

FIGURE 12.16: Example Net Promoter Score (NPS) slide with breakout of promoters, passives, and detractors for a moderated benchmark.

Appendix demographics

When the particular demographics of the participants aren't of particular interest (which is often the case with general population consumer benchmarks), we include them in the appendix for more reference. We'll even use fancy icons and graphics as seen in Figure 12.17.

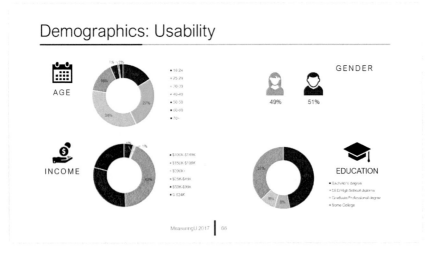

FIGURE. 12.17: Example demographics from a wireless SUPR-Q benchmark report (appears in an appendix).

UX Issues and Insights

While the emphasis of a UX benchmark is on the metrics, you should plan on including enough detail to explain the "why" behind the metrics as well as providing any of the more in-depth, advanced analysis techniques used in the study (as described in Chapter 11). Figure 12.18 shows an example of how participants used filters on one website benchmark.

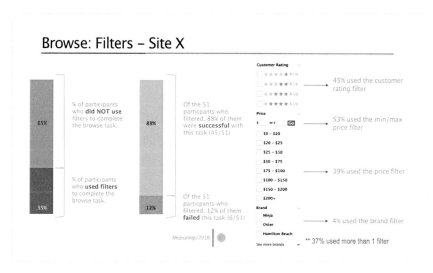

FIGURE 12.18: Example of filter usage from an unmoderated benchmark.

FIGURE 12.19: Example of a problem on checkout (some details changed) from a retail benchmark report.

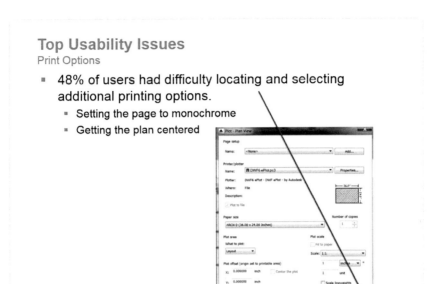

FIGURE 12.20: Example of a usability problem from a moderated benchmark.

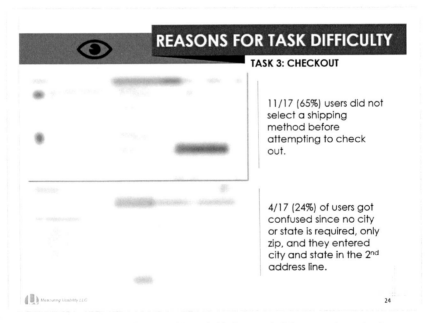

FIGURE 12.21: Examples of two problems (with frequencies) from a task on checkout on a retail website (from observing 17 session videos from an unmoderated benchmark).

Verbatim comments

Including verbatim participant comments in a benchmark report provides a human component to the numbers and, like videos, can really drive home a point. We display verbatim comments in two ways: We'll either pick a selection that is representative of common themes (see Figure 12.22), or we'll categorize the verbatim comments into groups and then graph the frequency of comments with selections as shown in Figure 12.23. For more on this approach, see "How to Code & Analyze Verbatim Comments" at measuringu.com/code-verbatim/.

What to improve: User Comments

- Pages are slow to load: *"The website tends to lag when trying to navigate."*
- Frequently have difficulty logging in: *"I always need additional security measures when trying to log-in."*
- Difficult to contact support: *"It could be hard to contact using a live chat"*
- Difficult to understand plans and pricing: *"It is not always clear what exactly you are getting with each deal."*
- Confusing: *"It is so confusing to see everything"*
- Some information is difficult to find: *"Some details couldn't be found on the website and had to call to get answers."*
- Cluttered design: *"The page is jumbled in my opinion. There is too much going on. It makes it less attractive."*

MeasuringU 2017 | 19

FIGURE 12.22: Example of selected verbatims from a wireless benchmark report.

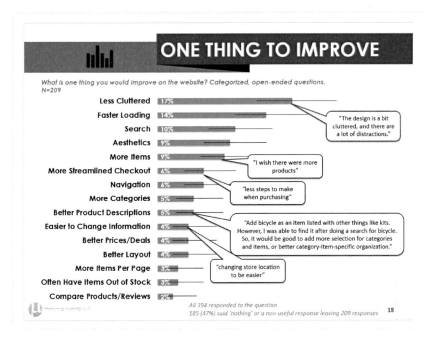

FIGURE 12.23: Example of categorized verbatim comments with confidence intervals.

RECOMMENDATIONS FOR BENCHMARK REPORTS AND PRESENTATIONS

We put together a lot of benchmark reports and have refined our presentation styles over the years based on client input. We're always looking to improve; here are some guidelines and recommendations from our experience to help make your reports more effective. Many of these recommendations are reflected in the figure examples in this chapter.

- **Start with the right template and the right style.** We've created reports for clients only to find out after an initial draft that our client wanted the information to be presented in a different template or a different style (less graphs and more explanations).

- **Add "bang" boxes.** For most slides we like to include, what we call, a "bang box" at the bottom of the slide that summarizes the key findings of the slide (leaning on the executive-friendly side).

- **Don't just report the bad news.** Include any suggestions, positive comments, and features that seemed to improve the user experience. While a development team will often want to know what's not working and get right to the problems, most will appreciate that users and usability professionals aren't all gloom and doom.

- **Report as double duty.** Keep in mind these reports typically do double duty, as stand-alone reports and as presentations to walk through. You need to balance providing enough information in the report so people know what it means without overwhelming viewers with dense graphs and text.

- **Use an appendix.** One of the best ways to keep reports informative without being overwhelming is to put a lot of the essential but not necessarily informative data, like second-tier demographics, additional cross tabs, and verbatims, into an appendix. By using an appendix, the flow of the presentation won't be derailed but will still cover the essentials for any unexpected questions.

- **Illustrate issues using screenshots and categorize problems.** Sorting problems into logical groups, such as "buttons," "navigation," and "labels," along with a good picture can really help with digesting a lot of issues. When possible, include how common the issue was encountered by participants.

- **Use highlight videos.** Small clips of the most common usability problems or illustrative examples are helpful for stakeholders who rarely have time to pore over hours of video; this can make a huge impact with little effort. When possible, we include short clips (usually under 30 seconds and under 5MB). While benchmark reports are all about the data, sometimes the best way to illustrate what the data says is not with a graph but with a gaffe.

- **Use call-outs appropriately.** While we have sections that detail problem areas, small call-outs on metric heavy/graph slides help answer a lot of immediate questions, such as "Why was the completion rate so low?"

- **Reference historical benchmarks.** Whenever possible, include a reference to a historical benchmark, such as the average task-level ease, average NPS for the industry, or average SUPR-Q score. See Chapter 6 for finding and referencing historical/industry-standard benchmarks.

- **Display statistical significance.** Find a way to communicate real differences versus sampling error in your presentation. We usually include confidence intervals, but there are other ways to display statistical significance (see the next section in this chapter).

How to Display Statistical Significance

Throughout Chapters 10 and 11 I've written a lot about the importance of understanding sampling error and using confidence intervals and *p*-values to understand the uncertainty in your benchmark data. Understanding and appreciating the consequences of sampling error and statistical significance in a benchmark analysis is one thing; conveying this concept to stakeholders is another challenge—especially if they are less quantitatively inclined.

Picking the "right" visualization is a balance between working with conventions, knowing your audience, and not overwhelming them. The following sections highlight recommended ways to indicate sampling error and statistical significance in your benchmark reports.

Confidence interval error bars

Confidence intervals are one type of error bar that can be placed on graphs to show sampling error. Confidence intervals visually show the reader the most plausible range of the unknown population average based on the available data (see the sidebar "Using Confidence Intervals with Benchmark Data" in Chapter 10 for more information on error bars). They are usually 90% or 95% by convention.

What's nice about confidence intervals is that they act as a shorthand statistical test, even for people who don't understand *p*-values. They tell you if two values are statistically different along with the upper and lower bounds of a value.

That is, if there's no overlap in confidence intervals, the differences are statistically significant at the level of confidence (in most cases). For example, Figure 12.24 shows the percent of participants that found items on two websites for different products along with 90% confidence intervals depicted as the black vertical line at the top of the error bars.

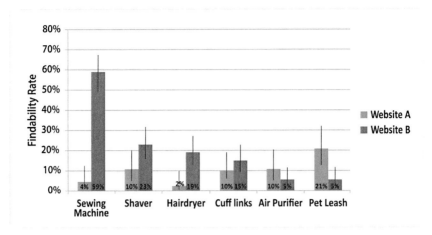

FIGURE 12.24: Findability rates (completion rates for finding products) for two websites. Black error bars are 90% confidence intervals.

Almost 60% of 75 participants found the sewing machine on Website B compared to only 4% of a different group of 75 participants on Website A. The lower boundary of Website B's findability rate (49%) is well above the upper boundary of Website A's findability rate (12%). This difference is statistically significant at $p = < .10$.

You can also see that the findability rate for Website A is unlikely to ever exceed 15% (the upper boundary is at 12%). This visually tells you that with a sample size of 75, it's highly unlikely (less than a 5% chance) that the findability rate would ever exceed 15%. Of course, a 15% findability rate is abysmally low (meaning roughly only 1 in 7 people will ever find the sewing machine).

This is my preferred method for displaying statistical significance in benchmark studies. But even experienced researchers with strong statistics backgrounds have trouble interpreting confidence intervals, and they aren't always the best option. You may think that the following recommendations may be better options for your study and audience.

Shaded graphs

Error bars of any kind can add a lot of "ink" to a graph, which can freak out some stakeholders. To avoid error bars on a visualization, you can differ the shading on the bars of a graph to show statistically significant findings. The dark red bars in Figure 12.25 show which comparisons are statistically significant. This shading can be done in color or in black-and-white to be printer friendly.

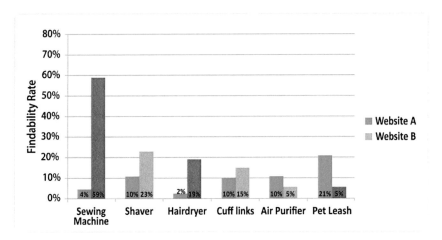

FIGURE 12.25: Findability rates for two websites; the dark red bars indicate differences that are statistically significant.

Asterisks

An asterisk (*) or other symbol can indicate statistical significance for a modest number of comparisons (shown in Figure 12.26). We've also seen (and occasionally use) multiple symbols to indicate statistical significance at two thresholds (often $p < .05$ and $p < .10$).

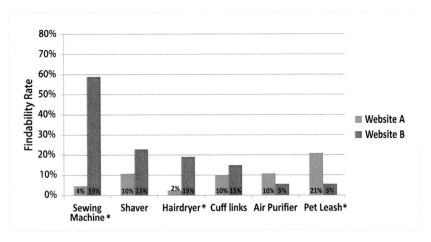

FIGURE 12.26: Findability rates for two websites; asterisks indicate statistically significant differences.

Notes

It's often the case that so many benchmark comparisons are statistically significant that any visual indication would be overwhelming (or undesired). In those cases, a note depicting significance is ideal. These notes can be in the footer of a table, the caption of an image (as shown in the caption for Figure 12.27), or in the notes section of slides in the benchmark report.

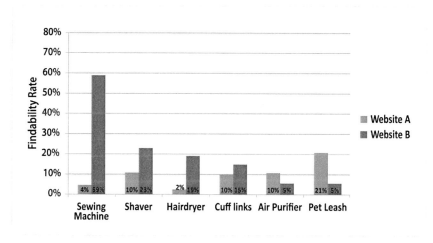

FIGURE 12.27: Findability rates for two websites. Sewing Machine, Hairdryer, and Pet Leash findability rates are statistically different.

Connecting lines and hybrids

When differences aren't contiguous, an alternative approach is to include connecting lines as shown in Figure 12.28. It shows eight conditions from a UX benchmark study using three measures (satisfaction, confidence, likelihood to purchase). Three differences were statistically different as indicated by the connecting lines. The graph also includes 95% confidence intervals and notes in the caption.

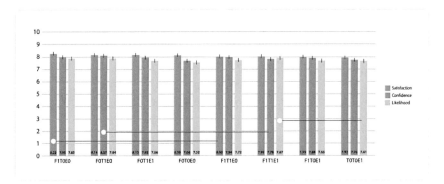

FIGURE 12.28: Mean satisfaction, confidence, and likelihood to purchase across eight conditions. Error bars are 95% confidence intervals. Connecting lines show statistical differences for conditions: satisfaction F1T0E0 vs. F1T1E0; confidence F0T1E0 vs F1T1E1; and likelihood to purchase F1T1E1 vs. T0T0E1.

CHAPTER SUMMARY AND TAKEAWAYS

In this chapter we've gone over the essentials of preparing a report for your clients/stakeholders. The most important factor when compiling your benchmark report is to use a format that meets their objectives—and expectations.

- Keep in mind a report does double duty—acting as a report and a presentation.

- Use appendices to document very detailed or less meaningful data that would otherwise interrupt the flow of the basic presentation.

- Start with task-completion rates and then proceed to task ease and task time when presenting task metrics.

- Include "bang boxes" to provide the clear takeaways for each slide.

- Include a section on UX insights and include screen shots and video clips to illustrate the "why" behind the metrics.

- Display statistical significance in a clear and concise way, such as using error bars, shaded graphs, asterisks, or notes, to ensure the readability of these complicated findings.

CHAPTER 13:

THE END OF THE BOOK— ALMOST

If there's one thing I hope you've taken away from this book is the value of benchmarking and the amount of detail that goes into planning, executing, and analyzing benchmark data. No single book can cover everything, especially with technology changing. The following sections provide a list of resources from MeasuringU and a reference list of the books that were discussed in this book. These resources will help you stay up to date on current trends in UX benchmarking and other UX methods, as well as provide background for the information in this book.

GOOD RESOURCES

MeasuringU.com Weekly Newsletter: Each week I write an article on UX measurement topics, including tips and best practices for benchmarking.

Benchmark Reports: Each quarter we benchmark the user experience of an industry (e.g., retail, consumer software, wireless websites, entertainment websites) that provide good reference points for benchmark studies. These can be found online at measuringu.com/products/.

UX Measurement Boot Camp: Each year I host a three-day boot camp on UX Metrics, Methods and Analysis. Participants get hands on training using the MUIQ platform and can design and analyze their own benchmarking study. For more information, see denverux.com.

UX Benchmark Course: In late 2017 I hosted a four-part UX benchmarking class under the auspices of the UXPA. A recording of this course is available online. See measuringu.com/events/benchmarking-the-user-experience/.

Custom Training: I have provided custom training to many companies on UX Benchmarking. A good model involves the MeasuringU team conducting an initial benchmark study, and then we train an internal team to continue collecting and analyzing data. Contact us at measuringu.com/contact/ for more information on custom benchmark training and services.

Excel Skills: To learn some essential Excel skills, see measuringu.com/excel-1/ and measuringu.com/excel-2/. A free benchmarking Excel package is available for download on the MeasuringU website: measuringu.com/benchmarkbook/.

GOOD READS

Albert, B., Tullis, T., & Tedesco, D. (2010). *Beyond the usability lab: Conducting large-scale online user experience studies* . Burlington, MA, USA: Morgan Kaufmann Publishers; Elsevier, Inc.

Brooke, J. (1996). SUS: A quick and dirty usability scale. In P. W. Jordan, B. Thomas, B. A. Weerdmeester & I. L. McClelland (Eds.), *Usability Evaluation in Industry* (pp. 189–194). London, UK: Taylor & Francis.

Brooke, J. (2013). SUS: A retrospective. *Journal of Usability Studies, 8*(2), 29–40.

Dumas, J. S., & Loring, B. (2008). *Moderating usability tests: Principles & practices for interacting.* Burlington, MA, USA: Morgan Kaufmann Publishers; Elsevier, Inc.

Dumas, J. S., & Redish, J. C. (1999). *A Practical Guide to Usability Testing.* Portland, OR, USA: Intellect Ltd.

Harris, D. F. (2014). *The complete guide to writing questionnaires: How to get better information for better decisions* London, UK: Insight & Measurement.

Lewis, J. R., & Sauro, J. (2012). *Excel & R companion to Quantifying the user experience: Practical statistics for user research (2nd Ed.).* Denver, CO, USA: Measuring Usability, LLC.

McGovern, G. (2010). *The stranger's long neck: How to deliver what your customers really want online*. London, UK: A & C Publishers.

Reichheld, F. (2011). *The ultimate question 2.0: How net promoter companies thrive in a customer-driven world*. Boston, MA, USA: Harvard Business School Publishing.

Rubin, J, & Chisnell, D. (2008). *Handbook of usability testing: How to plan, design, and conduct effective tests*. Indianapolis, IN, USA: Wiley Publishing, Inc.

Sauro, J. (2010). *A practical guide to measuring usability: Quantifying the usability of websites & software* . Denver, CO, USA: Measuring Usability, LLC.

Sauro, J. (2011). A *practical guide to the System Usability Scale: Background, benchmarks & best practices*. Denver, CO, USA: Measuring Usability, LLC.

Sauro, J., & Dumas J. S. (2009). Comparison of three one-question, post-task usability questionnaires. In *Proceedings of the Conference in Human Factors in Computing Systems (CHI 2009)* (pp. 1599–1608). Boston, MA, USA: ACM.

Sauro, J., & Kindlund E. (2005). A method to standardize usability metrics into a single score. In *Proceedings of the Conference in Human Factors in Computing Systems (CHI 2005)* (pp. 401–409). Portland, OR, USA: ACM.

Sauro, J., & Lewis J. R. (2009). Correlations among prototypical usability metrics: Evidence for the construct of usability. In *Proceedings of the Conference in Human Factors in Computing Systems (CHI 2009)* (pp. 1609–1618). Boston, MA, USA: ACM.

Sauro, J., & Lewis, J. R. (2016). *Quantifying the user experience: Practical statistics for user research (2nd Ed.)*. Cambridge, MA, USA: Morgan Kaufmann Publishers; Elsevier, Inc

Tullis, T., & Albert, B. (2008). *Measuring the user experience: Collecting, analyzing, and presenting usability metrics*. Burlington, MA, USA: Morgan Kaufmann Publishers; Elsevier, Inc.

The following appendices cover several common questions and include checklist for conducting a benchmark as well as reference relevant chapters for more details.

If you like what you read or have any questions, feel free to reach out at measuringu.com/contact/.

APPENDIX A:

A Checklist for Planning a UX Benchmark Study

I've discussed in detail the why and the how of conducting a benchmark study for a website, app, product, and so on. In this appendix, I discuss common points that go into the planning of a benchmark study before embarking on a benchmarking adventure.

WHEN SHOULD YOU CONDUCT A UX BENCHMARK STUDY?

There are usually two good times and reasons to conduct a benchmark study.

- **When you know you're going to make changes.** All too often we think that any change we make to an interface will improve it. And for some horrible interfaces, that might be the case. But even then, you should benchmark so that you understand which changes quantifiably help, hurt, or have little effect on the user experience. This is a key tenet in the framework for improving the user experience.

- **When you need to calculate a return on investment (ROI).** In order to know when your efforts to improve the interface are worth it (especially in terms of cost and time), benchmark the experience before and after changes.

HOW LONG DO BENCHMARK STUDIES TAKE?

Studies typically last between 4 and 12 weeks. At a minimum, it takes a week to plan the tasks, questions, and study details; a week or two to collect data; and a week to finalize a report with statistical analysis and insights into what's driving the numbers.

Often though, plan to take several weeks to get the tasks and questions right and to iterate them with the right stakeholders (it can be time consuming to get on everyone's calendar). For more complicated studies, it takes longer to be sure that the products are available and properly configured; it can also take longer to facilitate and then analyze results. See Chapter 4 for more detail on the factors that affect the length of studies.

SHOULD IT BE A COMPARATIVE OR A STAND-ALONE STUDY?

As I mention in Chapter 2, many benchmarking studies start as a stand-alone study to collect data for one experience, such as a single website or prototype, but sometimes it becomes clear that more data is needed. While benchmarking is an excellent way to get a pulse on your product or service experience, sometimes when we conduct an initial benchmark study, one of the first reactions we get to the data is, "Is that good or bad?" One way to help answer that is with external, industry-standard benchmarks that we provide from previous research using tools like the SUPR-Q, SUS, SEQ, and SUM. However, these benchmarks may not reveal if the data is "good" or "bad"—some tasks can be naturally more complicated—that's when you may want to consider a comparison study.

One of the best ways to understand if it's the task or the application that's less usable is to compare the same tasks with a competitor's product or service (or best in class comparison). If it takes twice as long to complete the same task on your product or service relative to the competition, then you can have more confidence that an improvement is needed and it's not the task complexity. This would be a reason to go with a comparative study. (See Appendix B for detail on making the most of a competitive benchmark.)

WHO ARE THE USERS?

If you're considering benchmarking, you probably have some idea who your users are. But be sure any assumptions you make about your users are substantiated with actual data (e.g., internal surveys or third-party reports). It doesn't make sense to spend all the effort on a benchmark study if you test with participants you think use your app instead of the users who actually do!

You'll also want to identify any meaningful subgroups of users. For example, teachers versus students, buyers versus sellers. If you want to generate precise metrics for each subgroup, this affects the sample size. Having personas and segments planned out before a benchmark can be helpful. However, it's often not necessary (or possible) to recruit strictly against every persona or customer segment.

WILL YOU BE ABLE TO GET ACCESS TO USERS?

For popular consumer websites, software, and apps, finding qualified users shouldn't be too difficult. For products or websites with specialized users, finding participants can be a challenge. For certain B2B products users are often highly technical, geographically spread out, and very unavailable. You'll want to identify the upper limits for the necessary sample size prior to conducting the study rather than going in with unrealistic expectations about the sample size. Chapter 9 provides details on recruiting participants for moderated and unmoderated benchmark studies.

WHAT WILL THE TASKS BE?

For task-based benchmarks you can rarely test an entire application; instead you'll want to narrow down your study to 5 to 10 tasks per benchmark (fewer when you go with a within-subjects study). It's difficult to ask even paid participants to be diligent for more than an hour for a moderated study and 30 minutes for an unmoderated study.

Focus on the tasks and functions that are most important to users. You can focus on less-used tasks if there is an expected change, if it's a known problem area, or you're benchmarking for that specific data. See Chapter 3 for a detailed discussion on selecting tasks for your benchmark.

WHAT METRICS WILL YOU COLLECT?

For most benchmarks, we typically start with our core set of task metrics (completion rates, time, and perceived ease of use) and study metrics (SUPR-Q or SUS), then work with stakeholders to convert business goals into the right metrics and approaches. The metrics cover both attitudes and actions; and with external benchmarks, we can compare the scores at the task and study level. Even though benchmarking primarily generates metrics, you'll also want to document the problems with the experience so you know what to fix. Metrics are covered extensively in Chapter 5.

WILL YOU (AND THE USERS) HAVE ACCESS TO THE INTERFACE?

For consumer websites, access shouldn't be an issue. But for more complicated software or hardware that requires customization, new versions, or working prototypes, it can be a challenge to get the right product. This is especially the case with a competitive benchmark. Be sure you know when and how you'll access your interfaces. See the section "Interface Access" in Chapter 3.

DO YOU NEED A MODERATED OR UNMODERATED STUDY?

For websites, web apps, and mobile apps, users can access these from anywhere in the world. This allows you to conduct an unmoderated study, which usually means you can collect data from a much larger sample size at a fraction of the cost of a moderated study. A moderated (remote or in-person) study limits the sample size because you'll need to schedule a facilitator with each participant. See the section "Different Modes of UX Benchmarking" in Chapter 1 for understanding the pros and cons of moderated and unmoderated studies.

WILL YOU CONDUCT A RETROSPECTIVE OR TASK-BASED STUDY?

Sometimes it's difficult to simulate a realistic task experience or get access to the right version of the product or find actual users. All is not lost. In such cases, you can generate a benchmark about the perception of the user experience. The user experience (like usability) is measured as a combination of attitudes and actions. If you can get half the equation then it's better than none of it.

You can assess attitudes toward UX by having your users answer a series of standardized questions (for example, the SUS or SUPR-Q) along with questions about specific features, task experiences, future intent, and branding. Use this retrospective study to understand where things are from a higher level, and then consider using a targeted task-based study or inspection method to understand the root causes of lower-level metrics. Measure using the same approach and look for changes that happen over time. Chapter 1 provides the pros and cons of these two types of benchmark studies.

HOW PRECISE DO YOU NEED TO BE?

One of the main motivations for benchmarking is to track changes over time. You therefore need a large enough sample size to differentiate random noise from real changes. After you've decided to make the study stand-alone or comparative (and if comparative, a within- or between-subjects study) and decided on the needed subgroups of users, you can compute the needed sample size.

There isn't a magic sample size (like 30 or 100) that will work for every benchmark study. Even if you can only run a few users—say 30—you can still detect differences, especially in a within-subjects study (if you're doing a comparative study). Keep in mind you're limited to only seeing very large differences (30%+) unless the variability in your metrics is low. See Chapter 6 for computing sample sizes.

APPENDIX B:

10 Best Practices for Competitive UX Benchmarking

Conducting a benchmark study is an excellent way to understand the quality of the website user experience. Adding a competitive component makes the benchmarking effort even more valuable. Having a comparison makes interpreting the subsequent data you collect easier to understand as you can immediately see how good or bad the experience was relative to relevant comparisons.

In a comparative study, the focus becomes less on absolute scores and more on relative comparisons. You can argue the tasks are artificial, but if the performance and attitudes for a competitor are consistently higher than your website, you have a compelling argument for change.

Here are 10 best practices and considerations we share with our clients, which you should consider next time you're ready to run a competitive UX benchmark study.

CONSIDER PRIOR EXPERIENCE

Prior experience with a website is one of the biggest influences on task metrics and overall attitudes. In general, participants with more experience rate the experience as higher quality and perform better (faster, higher completion rates). This is especially important in competitive studies. You don't want to declare one website as having a superior experience if all the participants had more experience on one site. You can control for prior experience by setting a quota of participants who have the same level of experience. Another alternative is to statistically control for prior experience. See Chapter 11 for more on analyzing differences in prior experience.

COLLECT DATA AT THE TASK AND STUDY LEVEL

You'll want to collect data about the overall experience (macro view) and the detailed task-level experience (micro view). Having participants attempt tasks, instead of just looking around the website, is the most effective way for exploring the nooks and crannies of your website. What's more, task-level metrics like completion rates, time, difficulty, and errors help diagnose interaction problems and generate ideas on what to improve.

Study-level metrics, like the SUS and SUPR-Q (Chapter 5), provide an overall impression of the website. While this impression is shaped by the task experiences encountered during the benchmark, participants also bring with them their experiences prior to the study and this is usually reflected in the study-level metrics. Both provide insights into the quality of the experience.

HAVE TASK SUCCESS CRITERIA

There's a lot you can learn from open-ended tasks scenarios where users are asked to search for products or information on their own volition. However, in unmoderated studies, such open-ended tasks often show little differentiation between websites. You'll want to include a closed-ended task that has clear success criteria, such as finding the right product, right price, or store location. If you're running a competitive benchmark, not all websites will have the same success criteria, but ensure that the level of difficulty is equivalent when creating the task and success criteria. See the "Determining Tasks Success in an Unmoderated Study" section in Chapter 7 for more information.

DECIDE ON AN APPROACH: BETWEEN- VS. WITHIN-SUBJECTS

While a between-subjects approach (different participants on each website) is the more familiar one to researchers, the within-subjects approach (same participants on all websites) has some important advantages. The right choice however is based on a few factors.

By far the biggest advantages to using a within-subjects approach is that you can use a much smaller sample size to detect the same differences as a between-subjects approach, and you have the ability to ask for participants' preferences. The cost of recruitment and honorariums are usually one of the biggest disadvantages faced in a study, so reducing the time and cost by choosing a within-subject approach for your study has a strong appeal. However, the disadvantage of a within-subjects approach is that you'll have carryover effects that can have an impact on attitude metrics as participants make relative judgments. But with the proper counterbalancing of tasks, you can reduce the carryover effects, and every within-subjects design contains a smaller between-subjects design given this proper counterbalancing (as explained in Chapter 2).

If you can't decide whether you need a within- or between-subjects approach, you can compromise by using a combination of the two. For example, all participants perform tasks on your website and one of three random competitors to compare. See the "Within vs. Between Subjects vs. Mixed" section in Chapter 2 for more information.

MEASURE PREFERENCE

Asking which website participants prefer is an excellent indicator of choice. It's most intuitive to ask this question in a within-subjects study where participants encounter all websites. However, you can still ask participants which website they prefer, assuming they have had some experience with them. You can then see how much the recent experience affected their preference. We like to measure both selection (which did a user prefer) and intensity (how much more did the user prefer). Chapter 11 has a discussion on analyzing preference data.

MEASURE WEBSITE AND BRAND ATTITUDES

Like prior experience, existing attitudes toward the website and brand have a lot to do with the measures you collect. Negative press can really influence people's attitudes, and those affect UX metrics. Collect those at the beginning of the study and you can also control for attitudes, such as prior experience, which allows you to hold constant existing attitudes while assessing actions and attitudes. With before and after data you can also measure brand lift to see whether the experience hurt or helped customer attitudes. Chapter 11 provides more detail on examining brand lift data.

USE STANDARDIZED MEASURES

While it's OK to come up with your own questions to ask participants, you get more accurate results when you use existing standardized questionnaires at the task and study level. Research has shown that standardized questionnaires provide a more reliable and valid view of the user experience than homegrown questionnaires.

For example, instruments like the SUPR-Q at the study level provide a picture of the quality of the website user experience in just eight items. It also highly correlates with SUS, which provides a view of website usability using 10 items and is comparable to about 500 other product experiences. The Single Ease Question (SEQ) asked after each task has been shown to discriminate well between poor and excellent tasks (see Chapter 5 for more standardized metrics).

COMPARE TO OTHER REPORTED METRICS

There's a plethora of published data for many industries, like airline, healthcare, and retail websites. Don't reinvent the wheel when coming up with tasks, metrics, or findings; your findings will end up being redundant. Use these existing data sources as a point of corroboration with your findings or to help take your study to a more focused level. We report regular industry benchmarks at MeasuringU.com.

HAVE A SUFFICIENT SAMPLE SIZE

To differentiate between random variations in scores, you need a sufficient sample size. Just because you find no difference doesn't mean UX website quality is the same. All too often I see competitive studies with insufficient sample sizes to detect even a large difference. Our sample sizes for competitive studies are usually between 150 and 300 participants per website when using an unmoderated between-subjects approach.

With a sample size this large we can detect differences of about 15 percentage points for completion rates (and smaller differences for continuous metrics). You can detect the same size of a difference with just 50 participants using a within-subjects approach. Before launching your study, review the sample size tables in Chapter 6 to ensure your sample size is sufficient to detect a meaningful difference.

RINSE AND REPEAT: COMPARE OVER TIME

Conducting a benchmark study involves a lot of effort and coordination. To make a line, you need at least two points. The same can be said for benchmark studies. If you conduct an initial benchmark study, even a competitive one, it becomes a lot more valuable when you can compare future data to it. Plan to conduct benchmarks at regular intervals (e.g., every year or quarter). One of the hallmarks of measuring the user experience is seeing whether design efforts actually make a quantifiable difference over time. A regular benchmark study is a great way to institutionalize that.

APPENDIX C:

5 Common Mistakes Made in
UX Benchmark Studies

In the last two appendixes I've provided some guidance on making a benchmark effort successful. A lot goes into a benchmarking study, and any of those things can go wrong. I've seen all sorts of problems. Here are five of the more common mistakes made when conducting benchmark studies, and what you can do to prevent them.

TESTING THE WRONG TYPE OF PARTICIPANT

Benchmarking studies need participants. A lot of services promise to deliver test participants quickly and easily. While they're great for getting general population participation, they're not ideal for obtaining participants with specific profiles; maybe you need accountants, IT administrators, radiological technicians, or people who have recently sold a home. But both domain knowledge and motivations specific to specialized tasks will have a major impact on benchmark data.

What to do: Understand the essential domain knowledge and skills of your users, and recruit accordingly using a good panel provider.

If you're unsure if you're using the right mix of participants, record each participant's skills and product/service knowledge so you can account for discrepancies between the actual and ideal participant profiles over time. For example, if your sample in Year 1 had a lot of experienced users and Year 2 had more novice participants, then you'll likely need to account for this discrepancy in the analysis. See Chapter 3 for more on defining the right participants for your benchmark.

USING THE WRONG TASKS

For a task-based benchmarking study, such as for a retail website, so many metrics are affected by the tasks you have participants perform. If you provide irrelevant tasks, then you'll get irrelevant results. But it's more complicated than just knowing what users are trying to accomplish on a site. You also have to effectively simulate these tasks and have the right type of validation. All too often I see tasks, especially in unmoderated studies, that are not representative of what users actually do on a site.

What to do: Don't pick tasks because they're easy or seem right. Use data from a top-tasks analysis and get stakeholder buy in. Answer the question: If most people fail this task, will the stakeholders care? Then be sure the success criteria are realistic (not too hard or easy). It takes pretesting and some experience to craft tasks that will provide meaningful data. See Chapter 3 for more on defining the right tasks for your benchmark.

NOT COLLECTING THE RIGHT OR ENOUGH METRICS

While the study should be scheduled for a manageable amount of time so participants don't get too fatigued, you still need to collect a sufficient amount of data to describe the user experience. This means you need to measure what participants are doing (behavioral metrics), what they think (attitudinal metrics), and who they are (experience and demographics). You don't want to spend the time and money it takes to complete a benchmark study only to discover that there is not enough data to analyze properly or, worse yet, the wrong data was collected.

What to do: Use multiple measures that address attitudes and actions at the task and test level. When possible, include questions that map to the company's key performance indicators (KPI). See Chapter 5.

HAVING TOO SMALL OF A SAMPLE SIZE

When budgets are tight, sample sizes are one the first things that get cut in benchmarking studies. It's understandable when the cost per user is very expensive. However, you should look at the cost of participants as the smaller incremental cost compared to the initial fixed cost of setting up and planning the benchmark.

It's a waste to build an expensive factory to churn out only 20 products. It likewise doesn't make sense to go through the trouble of planning a benchmark study only to collect data from a few participants. With too few participants you won't be able to differentiate real changes from chance. This is especially the case in competitive benchmarks.

What to do: Understand how much precision you need (based on a future comparison or a stand-alone study) and compute the sample size needed. See Chapter 6 for more on sample sizes.

NOT ACCOUNTING FOR SAMPLING ERROR

Just because you use a large sample size (whatever that means to your organization), you can't ignore the very real impact of sampling error on your data. Statistical comparisons allow you to differentiate real changes (the signal) from random chance (the noise) and should be used on any sized sample.

What to do: Use confidence intervals and the right statistical test (usually a two-sample t-test or two proportion test) to be sure you're not being fooled by randomness. See Chapter 10 for using confidence intervals and Chapter 11 for conducting the right statistical test.

APPENDIX D:

Example Project Booking Form for Hotel Comparison Study

The following is an example project booking form for the sample comparative hotel benchmark study (used throughout the book). While the information here is brief and informal, it serves as a starting place for the benchmark study design.

Hypothesize

What are the Hypothesis/Research Question(s) or goals of the study?

There is no significant difference in the user experience between the Best Western and Marriott websites.

Operationalize

1. What type of method are you using?
   Task-based comparative study

   a) Are there tasks? If so, what are they?
   Browse for hotel rooms
   Search for prices

   b) How will this be tested? [e.g., live site? Product, Prototype? Wireframes?]
   Desktop only
   Desktop, Mobile [Android and iOS?]

2. What are your metrics (how will success be measured)?
   Task Metrics: Completion, SEQ, time, and usability problems
   Study Metrics: SUPR-Q, NPS, Brand Attitude

3. Is this a stand-alone or comparative study?

    a) If this is a comparative study, is it between (different users in each group) or within subjects (same users in each group)? Between subjects

4. Who are the participants? [e.g., Geo, Membership, Age, Income, State (logged in or out) Tenor, etc.]
People who have booked a hotel online in the last year in the US

    a) Are there distinct subgroups [e.g., Account Holders vs. Prospects?]
General population (no brand haters)

5. What sample size will you use and why? Use the tablqes on the next pages to help with sample size planning.
Exploratory study: 30 participants in each group (function of time and budget)

APPENDIX E:

Example Study Script for an Unmoderated Study

The following is an example study script for the comparative hotel benchmark study used throughout this book.

HOTELS STUDY SCRIPT

Welcome Page:

Welcome! Thank you for participating in this evaluation.

You will be asked to perform a few tasks on a retail website. After you have read the task and are ready to proceed, click the "Start Task" button. The task instructions will also be shown in a small window on the bottom of your screen so you can refer to them throughout the task. Once you feel that you have completed the task successfully, click the "End Task" button.

Please remember that this is an evaluation of two websites and not you, so do the best you can to complete the tasks. Some tasks may be harder than others.

Have a piece of paper and pen ready as you will be asked to write down information during some tasks.

PRE-STUDY QUESTIONNAIRE:

1. Please select your gender:
   - Male
   - Female

2. Please select your income from the choices below:
   - 0–$24k
   - $25k–$49k
   - $50k–$74k
   - $75k–$99k
   - $100k+

3. Please select your age from the choices below:
   - Under 18 [SCREEN OUT]
   - 18–24
   - 25–34
   - 35–44
   - 45–54
   - 55–64
   - 65+

4. How would you describe your attitude toward the following companies? [1–7, Very Unfavorable – Very Favorable] [SCREEN OUT IF 1]
   - Hilton
   - Marriott
   - Holiday Inn
   - Best Western
   - Hyatt

5. In the past 12 months, how many times have you visited the following websites? [Marriott, Best Western, Hyatt, Hilton, Double Tree]
   - 0 Times
   - 1–3 Times
   - 4–6 Times
   - 7–9 Times
   - 10+ Times

Thank you for your responses. You qualify for this evaluation!

You will now be asked to perform a few tasks on a website. You will first be shown a description of the task. After you have read it and are ready to proceed, click the "Start Task" button. The relevant information you need to complete each task will then be shown in a small window on the bottom of your screen for you to refer to throughout the task.

Once you feel you're done with the task, click the "End Task" button to move on. This is an evaluation of a website and not you, so do the best you can to complete the tasks. Some tasks may be harder than others.

Have a piece of paper ready to write down information or copy it electronically, as you will be asked to recall information at the end of some tasks.

TASKS

MARRIOTT

Task 1: Search

Task Descriptions:

Task Description Full:

Start URL: http://www.marriott.com
Imagine you're scheduling a trip to Denver, Colorado and need to book a hotel for your stay. On the following website, find out how much it would cost to book a room (without fees or tax) with one king bed from November 27th – November 29th at the Denver Marriott City Center (use 'MEMBER RATE' pricing).

Please write down or remember the cost of the room as you will be asked for it later.

This information will be shown on the next screen.

Validation Question

1. How much was the cost of the hotel room (for all three nights)? *($224, $224)*
    a) $588
    b) $448
    c) $425
    d) $547
    e) $503
    f) Other:

Post Task Questions

1. How confident are you that you completed the task successfully? [1–7, Not at all Confident – Extremely Confident]
2. How easy or difficult was it to complete the task? [1–7, Very Difficult – Very Easy]
3. Briefly describe why you chose the number you did.

Task 2: Browse

Task Descriptions:

Start URL: http://www.marriott.com

Imagine you're booking one hotel room for a trip to Salt Lake City, Utah from October 15th to October 17th. On the following website, find a hotel in Salt Lake City, Utah that is pet friendly, has a pool, and has a user rating of at least 4.7 out of 5.

Please write down or remember the name of the hotel as you will be asked for it later.

This information will be shown on the next screen.

Validation Question:

1. What is the name of the hotel you found?
   a) Residence Inn Salt Lake City Cottonwood
   b) Residence Inn Salt Lake City Murray
   c) TownePlace Suites Salt Lake City-West Valley
   d) TownePlace Suites Provo Orem
   e) Other:

Post Task Questions

1. How confident are you that you completed the task successfully? [1–7, Not at all Confident – Extremely Confident]
2. How easy or difficult was it to complete the task? [1–7, Very Difficult – Very Easy]
3. Briefly describe why you chose the number you did.

BEST WESTERN

Task 1: Search

Task Descriptions:

Task Description

Start URL: https://www.bestwestern.com/

Imagine you're scheduling a trip to Denver, Colorado and need to book a hotel for your stay. On the following website, find out how much it would cost to book a room (without fees or tax) with one king bed from October 1st – October 4th at the Denver Tech Center Hotel (note: use the "Flexible Rate").

Please write down or remember the cost of the room as you will be asked for it later.

This information will be shown on the next screen.

Validation Question:

1. How much was the cost of the hotel room (for all three nights)?
    a) $474
    b) $490
    c) $419
    d) $509
    e) $521

Post Task Questions

1. How confident are you that you completed the task successfully? [1–7, Not at all Confident – Extremely Confident]
2. How easy or difficult was it to complete the task? [1–7, Very Difficult – Very Easy]
3. Briefly describe why you chose the number you did.

Task 2: Browse

Task Descriptions:

Task Description Full:

Imagine you're booking one hotel room for a trip to Salt Lake City, Utah from October 15th to October 17th. On the following website, find a hotel in Salt Lake City, Utah that is pet friendly, has a pool, and has at least 400 user ratings.

Please write down or remember the name of the hotel as you will be asked for it later.

This information will be shown on the next screen.

Validation Question:

1. What is the hotel you found?
   a) Landmark Inn & Pancake House
   b) Cotton Tree Inn
   c) Mountain View Inn
   d) High Country Inn
   e) Other:

Post Task Questions

1. How confident are you that you completed the task successfully? [1–7, Not at all Confident – Extremely Confident]
2. How easy or difficult was it to complete the task? [1–7, Very Difficult – Very Easy]
3. Briefly describe why you chose the number you did.

FINAL QUESTIONNAIRE

You are finished with the task portion of this study.

For the next series of questions, think about the entire experience you had while using the **Marriott** website today.

SUPR-Q/NPS

Please rate how well you agree or disagree with the following statements about the **Marriott** website you just visited. [1–5, Strongly Disagree – Strongly Agree]

1. The information on the **Marriott** website is credible.
2. The **Marriott** website is trustworthy.
3. The **Marriott** website has a clean and simple presentation.
4. I found the website to be attractive.
5. It is easy to navigate within the **Marriott** website.
6. The **Marriott** website is easy to use.
7. I will likely visit the **Marriott** website in the future.

8. How likely is it that you would recommend the **Marriott** website to a friend or colleague? [0–10, Not at all Likely – Extremely Likely]

   a) [IF Q8<7] Briefly describe why you chose the number you did.

9. If you have any comments about this evaluation or the websites you visited, please provide them below.

For the next series of questions, think about the entire experience you had while using the **Best Western** website today.

SUPR-Q/NPS

Please rate how well you agree or disagree with the following statements about the **Best Western** website you just visited. [1–5, Strongly Disagree – Strongly Agree]

1. The information on the **Best Western** website is credible.
2. The **Best Western** website is trustworthy.
3. The **Best Western** website has a clean and simple presentation.
4. I found the website to be attractive.
5. It is easy to navigate within the **Best Western** website.
6. The **Best Western** website is easy to use.
7. I will likely visit the **Best Western** website in the future.
8. How likely is it that you would recommend the **Best Western** website to a friend or colleague? [0–10, Not at all Likely – Extremely Likely]

   a) [IF Q8<7] Briefly describe why you chose the number you did.

9. If you have any comments about this evaluation or the websites you visited, please provide them below.

INDEX

A

ACSI (American Customer Satisfaction
  Index), 65
adding error bars, 184
administration, task, 134, 138
advertising, participant recruitment,
  52, 53, 155
Amazon
  example, 31, 62, 151
  Mechanical Turk, 52, 133, 144
analysis
  advanced, 222–258
  key drivers, 252
  logistic regression, 255
  regression, 252
  statistical, additional, 252
  verbatim, 233
analyzing data, 169, 177, 178
ANOVA (analysis of variance), 229,
  254, 255
assist
  what is an, 164
  when to, 165
  why, 164
assistance, moderator, 164
attitude
  customer, 64, 65
  measurement, 67
  negative, 67
  participant. *See* brand attitude
  positive, 68, 98, 102, 223

attributes
  participant, 30
  product, 66
  satisfaction, 67
Audible example, 235–239
authentication problems, 38
authenticity, participant, 98, 103
AutoCAD, 31, 134, 218
automated "bots", 170
average score computation, 198
Axure, 44

B

B2B (business to business), 4, 98, 101,
  234, 286
B2C (business to consumer), 4, 56
bang box, 273, 279
behavior, participant, 30, 147, 148
benchmark
  calculator, 181, 221
  defined, 2
  metrics, 10, 56–76
  modes, types of, 7
  report, parts, 259
  study, types of, 4–5
  training courses, 280
Benjamini–Hochberg procedure, 255
Best Buy example, 63
best practices, competitive benchmark,
  289–293

phone. *See* cell phone

PII (personally identifiable information), 39, 95

pilot study, 159

planning
  study, the, 12–20
  time factors for, 48

platforms, 21, 34, 37, 51
  analyzing data, for, 177
  programming, unmoderated study, 119

Plaza Research (recruiting company), 53

point estimates, 147

poor quality response, detecting, 170, 171

positive attitude, participant, 68, 98, 102, 223

post-study questions, 109, 116

post-task
  ease, 188
  metrics, 73, 108, 136
  questions, 116

Practical Guide to Measuring Usability: Quantifying the Usability of Websites & Software (Sauro), 113

Practical Guide to the System Usability Scale (Sauro), 58, 86, 218

Practical Guide to Usability Testing (Dumas and Redish), 113, 134

practice
  calculating comparison study sample sizes, 84

precision, 79, 288, 296

prediction, SUS score, 62

preference, 18, 116, 291
  analyzing, 222

prepaid debit card, 42

preparation, data collection, 119–131

presentation
  completion rate, 186
  post-task confidence, 201

post-task ease, 191
  preparation, 177
  recommendations, 273
  SUM, 206
  task time, 196

pre-study questions, 97, 107

pretest, study, 157–168

primacy effects, 16

prioritizing tasks, 27

privacy concerns, 22, 39, 95

probability, 249

probability panels, 147

product
  satisfaction, 66, 67
  selection, 41

professional participant, 148

professional service costs, 49

project booking form, 12, 93
  example, 297

promoters, 63

pros and cons
  interface, *24*
  mandatory responses, *131*
  retrospective vs. tasked based studies, *7*
  testing methods, *9*
  within- and between-subjects design, *18*

prospective customers, 67, 149

prototype, 23, 115

publication confidence level, 256

purchases, 39
  making, 41
  simulating, 40

p-values
  interpreting, 244
  output, 251

Q

qualification questions, 97

Qualtrics, 37

ROI (return on investment), 284
Roku, example, 22
roles, company, 98, 101
R statistical package, 178, 245

S

sample
   power, 16
   quality, *9*
   size, *9*, 16, 292
   size, comparison study, 81
   size, planning, 77
   size, precision, 84
   size, stand-alone study, *78*
   size too small, 295
sampling error, 249
   not accounting for, 296
   ways to indicate, 275
satisfaction
   attributes/features, 66
   customer, 64, 65
   product, 66
Satmetrix Systems, 64
scenarios, task, 5, 107, 110
screening questions, 98
screen recording software, 37, 38, 51
screenshots, 115, 274
script
   moderated study, 104
   unmoderated study, 94
selection, participant, 30, 35
SEQ (Single Ease Question), 10, 72
   example, *266*
   general satisfaction, 65
   post-task, 188
sequence effects, 16, 135
session recordings, 115, 137, 138, 172, 239
shaded graphs, 276
sidebars
   confidence intervals, 185

Excel error bars, 184
   insufficient sample size, 82
   noting errors, 209
   sample size, 77
similar variables. *See* cross tabbing
Simple Startup tool, 119
simulated purchasing, 43
soft launch, study, 157–164
software, 22, 287
   in-person, moderated study, 38
   logging, 51
   remote, moderated study, 37
   screen recording, 51
   video editing, 51
software examples
   AutoCAD, 31, 134, 218
   Axure, 44
   BlueJeans, 37
   Camtasia, 38, 137
   GoToMeeting, 7, 37, 138, 158
   InVision, 44
   join.me, 37, 138
   Morae, 38, 51, 137, 138
   WebEx, 7, 37, 138, 218
speeders, detecting, 169, 171
SPSS (Statistical Package for the Social Sciences), 177, 178, 229
stakeholder buy-in, 45
stand-alone study, 14, 78, 285
   sample size, planning, 80
standardized
   database, SUPR-Q, 61
   measures, 292
statements of confidentiality, 95
statistical
   analyses, additional, 252
   power, 82, 84, *86*, 175
   significance, 223, 275
   significance, displaying, 275
   test, between subjects, 244
   test, output, 250

recruitment, 144, 155, 161

recruitment costs, 52

scripts, 94, 299

task success, 113

task validation, 113

technology costs, 50

testing, 7

welcome message, 94

URL, redirect link example, *145*

Usability Datalogger, *136*

usability issue example, *271*

user experience, defined, 1

UserFocus, 136

user interface. *See* interface

users

access to, 286

defining, 285

UserTesting, 34, 35, 161

UserZoom, 7, 34, 35

UX metrics, panel variation, 147

V

Validately, 34, 96

variability, 78, 81, 86, 176

variables

collapsing, 226

cross tabbing, 225

examining, 225

logistic regression for, 255

prior experience, 228

regression analysis for, 252

verbatim

analysis, 233

comments, *272, 273*

verify task success, 180

video

clip reference example, 241

editing software, 51

highlights, 274

recordings, 239

visualizations, click behavior, 235

VPN (virtual private network), 25

W

Walmart, example, 4, 22

WebEx, 7, 37, 138, 218

website

checkout problem example, *270*

consumer, 22, 286

filter usage example, *270*

intercept, 150

problems, diagnosing, 242

satisfaction, 66

weighted *t*-test

about, 230

using, 230

welcome message, 94, 105

example, 105

Wi-Fi, 38

within-subjects design, 15, 290

comparisons, 247

pros and cons, *18*

sample size planning, *81, 84*

statistical test, 245

Word, Microsoft, example, 27, 220

Z

Zazelenchuk, Todd, 136

Made in the USA
San Bernardino, CA
20 July 2018